PUBLISHED            ol Library

Drama Criticism: *Developments since Ibsen*   ARNOLD P. HINCHLIFFE
*Poetry of the First World War*   DOMINIC HIBBERD
*Tragedy: Developments in Criticism*   R. P. DRAPER
*The English Novel: Developments in Criticism since Henry James*   STEPHEN HAZELL
*The Romantic Imagination*   JOHN SPENCER HILL

TITLES IN PREPARATION INCLUDE

Henry James: *'Washington Square' and 'Portrait of a Lady'*   ALAN SHELSTON
Keats: *Narrative Poems*   JOHN SPENCER HILL
O'Casey: *'Juno and the Paycock', 'The Plough and the Stars' and 'The Shadow of a Gunman'*   RONALD AYLING
Shakespeare: *A Midsummer Night's Dream*   ANTONY W. PRICE
Wilde: *Comedies*   WILLIAM TYDEMAN

*The Auden Group*   RONALD CARTER
*Comedy: Developments in Criticism*   D. J. PALMER
*Elizabethan Lyric and Narrative Poetry*   GERALD HAMMOND
*Poetry Criticism: Developments since the Symbolists*   A. E. DYSON

# Conrad

## *Heart of Darkness*
## *Nostromo*
## and *Under Western Eyes*

A CASEBOOK

EDITED BY

## C. B. COX

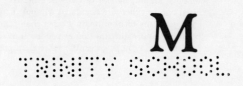

M

TRINITY SCHOOL

*First edition 1981*
*Reprinted 1982*
*Published by*
THE MACMILLAN PRESS LTD
*London and Basingstoke*
*Associated companies in Delhi Dublin*
*Hong Kong Johannesburg Lagos Melbourne*
*New York Singapore and Tokyo*

*Printed in Hong Kong*

**British Library Cataloguing in Publication Data**

Conrad, 'Heart of darkness', 'Nostromo' and
   'Under Western eyes'. – (Casebook series).
   1. Conrad, Joseph. Heart of darkness –
   Addresses, essays, lectures
   2. Conrad, Joseph. Nostromo – Addresses,
   essays, lectures
   3. Conrad, Joseph. Under western eyes –
   Addresses, essays, lectures
   I. Cox, Charles   II. Series
   823'.9'12          PR6005.04H479

   ISBN 0-333-26823-7
   ISBN 0-333-26824-5   Pbk

# CONTENTS

# ACKNOWLEDGEMENTS

The editor and publishers express their thanks for the use of the following material in copyright: John Buchan, review of *Nostromo* (19 Nov. 1904) by permission of the Editor of the *Spectator*; C. B. Cox, extract from *Joseph Conrad; The Modern Imagination* (1974), by permission of J. M. Dent & Sons Ltd.; H. M. Daleski, extract from *Joseph Conrad: The Way of Dispossession* (1977), by permission of Faber & Faber Ltd.; Avrom Fleishman, extract from *Conrad's Politics* (1967), by permission of the Johns Hopkins University Press; Edward Garnett, extracts from reviews in *Academy and Literature* (9 Dec. 1902), the *Speaker* (12 Nov. 1904) and the *Nation* (21 Oct. 1911), by permission of David Garnett; Albert J. Guerard, extract from *Conrad the Novelist* (1958), by permission of Harvard University Press, copyright © 1958 by the President and Fellows of Harvard College; James Guetti, essay '*Heart of Darkness* and the Failure of the imagination', *Sewanee Review*, 73 (Summer 1965), copyright © 1965 by the University of the South, reprinted by permission of the Editor; Douglas Hewitt, extract from *Conrad: A Reassessment* (1952), by permission of Bowes and Bowes Publishers Ltd.; Bruce E. Johnson, extract from *Conrad's Models of Mind* (1971), copyright © 1971 by the University of Minnesota, by permission of the University of Minnesota Press; Thomas Moser, extract from *Joseph Conrad: Achievement and Decline* (1957), by permission of Harvard University Press; Royal Roussel, extract from *The Metaphysics of Darkness* (1971), by permission of the Johns Hopkins University Press; K. K. Ruthven, extract from 'The Savage God: Conrad and Lawrence', *Critical Quarterly*, 10, nos 1 & 2 (Spring & Summer 1968), by permission of the author; Dr Tony Tanner, essay 'Nightmare and Complacency: Razumov and the Western Eye', *Critical Quarterly* 4, no. 3 (1962), by permission of the author; Lionel Trilling, extract from *Beyond Culture* (1965), by permission of Harcourt Brace, Jovanovich, Inc.

# GENERAL EDITOR'S PREFACE

The Casebook series, launched in 1968, has become a well-regarded library of critical studies. The central concern of the series remains the 'single-author' volume, but suggestions from the academic community have led to an extension of the original plan, to include occasional volumes on such general themes as literary 'schools' and genres.

Each volume in the central category deals either with one well-known and influential work by an individual author, or with closely related works by one writer. The main section consists of critical readings, mostly modern, collected from books and journals. A selection of reviews and comments by the author's contemporaries is also included, and sometimes comment from the author himself. The Editor's introduction charts the reputation of the work or works from the first appearance to the present time.

Volumes in the 'general themes' category are variable in structure but follow the basic purpose of the series in presenting an integrated selection of readings, with an Introduction which explores the theme and discusses the literary and critical issues involved.

A single volume can represent no more than a small selection of critical opinions. Some critics are excluded for reasons of space, and it is hoped that readers will pursue the suggestions for further reading in the Select Bibliography. Other contributions are severed from their original context, to which some readers may wish to turn. Indeed, if they take a hint from the critics represented here, they certainly will.

A. E. DYSON

# INTRODUCTION

In his first novels, *Almayer's Folly* (1895), *An Outcast of the Islands* (1896) and *The Nigger of the 'Narcissus'* (1897), Conrad narrates the story in the usual nineteenth-century manner, as if he were the omniscient author who is in charge of the plot. After his marriage in 1896 he was desperate to make money by his writing, but he found it very difficult to make progress when using such conventional forms. He was frustrated and bogged down by *The Rescuer*, which he didn't manage to finish until twenty years later (then called *The Rescue*).

When writing the short story, 'Youth', published in *Blackwood's Magazine* in 1898, he for the first time invented a character called Marlow to act as a narrator. Marlow is supposed to be recounting his memories to a group of companions, all ex-merchant seamen, on a convivial occasion. The device appealed to Conrad, and he immediately used Marlow again, in a much more complex role, first in *Heart of Darkness* (1899; issued in book form in 1902), and then in *Lord Jim* (1900).

*Heart of Darkness*, based on Conrad's memories of his own trip down the Congo in 1890, was written very quickly, and undoubtedly the indirect mode of narration liberated him from the impotent state he had fallen into while trying to write *The Rescuer*. The other two novels considered in this Casebook, *Nostromo* (1904) and *Under Western Eyes* (1911), also depend on unusual methods of narration. *Nostromo* begins with a series of shifts backwards and forwards in time which contemporary readers found difficult to follow. *Under Western Eyes* is narrated by an English teacher of languages, to whose Western eyes the violence and passion of Russian lives are supposed to be almost beyond comprehension.

During this period from *Heart of Darkness* in 1899 to *Under Western Eyes* in 1911, Conrad's extraordinary innovations in technique helped him to explore deep-seated personal problems, and to link these to the cultural crises of the time which eventually produced such great works of modernism as Kafka's

*The Trial* or T. S. Eliot's *The Waste Land*. In *Joseph Conrad: The Way of Dispossession* (1977), H. M. Daleski follows Thomas Moser in arguing that Conrad's major achievement is to be found in this period, and this view is probably now held by a majority of critics. In his important biography, *Joseph Conrad: The Three Lives* (1979), Frederick R. Karl says that the completion of *Under Western Eyes* marked the end of an era. Afterwards, little of Conrad's fiction was again so intensely personal:

Conrad had, in fact, reached out for what every artist must do or try to do: to dip so deeply into his psyche for what he fears most that he endangers himself: and then, once close to extinction, having discovered what he can do, he either frees himself or cracks up. Only a major artist can perform this way, since the journey into himself must be intense. (Karl, p. 678)

Daleski believes that in this great period Conrad's central theme was the search for self-possession. In his two lives, as seaman and artist, he often experienced a personal insecurity, a radical uncertainty about his own identity. He had a positive horror of losing his self-possession. In his *Conrad: A Psychoanalytic Biography* (1967), Dr Bernard Meyer argues that 'it would appear certain that the tenuousness of the sense of self and the reparative reliance on fetishism pervading Conrad's fiction was a projection of identical elements in his own personality'. Conrad's fascination with spiritual disintegration can be seen in his treatment of Kurtz in *Heart of Darkness*, Charles Gould in *Nostromo* and Razumov in *Under Western Eyes*.

Already in his youth when at Marseilles in 1878 Conrad had tried to commit suicide. In his letters words such as 'weariness', 'depression', 'paralysis' and 'suicide' crop up again and again, giving evidence to his continual struggle against the urge to self-destruction. Suicide often occurs in his fiction. In *The Great Tradition* (1948), F. R. Leavis argues that in *Nostromo* Conrad was instinctively sympathetic towards Decoud's radical scepticism which eventually leads to his decision to kill himself.

After completing *Under Western Eyes* at the start of 1910, Conrad was laid up with nervous tension for three months. His wife Jessie's description of his condition is printed in Part One below. There is a growing consensus among students of the

novelist that after this terrifying breakdown Conrad repressed
the sensitive, imaginative side of his nature, and forced his mind
into safer, more normal channels of thought. F. R. Leavis's
admiration for *Chance* (1913) and *Victory* (1915) is not now shared
by many readers. Among later novels only *The Shadow-Line*
(1917) stands comparison with his major achievements. The
treatment of sexual love in his later works is superficial, and in
*The Arrow of Gold* (1919), *The Rescue* (1920), *The Rover* (1923) and
*Suspense* (1925) he indulges in sentimental evasions. Dr Bernard
Meyer argues that after Conrad's breakdown in 1910 his fiction
changed radically. The most striking manifestation of this
change, he says, is 'an exteriorisation of the source of suffering'.
The poignant inner mental conflicts of Decoud or Razumov are
replaced by conflict with the outer world, where more innocent
creatures like Peyrol in *The Rover* struggle with indifferent success
against external influence or accident. In contrast, in novels such
as *Heart of Darkness*, *Nostromo* and *Under Western Eyes*, Conrad
grapples courageously with his personal neuroses, with his sense
of alienation and his longing for commitment, and thereby
creates great fictions that explore all the central problems of
modern art.

☆

Conrad was fortunate to have in Edward Garnett a friend whose
highly perceptive reviews were most influential. The first reviews
of a book often mould the opinions of later faint-hearted critics
who distrust their own judgement, and this seems to have
occurred after Garnett had praised *Heart of Darkness* as an
'amazing, a consummate piece of artistic *diablerie*', 'the high-
water mark of the author's talent'. Garnett recognised *Heart of
Darkness* as a 'psychological masterpiece' and later in 1904 said
that in *Nostromo* Conrad 'had achieved something which it is not
in the power of any English contemporary novelist to touch'.
Garnett particularly stressed Conrad's power in creating 'a
special poetic sense of *the psychology of scene*', and was the first to
realise how in *Nostromo* descriptions of Nature make 'the tiny
atom of each man's individual life' seem frighteningly precarious
and vulnerable. Although Garnett was distressed by the criticism
of Russian exiles in *Under Western Eyes*, his review shows insight

into the 'pathological truth' of Conrad's depiction of Razumov and the artistic intensity with which the Russian atmosphere is created.

The most important event in Conrad's literary career was probably his meeting with Ford Madox Hueffer in 1898. Both were absorbed by problems of narrative technique and both were steeped in French literature, particularly Flaubert and Maupassant. Only a few months after their first meeting Conrad was writing *Heart of Darkness* with amazing rapidity, and their friendship lasted until they quarrelled in 1909. It is true that Conrad's great period is mostly confined to the time of his association with Hueffer. What mattered was not so much their collaboration on two unsuccessful novels, *The Inheritors* (1901) and *Romance* (1903), as the constant stimulus of Hueffer's criticism and conversation. The originality of Hueffer can be seen in his comments on *Under Western Eyes*, written after the quarrel. A portion of this review is presented in Part One below.

Conrad ought to have been stimulated and encouraged by the support of friends such as Garnett and Hueffer. Unfortunately, although his genius was early recognised, he remained to his dismay comparatively unpopular with the general reader until the success of *Chance* in 1913. The reasons for this can be seen in some of the other reviews printed in Part One. The reviewer of *Heart of Darkness* in the *Times Literary Supplement* thought the poetic rhetoric indulgent. Much to Conrad's annoyance, John Masefield said he preferred the vigorous, effective narrative of Kipling and Stevenson. Clearly many readers failed to understand the ambiguities of the story and the amazing success of Conrad in finding a new language and symbolism to reflect the uncertain nature of reality.

When *Nostromo* was appearing in serial form in *T.P.'s Weekly*, many readers wrote to protest indignantly about so much space being taken up by such unreadable stuff. The reviewer in the *Times Literary Supplement* thought that the novel was far too long, and that the material ought to have been compressed into a short story. This reviewer felt that Conrad's retrospective mode of narration was a failure, while John Buchan in his comments, also included in Part One, demanded more pruning and selection to impose coherence on this 'topsy-turvy' novel.

Readers tended to prefer simple narratives such as *Typhoon*

(1902). In his Author's Note to *Nostromo* Conrad tells us that, after he finished his *Typhoon* volume, it seemed somehow that there was nothing more in the world to write about. He had almost exhausted the material offered by his own experiences, and could no longer draw on colourful memories. The three major works which followed – *Nostromo*, *The Secret Agent* (1907) and *Under Western Eyes* – were written with much anxiety and self-doubt, and Conrad considered them all to have been failures with his public. Richard Curle's review shows how even a sympathetic reader could be bemused by Conrad's originality, and hanker after a return to simple exotic romance.

☆

After Conrad's death in 1924, Richard Curle, in various books and articles, and G. Jean-Aubry, who published his *Life and Letters of Joseph Conrad* in 1927, endeavoured to keep interest in the fiction alive. Edward Crankshaw's *Joseph Conrad: Some Aspects of the Novel* (1936; new edition 1976) gave a good account of his greatness, but by and large Conrad's pessimistic conservatism was not in vogue in the 1930s. M. C. Bradbrook's *Joseph Conrad: England's Polish Genius* (1941) attracted some attention, but the new post-war enthusiasm for Conrad was undoubtedly initiated by F. R. Leavis's *The Great Tradition*. Leavis asserted that the great English novelists are Jane Austen, George Eliot, Henry James, Conrad and D. H. Lawrence.

Leavis devotes almost ten pages to *Heart of Darkness*, but this famous section in *The Great Tradition* has become as well known for its reservations as for its praise. Leavis admires the concrete particular details of the early sections of the novel, 'this art of vivid essential record', whereby a series of 'objective correlatives' communicate to us the lunatic greed and moral squalor of the Europeans. He mentions specifically the gunboat dropping shells into Africa and the black figures in the grove of death. He begins this section, however, by recalling E. M. Forster's criticisms of Conrad printed in *Abinger Harvest* (1936):

What is so elusive about him is that he is always promising to make some general philosophic statement about the universe, and then refraining

with a gruff disclaimer. . . . These essays [Forster is reviewing Conrad's
*Notes on Life and Letters* (1921)] do suggest that he is misty in the middle
as well as at the edges, that the secret casket of his genius contains a
vapour rather than a jewel; and that we needn't try to write him down
philosophically, because there is, in this direction, nothing to
write. . . . (pp. 134–5)

Leavis proposes to support Forster's argument by close analysis.
He says that in *Heart of Darkness* words such as 'inscrutable',
'inconceivable' and 'unspeakable' are overworked, and that
nothing is added to the mystery of the Congo by sentences such as
'It was the stillness of an implacable force brooding over an
inscrutable intention'. Leavis comments:

The same vocabulary, the same adjectival insistence upon inexpressible
and incomprehensible mystery, is applied to the evocation of human
profundities and spiritual horrors; to magnifying a thrilled sense of the
unspeakable potentialities of the human soul. The actual effect is not to
magnify but rather to muffle. (p. 177)

For Leavis the mystery of the Congo remains inconceivable.
    There have been many attempts to refute Leavis's criticism. In
*Scene and Symbol from George Eliot to James Joyce* (1969), Peter K.
Garrett contrasts two forms of narrative in *Heart of Darkness*. At
first the sordid farce of imperialism is presented in an imagistic
manner, but as the narrative progresses the centre of attention
shifts to the wilderness. Imperialist corruption is anatomised in
sharp, visual images, and a clear moral viewpoint is presented, a
scheme of values preserved by Marlow in his devotion to the work
ethic. In contrast, the wilderness is evoked in portentous,
rhetorical language which creates an indefinitely metaphysical
meaningfulness, an inner 'reality' which threatens all moral
significance. The tale represents an unresolved tension between
the two.
    A growing understanding of Conrad's attitude to language has
characterised much criticism of recent years. Jeremy Hawthorn's
*Joseph Conrad: Language and Fictional Self-Consciousness* (1979)
makes this its central theme. James Guetti's treatment of *Heart of
Darkness* (in his essay of 1965, presented in Part Two below) has
been highly influential. Guetti answers Leavis by showing that

the concrete particulars of language used by Marlow in the early sections are inadequate as a means of penetrating the reality, the wilderness, the darkness, at the centre of man's consciousness. Language itself is part of the exteriors of experience, giving an illusion of order and coherence. In a brilliant article, 'Conrad and Nietzsche'–in Norman Sherry's *Joseph Conrad: A Commemoration* (1976) – Edward W. Said argues that these two writers share a set of working attitudes to language:

And of these attitudes the one seeing utterance as inevitably and endlessly leading to another, without recourse to a single originating or unequivocally privileged first fact – that is, I think, the major point in common. . . . Kurtz and Jim and Nostromo are finally no more important than the meditation and the reflection and the language they stimulate. They are posited in a way as fundamentally unknowable. It is left for the narrative to deliver them, not in themselves, but as they are from many perspectives. Narrative does not explain, it introduces plural meanings where none had been before – at the heart of darkness. (pp. 69–70)

The indirect method of narration devised by Conrad in the late 1890s was an essential element in his creation of this type of narrative which 'does not explain'.

How then are we to react to Kurtz? Lionel Trilling thinks of him as 'a hero of the spirit'. K. K. Ruthven sees him as a Faustian figure, a man with the courage to reject the obsolete values of European civilisation. In contrast, for a left-wing radical such as Jonah Raskin in *The Mythology of Imperialism* (1971), *Heart of Darkness* is about the decay of European civilisation, and Kurtz is the quintessence of Western man, capitalism personified. A. J. Guerard talks of Kurtz as hollow at the core, an evil man, and in the chapter printed in this volume proposes a Jungian interpretation of the story. The adventure down the Congo has also been analysed as a Freudian voyage into the wilderness of sex, a discovery of the Id. Marlow penetrates down a narrow channel to find in the darkness an orgiastic experience.

The writings of James Guetti and Edward Said offer a reconciliation of these conflicting views. *Heart of Darkness* is a typical work of modernism, resistant to conventional interpretations. The story offers to us multiple perspectives, which criticism has tended to simplify. At the end, as Marlow finishes his story, he can produce no coherent explanation of the enigma of Kurtz.

☆

Neither *Nostromo* nor *Under Western Eyes* has provoked the same amount of controversy as *Heart of Darkness*. Leavis sees the main theme of *Nostromo* as the relation between moral idealism and 'material interests', and believes the novel is Conrad's most considerable work: 'the whole book forms a rich and subtle but highly organised pattern'. Leavis is particularly acute in his analysis of Decoud, whose consciousness, he suggests, permeates and even dominates the novel. Another excellent piece of analytical criticism is Robert Penn Warren's article in his *Selected Essays* (1958).

The main disagreement over *Nostromo* concerns how far it should be interpreted as a political novel. Several books have considered the interest of *Nostromo* to be essentially in its treatment of politics. In *The Political Novels of Joseph Conrad* (1963) Eloise Knapp Hay argues that in *Nostromo* Conrad is lamenting 'the loss of individual self-control and the defeat of will power by anonymous social forces, whether blind or directed by the menacing ingenuity of "representative" leaders'. She believes that when Conrad was forced to write fiction based on his reading of books rather than on his own memories, when his sea career was definitely finished, he became absorbed more by historical process than by private experience. She disagrees with Irving Howe's *Politics and the Novel* (1957), in which he rates Conrad below Dostoevsky as a political novelist by reading in the themes of *Nostromo* and *Under Western Eyes* an ultimate retreat from political engagement to 'the resources of private affection and gentleness'. Avrom Fleishman's searching analysis of the political dimensions of the novel, included in this Casebook, shows that Conrad had an astonishing insight into the relations between the individual and his community.

Bruce E. Johnson tells us that he inclines to take the side of Irving Howe against that of Mrs Hay. His chapter, reprinted here, takes a diametrically opposed view to that of Fleishman. 'Charles Gould is essentially apolitical', he says, arguing that the whole story uses politics as 'an aesthetic means to an end'.

Johnson considers that the novel 'is a study of identity and self-image as a source of value'.

In his biography, already mentioned, Frederick Karl also opposes those who theorise about Conrad's politics:

Various theorists about Conrad's politics – whether those who see him in a Burke–Mill liberal tradition (Fleishman), in the Polish romantic gentry tradition (Najder) [*], or as an antiliberal who argues for the status quo (Howe) – often ignore what the fiction tells us. As a creative artist, Conrad intertwined his politics with matters of tone, texture, irony, all of them indescribable matters. These qualities not only affect his politics, they *are* his politics. (p. 568)

This is also the view of Royal Roussel, who brilliantly analyses *Nostromo*'s landscapes. In *The Metaphysics of Darkness* (1971), an excerpt from which is reproduced below, he argues that in his work at the silver mine Charles Gould is trying to conquer matter, to make its hard intransigence his servant. If he succeeds, he will prove consciousness is not a passing shadow, but capable of imposing its values on the material world. His confidence is treated with bitter irony, for in the battle between matter and mind, the former always wins. At the end he is destroyed, and the silver reigns supreme. The real movement of history is not linear but cyclical, for all civilisations will inevitably disintegrate. Historical progress is an illusion. For Roussel, the prime concern of the novel is with this metaphysical dimension.

The one element that unites recent critics of *Nostromo* is that it is now generally agreed that Leavis was right to declare *Nostromo* 'one of the great novels of the language'.

☆

Leavis admires *Under Western Eyes*, but believes it is not such a great novel as *Nostromo* or *The Secret Agent*. Many critics have felt that the compelling intensity of the opening description of Razumov's betrayal of Haldin is not sustained, and that at times the scenes in Geneva are tedious. As usual Conrad is not successful in portraying women characters such as Natalia Haldin. Thomas Moser's analysis of Conrad's treatment of love is

[*] In *Conrad's Polish Background* (1964).

definitive, and the relevant section of his *Joseph Conrad: Achievement and Decline* (1957) is included in this Casebook.

Douglas Hewitt's *Conrad: A Reassessment* (1952) repeats the view of some of Conrad's contemporaries that the novel reflects his hatred of Russia, and that he is insufficiently detached. Hewitt believes Conrad is in general agreement with the narrator's judgements, and that whatever irony is directed against the fussy English teacher of languages is very mild. Tony Tanner takes a very different view. He argues that, as elsewhere in Conrad's fiction, the introduction of a narrator makes possible a challenging interplay of two frames of reference. Conrad, Tanner argues, is just as critical of the narrator's Western complacency as of the violence of the Russians. These contrasting viewpoints are exemplified in our selection.

Conrad's brilliant analysis of Razumov's psychology ends with the young man's decision to confess his crime to the woman he loves, Natalia, and to the revolutionaries. H. M. Daleski, in the study excerpted below, believes that this novel is even less political than *Nostromo*, and that its main concern is with Razumov's spiritual crisis. Razumov does not abandon himself to despair. He assumes responsibility for his crime, and by his confession liberates himself into a new state of true self-possession. By this symbolic act he overcomes that isolation so typical of Conradian heroes.

Yet Razumov lives on as a deaf man. His confession marks an attempt to achieve a new relation with the community, yet afterwards he can only exist as a cripple, ill, getting weaker every day, in a condition of withdrawal and impotence. Confession may heal his anguish, but only by a process that seems self-destructive. Is Daleski right to think of him as achieving true self-possession? As Tony Tanner says, Conrad's great fictions are intended to disturb his readers, to force them to go on asking questions.

## PART ONE

# Comments by Conrad and Contemporary Reviewers

# 1. COMMENTS ON *HEART OF DARKNESS*

*Heart of Darkness* first appeared in 1899 in *Blackwood's Magazine* ('Maga') in the February, March and April issues. William Blackwood had been editor for twenty years. On 30 December 1898 he wrote to Conrad: 'I am hoping to have the pleasure of seeing your hand in Maga again soon, and I should be specially pleased if you had anything on the stocks, or nearly ready, to send me for Maga's Thousandth number. . . .' Conrad replied the next day.

CONRAD to WILLIAM BLACKWOOD, 31 December 1898

Dear Mr Blackwood,

Come this moment to hand is your good letter whose kind wishes, believe me, I reciprocate with all my heart.

Your proposal delights me. As it happens I am (and have been for the last 10 days) working for Maga. The thing is far advanced and would have been finished by this only our little boy fell ill, I was disturbed and upset and the work suffered. I expect to be ready in a very few days. It is a narrative after the manner of *youth* [sic] told by the same man dealing with his experience on a river in Central Africa. The *idea* in it is not as obvious as in *youth* – or at least not so obviously presented. I tell you all this, for tho' I have no doubts as to the *workmanship* I do not know whether the *subject* will commend itself to you for that particular number. Of course I should be very glad to appear in it and shall try to hurry up the copy for that express purpose, but I wish you to understand that I am prepared to leave the ultimate decision as to the date of appearance to your decision after perusal.

The title I am thinking of is '*The Heart of Darkness*' but the narrative is not gloomy. The criminality of inefficiency and pure selfishness when tackling the civilising work on Africa is a justifiable idea. The subject is of our time distinctly – though not topically treated. It is a story as much as my [*An*] *Outpost of*

*Progress* was but, so to speak, 'takes in' more – is a little wider – is less concentrated upon individuals. I destine it for the vol: which is to bear your imprint. Its length will be under 20,000 words as I see it now. . . . [Source: William Blackburn (ed.), *Joseph Conrad: Letters to William Blackwood and David S. Meldrum*, Durham, N. Car. (1958), pp. 36–7.]

In fact, the final version of *Heart of Darkness* turned out to be just under 40,000 words. Blackwood's invitation encouraged Conrad to finish the story quickly, and the final draft was ready within a few weeks. Considering how difficult at times Conrad found literary composition, it is interesting that this story flowed so easily from his pen. After the February instalment appeared he received an enthusiastic letter from his friend R. B. Cunninghame Graham – traveller, socialist, Scottish laird, writer: one of the personalities of the time. Conrad replied gratefully, but with a word of caution.

CONRAD to CUNNINGHAME GRAHAM, 8 February 1899

Cherissime ami,

I am simply in the seventh heaven, to find you like the *H of D* so far. You bless me indeed. Mind you don't curse me by and bye for the very same thing. There are two more instalments in which the idea is so wrapped up in secondary notions that You – even You! – may miss it. And also you must remember that I don't start with an abstract notion. I start with definite images and as their rendering is true some little effect is produced. So far the note struck chimes in with your convictions – mais après? There is an après. But I think that if you look a little into the episodes you will find in them the right intention though I fear nothing that is practically effective. . . . [Source: C. T. Watts (ed.), *Joseph Conrad's Letters to R. B. Cunninghame Graham*, Cambridge (1969), p. 116.]

*Heart of Darkness* was published in book form in 1902, together with 'Youth' and 'The End of the Tether', in a volume called *Youth: A Narrative and Two Other Stories*. In the summer of 1900 he wrote to Cunninghame Graham about this collection. His comments here on his mental condition show how he was often on the verge of breakdown.

## CONRAD to CUNNINGHAME GRAHAM, 28 July 1900

. . . *Youth, Heart of darkness* [sic] and some story of the same kind which I shall write before long are to form a vol. of Tales which (unless forbidden) it is my intention to dedicate to You.

My brain reduced to the size of a pea seems to rattle about in my head. I can't rope in a complete thought; I am exhausted mentally and very depressed.

Pity I miss you. It would have done my heart good to see and hear you – the most alive man of the century.

I am awfully sickened by 'public affairs'. They made me positively ill in Feby last. Ten days in bed and six weeks of suspended animation. . . . [Source: ibid., p. 135.]

The early reviews of this collection of stories were encouraging, though several concentrated on 'Youth' and neglected *Heart of Darkness*. The most perceptive review was written by Edward Garnett, the influential critic and publisher's reader who, in 1895, had recommended publication of Conrad's first novel, *Almayer's Folly*.

## EDWARD GARNETT on *Heart of Darkness* (1902)

The publication in volume form of Mr Conrad's three stories, 'Youth', 'Heart of Darkness', 'The End of the Tether', is one of the events of the literary year. These stories are an achievement in art which will materially advance his growing reputation. Of the stories, 'Youth' may be styled a modern English epic of the Sea; 'The End of the Tether' is a study of an old sea captain who, at the end of forty years' trade exploration of the Southern seas, finding himself dispossessed by the perfected routine of the British empire overseas he has helped to build, falls on evil times, and faces ruin calmly, fighting to the last. These two will be more popular than the third, 'Heart of Darkness', a study of 'the white man in Africa' which is most amazing, a consummate piece of artistic *diablerie*. On reading 'Heart of Darkness' on its appearance in *Blackwood's Magazine* our first impression was that Mr Conrad had, here and there, lost his way. Now that the story can be read, not in parts, but from the first page to the last at a sitting, we retract this opinion and hold 'Heart of Darkness' to be the high-water mark of the author's talent. It may be well to analyse this story a little so that the intelligent reader, reading it very deliberately, may see better for himself why Mr Conrad's book enriches English literature.

'Heart of Darkness', to present its theme bluntly, is an impression, taken from the life, of the conquest by the European whites of a certain portion of Africa, an impression in particular of the civilising methods of a certain great European Trading Company face to face with the 'nigger'. We say this much because the English reader likes to know where he is going before he takes art seriously, and we add that he will find the human life, black and white, in 'Heart of Darkness' an uncommonly and uncannily serious affair. If the ordinary reader, however, insists on taking the subject of a tale very seriously, the artist takes his method of presentation more seriously still, and rightly so. For the art of 'Heart of Darkness' – as in every psychological masterpiece – lies in the relation of the things of the spirit to the things of the flesh, of the invisible life to the visible, of the subconscious life within us, our obscure motives and instincts, to our conscious actions, feelings and outlook. Just as landscape art implies the artist catching the exact relation of a tree to the earth from which it springs, and of the earth to the sky, so the art of 'Heart of Darkness' implies the catching of infinite shades of the white man's uneasy, disconcerted, and fantastic relations with the exploited barbarism of Africa; it implies the acutest analysis of the deterioration of the white man's *morale*, when he is let loose from European restraint, and planted down in the tropics as an 'emissary of light' armed to the teeth, to make trade profits out of the 'subject races'. The weirdness, the brilliance, the psychological truth of this masterly analysis of two Continents in conflict, of the abysmal gulf between the white man's system and the black man's comprehension of its results, is conveyed in a rapidly rushing narrative which calls for close attention on the reader's part. But the attention once surrendered, the pages of the narrative are as enthralling as the pages of Dostoevsky's *Crime and*

*Punishment.* The stillness of the sombre African forests, the glare of
sunshine, the feeling of dawn, of noon, of nights on the tropical
rivers, the isolation of the unnerved, degenerating whites staring
all day and every day at the Heart of Darkness which is alike
meaningless and threatening to their own creed and conceptions
of life, the helpless bewilderment of the unhappy savages in the
grasp of their flabby and rapacious conquerors – all this is a page
torn from the life of the Dark Continent: a page which has been
hitherto carefully blurred and kept away from European eyes.
There is no 'intention' in the story, no *parti pris*, no prejudice one
way or the other; it is simply a piece of art, fascinating and
remorseless, and the artist is but intent on presenting his
sensations in that sequence and arrangement whereby the
meaning or the meaninglessness of the white man in uncivilised
Africa can be felt in its really significant aspects. If the story is too
strong meat for the ordinary reader, let him turn to 'Youth',
wherein the song of every man's youth is indeed sung. . . .
[Source: review in *Academy and Literature*, 6 December 1902]

> The reviewer in the *Times Literary Supplement* preferred 'The
> End of the Tether', and was typical of many readers of the
> time in not appreciating the originality of its companion
> story with an African theme.

ANONYMOUS on *Heart of Darkness* (1902)

Telling tales, just spinning yarns, has gone out of fashion since the
novel has become an epitome of everything a man has to say
about anything. The three stories in *Youth* by Joseph Conrad are
in this reference a return to an earlier taste. The yarns are of the
sea, told with an astonishing zest; and given with vivid accumu-
lation of detail and iterative persistency of emphasis on the
quality of character and scenery. The method is exactly the
opposite of Mr Kipling's. It is a little precious; one notes a tasting
of the quality of phrases and an occasional indulgence in poetic
rhetoric. But the effect is not unlike Mr Kipling's. In the first
story, 'Youth', the colour, the atmosphere of the East is brought
out as in a picture. The concluding scene of the 'Heart of
Darkness' is crisp and brief enough for Flaubert, but the effect – a

woman's ecstatic belief in a villain's heroism – is reached by an indulgence in the picturesque horror of the villain, his work and his surroundings, which is pitiless in its insistence, and quite extravagant according to the canons of art. But the power, the success in conveying the impression vividly, without loss of energy, is undoubted and is refreshing. 'The End of the Tether', the last of the three, is the longest and best. Captain Whalley is racy of the sea, and an embodiment of its finest traditions; and the pathos of his long-drawn wrestle with the anger of circumstance is poignant to the end. Mr Conrad should have put him in the forefront of the book. There are many readers who would not get beyond the barren and not very pretty philosophy of 'Youth'; more who might feel they had had enough horror at the end of the 'Heart of Darkness'. But they would miss a great deal if they did not reach 'The End of the Tether'. It has this further advantage over the other two tales, that it is much less clever, much less precious. [Source: unsigned review in the *Times Literary Supplement*, 12 December 1902.]

Another comparatively hostile review came from a future Poet Laureate, then at the threshold of his literary career.

## JOHN MASEFIELD on *Heart of Darkness* (1903)

Mr Conrad's stories, excellent though they are, leave always a feeling of disappointment, almost of regret. His is a rare temperament, an exotic, a poetic temperament, and its artistic expression, though tense, nervous, and trembling with beauty, is always a little elusive, a little alien, of the quality of fine gum from Persia, or of precious silk from China.

In this volume Mr Conrad gives us three stories, and in each shows a notable advance upon the technique and matter of his former work. His manner, indeed, shows a tendency towards the 'precious', towards the making of fine phrases and polishing of perfect lines. He has filled his missal-marge with flowerets; he has planted his forest full of trees; till both prayer and forest are in some danger of being hid. In the story called 'Youth', and still more in the story called 'Heart of Darkness' (both of them stories written as told by one Marlow to a company of friends), he has set down page after page of stately and brilliant prose, which is fine writing, good literature, and so forth, but most unconvincing narrative. His narrative is not vigorous, direct, effective, like that of Mr Kipling. It is not clear and fresh like that of Stevenson, nor simple, delicate, and beautiful like that of Mr Yeats. It reminds one rather of a cobweb abounding in gold threads. It gives one a curious impression of remoteness and aloofness from its subject. Often it smells very palpably of the lamp, losing all spontaneity and becoming somewhat rhetorical. . . . [Source: review in the *Speaker*, 31 January 1903.]

Masefield's feeling that Conrad's narrative gives an impression of remoteness and aloofness from its subject was to be often repeated. The reasons for this apparent 'elusive' quality, as E. M. Forster called it in his *Abinger Harvest* (1936), have preoccupied much recent criticism.

# 2. COMMENTS ON *NOSTROMO*

*Nostromo* first appeared in T. P. O'Connor's periodical *T.P.'s Weekly* from 29 January to 7 October 1904. The book version, with considerable revisions, appeared on 14 October. During 1903, while he was writing the novel, Conrad was often in bad health. He had financial worries, and there is no doubt that he was once again suffering from considerable nervous strain.

CONRAD to CUNNINGHAME GRAHAM, 8 July 1903

... I am dying over that cursed *Nostromo* thing. All my memories of Central America seem to slip away. I just had a glimpse 25 years ago – a short glance. That is not enough pour bâtir un roman dessus. And yet one must live. . . . [Source: C. T. Watts (ed.), *Joseph Conrad's Letters to R. B. Cunninghame Graham*, op. cit., p. 145.]

Six weeks or so later he was complaining to a fellow novelist and friend that he felt a 'mental and moral outcast'.

CONRAD to JOHN GALSWORTHY, 22 August 1903

Dearest Jack,
The book is, this moment, half done and I feel half dead and wholly imbecile.
If you want to do your part by a man, for whom you have done so much already, then do not fail to come down here the first day you can spare.
To work in the conditions which are, I suppose, the outcome of my character mainly, is belittling – it is demoralising. I fight against demoralisation, of which fight I bear the brunt and my friends bear the cost. . . .
I didn't write to you because, upon my word, I am ashamed to

tell anybody. I feel myself strangely growing into a sort of outcast. A mental and moral outcast. I hear of nothing – I think of nothing – I reflect upon nothing – I cut myself of – and with all that I can just only keep going, or rather keep on lagging from one wretched story to another – and always deeper in the mire'. . . . [Source: G. Jean-Aubry, *Joseph Conrad: Life and Letters*, (London, 1927), I, 317.]

But a letter he sent on the same day to his literary agent reveals that Conrad knew how good Nostromo was going to be.

CONRAD to J. B. PINKER, 22 August 1903

. . . I have never worked so hard before – with so much anxiety. But the result is good. You know I take no credit to myself for what I do – and so I may judge my own performance. There is no mistake about this. You may take up a strong position when you offer it here. It is a very genuine Conrad. At the same time it is more of a Novel pure and simple than anything I've done since *Almayer's Folly*. . . . [Source: ibid., I, 316.]

In his autobiographical reminiscences, *A Personal Record*, he recalled the strain of those days.

CONRAD on 'the everlasting sombre stress'

. . . I was just then giving up some days of my allotted span to the last chapters of the novel *Nostromo*, a tale of an imaginary (but true) seaboard, which is still mentioned now and again, and indeed kindly, sometimes in connection with the word 'failure' and sometimes in conjunction with the word 'astonishing'. I have no opinion on this discrepancy. It's the sort of difference that can never be settled. All I know is that, for twenty months, neglecting the common joys of life that fall to the lot of the humblest on this earth, I had, like the prophet of old, 'wrestled with the Lord' for my creation, for the headlands of the coast, for the darkness of the Placid Gulf, the light on the snows, the clouds on the sky, and for the breath of life that had to be blown into the shapes of men and women, of Latin and Saxon, of Jew and Gentile. These are, perhaps, strong words, but it is difficult to characterise otherwise the intimacy and the strain of a creative effort in which mind and will and conscience are engaged to the full, hour after hour, day after day, away from the world, and to the exclusion of all that makes life really lovable and gentle – something for which a material parallel can only be found in the everlasting sombre stress of the westward winter passage round Cape Horn. . . . [Source: extract from Conrad's *A Personal Record* included in the Dent Collected Edition with *The Mirror of the Sea* (London, 1946), pp. 98–9. These recollections by Conrad were first published in 1912 with the title *Some Reminiscences*.]

> The reviews of *Nostromo* included much praise, but there was also adverse criticism, and Conrad was disappointed. He wrote to Pinker on 31 October 1904 that the book 'had a bad sendoff'. Like many subsequent readers, some contemporary reviewers found the narrative's dislocations difficult to follow.

ANONYMOUS on *Nostromo* (1904)

We have heard it urged by fairly intelligent judges against *Lord Jim*, which we consider Mr Conrad's finest novel, that its unwinding is intolerable. For ourselves it is more than tolerable, such is the fascination of Mr Conrad's conscientious method when applied to such a problem as Jim presented. But what shall we reply when the same critics impugn the unwinding of his new book, *Nostromo*, we dare not think; for its defence, even among Mr Conrad's most stalwart upholders, will not be easy. The fact is that in *Nostromo* Mr Conrad has definitely succumbed to a danger which must often have beset him – he has made a novel of a short story. When he began *Lord Jim*, we understand, he intended it to run through a number or so of *Blackwood* and come out the length of his 'Typhoon' or thereabouts; and behold it grew under his hands, became worthier and yet more worthy of the expenditure of his genius, until it stands now secure in its place as one of the finest (and longest) of our later novels. In *Nostromo* the very reverse has happened; Mr Conrad has written and written his five hundred pages, only to discover that it was in essence a short story after all. In the result the book is rather like one of those modern scenic plays where the drama is overwhelmed by machinery. We do not object to an author's finding his way by first losing it, or at any rate by first trying many others – probably it is the safest means – but we do object to being taken with him on the search. In other words, we think that the publication of this book as it stands is an artistic mistake. Let Mr Conrad write his way in as he will, but let us be called upon to join him only when he has found it. The first third of *Nostromo* should have been compressed into a few pages. The story – another of Mr Conrad's studies in self-respect – tells us how a Genoese sailor, a slave to the good opinion of others, in a South American port sinks to theft and his own contempt. The actual relation of Nostromo's tragedy, which occupies less than half of the book, is always strong and moving; Mr Conrad's hand there is sure, his sympathy lively. There is a scene, in his best manner, of three men at night on a lighter, in imminent peril of being run down by a steamer; a scene, in his best manner – a manner quite unique – of two men fencing intellectually by the dead body of a third; and in each of these scenes it is, we feel, the presence of Nostromo that nerves the author to do greatly. The book has other passages that are fine, but for the most part the narrative is allegation rather than proof – a long and not too absorbing history of revolutions and revolutionary motives, of plot and counter-plot. The drama of Nostromo, and his friends the Violas, is apart, although it is in reality the only matter. What we maintain is that a writer of Mr Conrad's genius, in order to introduce Nostromo's case, should not have to ask us to accompany him, backwards and forwards, through such a labyrinth of South American politics and into the careers of so many persons. Mr Conrad's retrospective habit has always been a little difficult to follow; but in *Nostromo* there are moments when it is impossible to feel sure whether the past or the present is being described. All this, which is at its worst in the first two hundred pages of the book, before the narrative really becomes single, ought, we think, to have been ruthlessly cut. Many readers will never survive it. Yet Mr Conrad is Mr Conrad, his mind is his own, and always curiously interesting. Hence *Nostromo*, although a shapeless work, is yet a shapeless work by a man of genius, satisfying only occasionally, but never undistinguished. Shapelessness is its only fault. The writing is always good, the character drawing is always subtle, and now and then the author gives us an unforgettable figure: the old Garibaldino [Viola], Nostromo himself, the dispirited and disillusioned Dr Monygham, and Martin Decoud of the Parisian boulevards, who would overthrow a State for the fun of it. But as a whole *Nostromo* is disappointing. It is not on a level with Mr Conrad's best work. [Source: unsigned review in *Times Literary Supplement*, 21 October 1904.]

A review by one of the younger generation of writers included some praise, but its reservations also stressed the difficulty of following the narrative.

## JOHN BUCHAN on *Nostromo* (1904)

Mr Conrad's new book shows in the highest relief the characteristic merits and defects of his work. He has a greater range of knowledge – subtle idiomatic knowledge – of the strange ways of the world than any contemporary writer. He has an imaginative force which at times can only be paralleled among the greatest; he has a profound sense of drama, and the logic of events which lesser people call fate; and he has a style which is often careless, involved, and harsh, but, like all true style, has moments of superb inspiration. On the other hand, he is burdened with the wealth of his equipment. A slender talent finds it easy to be lucid and orderly; but Mr Conrad, seeing his people before him with such tremendous clearness, and entering into their loves and hates with such gusto, does not know where to begin or to end their tale. His characters crowd upon him, demanding that each have his story told with the same patient realism, till the great motive is so overlaid with minor dramas that it loses much of its appeal. His books, in consequence, tend to be a series of brilliant episodes connected by a trickle of narrative, rather than romance with the stream of story running strongly to the close. And the misfortune is that the drama which is pushed into the background is nearly always of exceptional power, capable, were the rest only duly subordinated to it, of raising the work to the highest level of art. In the book before us the story, which gives the title to the whole, is of one Nostromo, an Italian sailor, who becomes Capataz de Cargadores in the service of a steamboat company at a port in a South American republic. He is the masterly egotist, the leader among his own class, trusted and used by his masters, happy in his second-rate greatness. But there come events which show, or seem to show, that he is a tool rather than a principal. His pride takes fire, he is all but in revolt, but his egotism comforts itself, and he does heroic work for his masters. And then somehow the story ebbs away. We see Nostromo an embryo revolutionary, spending himself in amours and a hurry to get rich, and killed at last by an accident. And the reason is that another and stronger drama comes athwart his. An Englishman and his wife have taken upon themselves the regeneration of the Republic of Costaguana by means of the silver industry which they control. The story of the regeneration, the revolution, and the creation of the Occidental Republic is the compelling interest of the book, and Nostromo comes in only as a handy *deus ex machina* in the greater story. The true story ends with the reminiscences of old Captain Mitchell, and the bitter reflection of Dr Monygham that some day it would have to be done all over again – the justification of the moral on the title-page: 'So foul a sky clears not without a storm.' The last two chapters belong to Nostromo's story alone, and are therefore irrelevant to the main drama; and a narrative which at times is profoundly moving and inspired with a kind of cosmic dignity ends bewilderingly with a mishap to a minor character. Either the politics of Sulaco should have been a mere background to Nostromo's tragedy, or his career should have been merely an episode in the story of the Republic. The separate interests are too potent to harmonise within one romance.

But though the construction of the book is topsy-turvy, beginning in the middle and finishing at the start, the story, considered even as narrative, is of surpassing interest. Mr Conrad has flung around his work the mystery of a cloud-covered sea and high remote mountains. All his characters, in spite of the close realism of his method, are invested with the glamour of romance. No one is perfunctorily treated; each is a living man or woman, adequately understood, drawn with firm, clean strokes. He has gone for many to the backways of life, but, strange as some are, the human blood of each is unmistakable. The most elaborate study is Nostromo, who misses being a masterpiece because of his habit of suddenly becoming a puppet in the development of another tale. But in the scene where he is adrift alone with Decoud and the treasure, in the fog, listening to the beat of the enemy's screws, there comes one of those intense moments of natural self-revelation which are the triumph of the psychologist. Mrs Gould is an exquisite figure, the good angel of a troubled time; and if any one desires proof of Mr Conrad's genius, let him turn to those wonderful scenes during the Revolution when she sees for the first time the defects of her husband's regenerating policy, and shuts her lips to accept the second-best. But the greatest achievements are in the minor personages: Decoud, the cynical and belated nationalist; Antonia; Hernandez, the brigand; the old Garibaldist Viola and his daughter; and the amazing crowd of schemers and swaggerers who play at politics in those Republics. We have said that every character is an adequate portrait. But Mr Conrad's achievement is still greater, for he has managed to make clear the strife of ideals in a sordid warfare, and to show the core of seriousness in mock-heroics. It is not a book which the casual reader will appreciate. The sequence of events has to be sought painfully through the mazes of irrelevancy with which the author tries to mislead us. But it is a book which will well repay those who gave it the close attention which it deserves. It shows signs of haste both in style and construction, and we trust that this may be the explanation of the main defects. It would be a thousand pities if an author who has few equals in talent should habitually spoil his work by an inability to do the pruning and selecting which his art demands. [Source: review in the *Spectator*, 19 November 1904.]

As usual, Edward Garnett wrote a perceptive review, but even he found the last two chapters, describing Nostromo's death, an unnecessary piece of melodrama.

EDWARD GARNETT on *Nostromo* (1904)

In *Nostromo* . . . Mr Conrad has achieved something which it is not in the power of any English contemporary novelist to touch. His genius, that rose to the consummate art of 'The Heart of

Darkness' and the beauty of 'Youth', has in *Nostromo* descended a step or two to a lower plane to weave [a] more orthodox, structured novel, with a plot and a *dénouement*. For we cannot disguise that the worst thing about the modern novel is the conventionalised plan of its structure. Happily, however, Mr Conrad's gifts have triumphed over the regular form prescribed for the public's consumption: *Nostromo* is not particularly orthodox in its structure, and the larger canvas Mr Conrad has chosen on this occasion gives him more elbow room to show the working unity and harmonious balance of his fascinating gifts.

We draw attention to the harmonious balance of the author's vision in *Nostromo*, for to speak frankly we did not expect that the creator of *Lord Jim* would have threaded the mazes of the situation exposed in *Nostromo* with such unerring and easy steps, or would have so clearly shaped the minor clues that lead us to the broad main issue. If we put aside the somewhat lengthy handling of the early history of the San Tomé silver mine and the abrupt and hurried final chapters that describe Nostromo's death, which are artistically too violent, there is scarcely a line in the book that is not essential to the development of this dramatic pageant of life in a South American state. For the book's theme is not, indeed, the life and death of the hero Nostromo, El Capataz de Cargadores, as Mr Conrad no doubt originally conceived it, nor is it the story of the vicissitudes of the great San Tomé silver mine and of the Europeans who develop it in Sulaco, as in Part I it threatens to become. Mr Conrad's artistic instinct has perhaps unconsciously led him to clear the reefs of these subsidiary issues, and has brought him and his readers safe into the open sea, whence they can look back at the Costaguanan coast, the placid waters of the Golfo Placido, and realise that his subject is the great mirage he has conjured up of the life and nature of the Costaguanan territory lying under the shadow of the mighty Cordilleras. . . .

The critic, pressed for an explanation of Mr Conrad's special power by which he accomplishes artistic feats beyond his rivals, may boldly declare that he has a special poetic sense for *the psychology of scene*, by which the human drama brought before us is seen in its just relation to the whole enveloping drama of Nature around, forming both the immediate environment and the distant background. In Mr Conrad's vision we may imagine

Nature as a ceaselessly-flowing infinite river of life, out of which the tiny atom of each man's individual life emerges into sight, stands out in the surrounding atmosphere, and is lost again in the infinite succession of the fresh waves of life into which it dissolves. The author's pre-eminence does not lie specifically in his psychological analysis of character, but in the delicate relation of his characters to the whole environment – to the whole mirage of life in which their figures are seen to move. Thus, the character drawings *per se* of Mrs Gould and Dr Monygham, Captain Mitchell and Old Viola, though admirable studies, cannot be called deeply original creations, but their human significance is very great if we consider them as figures which serve as arresting points by which we can focus the character of the national drama around them and so penetrate to the larger drama of Nature. Thus, while the psychology of certain characters, such as Charles Gould, Decoud, and Nostromo himself, is indeed not always clear and convincing, when we take the figure of Mrs Gould and analyse the effect made on us by the vision of her exquisite and gracious nature – moving 'with her candid eyes very wide open, her lips composed into a smile', amid the electric and sullen atmosphere of this South American town, weighed down by the ever-hanging menace of her husband's danger, ministering to all the world in turn seeking her ear, while conscious in secret that her husband, in his fanatical devotion to the interests of the San Tomé mine, has surrendered, merged, and lost sight of his love for her – if we consider the spirit of this woman we shall recognise how exquisitely just is the author's sense of perspective which has led him to place her so that, like a figure in a landscape, she serves as the gleam of light against the sombre and threatening horizon. And so against the devotion to duty of Giorgio Viola, the old Garibaldian hero, the Spanish-American revolutionary rabble of Sulaco shows up 'sullen, thievish, vindictive, and bloodthirsty'. And thus against the wooden-headed unimaginativeness of the Britisher, Captain Mitchell, the hard-headed idealism of Charles Gould, and the gloomy disillusionment of Dr Monygham, the whole racial genius of this captivating and gracious South American land, semi-barbarous, with its old-world, Spanish traditions and its 'note of passion and sorrow', stands forth triumphantly; and its atmosphere, which is, indeed, an artistic quintessence from both Central American and South American states, penetrates home to our European consciousness. And if this is so – and if in Mr Conrad's art the whole mirage of Nature be everything, and the series of flowing scenes in which are reflected the subtly shifting tides of human emotion and human passion – we shall see why it is that the artistic imperfections of some of his figures seem of curiously little importance. It is because with most writers the whole illusion of the scene is centred in their characters, but with Mr Conrad the central illusion is the whole mirage of Nature, in which the figures are, strictly speaking, the human accessories. Thus in the 'Heart of Darkness', that sinister presentment of the imbecility, the cruelty and rapacity of the white man in the Dark Continent, the effect is got by the tropical atmosphere of a savage environment dominating the white man's *morale*, and sapping him, body, mind and soul; thus in *Lord Jim*, Jim's actions and words and thoughts are not nearly so convincing in themselves as is the poetic conception of his figure placed by fate, and by the force of his one great *défaillance*, in the environment of the wanderer of the Eastern seas. It is not, indeed, essential to the author's spell over us that they should be. This great gift of Mr Conrad's – his special sense for the *psychology of scene*, that he shares with many of the great poets and the great artists who have developed it each on his own chosen lines – it is that marks him out for pre-eminence among the novelists. His method of poetic realism is, indeed, intimately akin to that of the great Russian novelists; but Mr Conrad, inferior in the psychology of character, has outstripped them in his magical power of creating the whole mirage of Nature. It is for this reason that we regret that the last two chapters describing Nostromo's death are included in the novel. Their touch of melodrama does violence to the evening stillness of the close. The narrative should have ended with the monologue of Captain Mitchell and the ironic commentary of Dr Monygham on the fresh disillusionment in store for the *régime* of 'Civilisation' planted by European hands on the bloodstained soil of the Republic of Costaguana. [Source: review in the *Speaker*, 12 November 1904.]

# 3. COMMENTS ON *UNDER WESTERN EYES*

Conrad in 1908 began a story which he at first called 'Razumov'. The final version of *Under Western Eyes* was completed by January 1910. Immediately afterwards he suffered a complete breakdown and was laid up for three months. Early in February his wife was writing hastily and in great anxiety to a London literary adviser.

JESSIE CONRAD to DAVID MELDRUM, 6 February 1910

. . . The novel is finished, but the penalaty [sic] has to be paid. Months of nervous strain have ended in a complete nervous breakdown. Poor Conrad is very ill and Dr Hackney says it will be a long time before he is fit for anything requiring mental exertion. I know both you and dear Mrs Meldrum will feel every sympathy with him. There is the MS complete but uncorrected and his fierce refusal to let even I touch it. It lays on a table at the foot of his bed and he lives mixed up in the scenes and holds converse with the characters.

I have been up with him night and day since Sunday week and he, who is usually so depressed by illness, maintains he is not ill, and accuses the Dr and I of trying to put him into an asylum. . . . [Source: Blackburn (ed.), *Letters to William Blackwood* etc., op. cit., p. 192.]

*Under Western Eyes* appeared in serial form in the *English Review* between December 1910 and October 1911, when the book version was published. The book was about 30,000 words shorter than the serial text, and Conrad wrote to Galsworthy that he had revised too recklessly, striking out passages he was too ill to reconsider. The reviews were again mixed, with emphasis this time on Conrad's foreignness. The *Athenaeum* reviewer (21 October 1911) said that 'the book reads like a translation from some other tongue'.

Edward Garnett, a sympathiser with Russian revolutionaries and exiles, accused Conrad in a letter of putting
hatred of Russia into the novel. Conrad replied by insisting
that he was 'concerned with nothing but ideas, to the
exclusion of everything else, with no arrière pensée of any
kind'. Garnett's actual review was characteristically
sensitive.

EDWARD GARNETT on *Under Western Eyes* (1911)

. . . It is in [the] scenes of Razumov's life and moral struggles in
Geneva that the irony of Mr Conrad's method gathers weight
and velocity, like a wheel set rolling down-hill. In Parts I and II
we see him skilfully arranging his chess board; in Part III the
drama of Razumov's 'moral revolt' coalesces with a corrosively
bitter etching of types of the revolutionary party, such as the
famous Feminist, Peter Ivanovitch; his companion, Madame de
S——; Laspara, the philosophic anarchist; the sinister Nikita,
slayer of gendarmes and spies, but himself another Azev; and so
on. This merciless picture, which is as formidable in its indict-
ment of the revolutionists' claims as the figures of Prince K——,
General T—— and Councillor Mikulin are destructive of the
Autocracy's pretensions, would seem vindictive art, had not the
author introduced into the group the admirable figure of Sophia
Antonovna, a woman Nihilist of the old school, who recalls the
heroines of the early 'eighties. Razumov, in his unwilling
intercourse with these chiefs of the circle, is ravaged by a whirling
anxiety of fear, contempt, hatred, malice, and self-loathing. It is
a psychological study of cynical pride sustaining the hollowness
of self-disillusionment, and throwing up volcanic, fresh defensive
waves of lava, that is offered to us in Razumov's portrait. The
study is very special, and to the English reader, who knows nought
of Dostoievsky, and is touchingly ignorant of his own soul's dark
places, may seem a nightmare of hallucination; but in fact,
within its narrow lines, it is illuminating in its pathological truth.
The artistic intensity of the novel lies, however, less in the
remarkable drawing of characteristic Russian types than in the
atmospheric effect of the dark national background. With almost
uncanny adroitness, Mr Conrad has both relieved and increased

the blackness of his picture by the rare, precious figure of Natalia Haldin. How he has managed to concentrate in a few 'impressions', conversations and confidences the essence, profoundly spiritual, of this exquisite type of Russian womanhood, is worth the closest examination; but he has attained a degree of fineness that is extraordinary. . . . [Source: review in the *Nation*, 21 October 1911.]

> Garnett later changed his mind, and came to think of Miss Haldin as the weakness in the book. A critic who later became a close friend of Conrad regretted that psychology was replacing romantic realism.

## RICHARD CURLE on *Under Western Eyes* (1911)

A new work by Mr Conrad is a literary event of the first importance. It is now three years since *A Set of Six* – that volume of stories which marked so distinct a change in his technique – was published, and one must not therefore be surprised to find that *Under Western Eyes* carries us still further on the fresh path. One need expect no longer, save in occasional sentences, the exuberant and monotonous vocabulary, that sea-like and sonorous ebb and flow. No; for that exotic style he has exchanged one very distinguished, it is true, very expressive, very artistic, but altogether less striking. It is the atmosphere which we miss (that impalpable thing which has no necessary relation to place), the atmosphere from which emerged people of an invincible reality, the atmosphere which gave us Jim, Mrs Gould and Winnie Verloc. It was in his tropical books especially that it became so enthralling. The strange glow which hung over the tropics hung over his figures as well; the languor of Southern nights which stole into his words stole into the hearts of his people. Everything seemed surrounded by a mysterious and patient force, amidst which life, dimly conscious of it all, went on increasingly with an ironical intensity of joy and suffering. An immense power appeared to brood over the vanities and struggles of men, an impassive and relentless purpose to await them at every step. The fleetingness of individual life, the disenchantment of desire, the passing away of hope, were contrasted with the stillness of the forest, the might of the ocean, the teeming prodigality of the earth. Such is the kind of atmosphere of novels like *Lord Jim* and *Nostromo*, of stories like 'Heart of Darkness', 'Youth', 'An Outpost of Progress' and 'The End of the Tether'. It was a romantic idealism, colouring life with an extraordinary vividness. And such is not the atmosphere of *Under Western Eyes*. It is not simply that it is a novel of Europe instead of the tropics, for the typical Conrad atmosphere can be seen in European tales such as 'The Return', 'To-morrow' and *The Secret Agent*. It is something much more. *Under Western Eyes* is the work of a great writer for whom psychology is swallowing romance, of a great artist for whom form is becoming more and more impersonal, of a great creator whose creations are beginning to lack energy. The sentences are perfectly modulated, the whole style is exact and finished, but there is something lacking which used not to be lacking. There are probably in this book a greater mastery of the detail of language, a nearer approach to complete avoidance of exaggeration, than in any of his books, but there is less of original genius. It is curiously as if he had been trying to model himself on Henry James, and in the effort had lost part of his own personality. . . . [Source: review in the *Manchester Guardian*, 11 October 1911.]

> Ford Madox Hueffer, who had collaborated with Conrad in the writing of two novels (and who subsequently changed his name to Ford Madox Ford), wrote provocatively about the alien qualities of Conrad's concept of honour.

FORD MADOX HUEFFER on *Under Western Eyes* (1912)

. . . If you consider the case of the sham escape of Razumov from the police you will see very plainly what I mean. Razumov is in league with – or let us say he is under the obsession of – the Russian secret police. He has to gain the confidence of the revolutionaries, so, to add a touch of verisimilitude, as it were, to advertise his escape, he goes to a madcap boy and announces his desire to borrow money in order to pay the expenses of escape. The boy has no money; he must rob his father in order to find it. This he does. He comes to Razumov with the money:

Razumov nodded from the couch, and contemplated the hare-brained fellow's gravity with a feeling of malicious pleasure.

'I've made my little sacrifice', sighed mad Kostia, 'and I've to thank you, Kirylo Sidorovitch, for the opportunity.'

'It has cost you something?'

'Yes, it has. You see the dear old buffer really loves me. He'll be hurt.'

'And you believe, all they tell you of the new future, and the sacred will of the people?'

'Implicitly! I would give my life. . . . Only you see, I am like a pig at a trough. I am no good. It's my nature.

Razumov, lost in thought, had forgotten his existence till the youth's voice, entreating him to fly without loss of time, roused him unpleasantly.

'All right. Well – good-bye.'

That is just all that Razumov had to say. He had forgotten the youth's existence, though he had made the boy rob his father in order to advertise his escape to the revolutionaries.

When dawn broke, Razumov, very still in a hot, stuffy railway car . . . rose quietly, lowered the glass a few inches, and flung out on the great plain of snow a small brown paper parcel.

It was the stolen money. He was too disdainfully honourable a man to use stolen money. He could not have done it.

And this same unimaginative cruelty of a man blindly pursuing his lost honour dignifies Razumov to the end. It pursues him into the room and into the presence of the sister of the man he betrayed to death – the woman with the trusting eyes who loves him, and whom he loves. He tells her with the fewest possible words: ' "It ends here – on this very spot." He pressed a denunciatory finger to his breast with force and became perfectly still.'

You observe those are the fewest possible words in which he could tell her that he was the traitor. Razumov is so set upon regaining his lost honour that even for the sake of the woman with the trusting eyes he cannot take the trouble to prepare her for the revelation he has to make. Then he goes to the revolutionaries in council, denounces himself to them as a police spy, receives his terrible punishment, and his soul is at peace.

It is here that Conrad differentiates himself from the

Elizabethans, for they could never have worked themselves up to the pitch of subtlety. They could, as it were, have conceived a Judas, and even the remorse of such an Iscariot. They had very certainly the conception of an avenging providence. But they could not prize honour quite so high. For here is the comment of the wise woman revolutionist on the case of Razumov:

'There are evil moments in every life. A false suggestion enters one's brain and then fear is born – fear of oneself, fear for oneself. Or else a false courage – who knows? Well, call it what you like; but tell me how many of them would deliver themselves deliberately up to perdition (as he himself says in that book) rather than go on living, secretly debased in his own eyes? How many? . . . And please mark this – he was safe when he did it. It was just when he believed himself safe and more – infinitely more – when the possibility of being loved by that admirable girl first dawned upon him, that he discovered that his bitterest railings, the devil work of his hate and pride, could never cover up the ignominy of the existence before him. There's character in such a discovery.'

Of course this labouring of, this preoccupation with, the idea of the point of honour is very foreign – so foreign that it has obviously come to this author with his foreign blood. It is a thing wholly individualistic and wholly of the aristocrat. And that is what the Poles are – aristocrats and individualists; that is why their land is harried and held down in this age of limited companies and democracy. . . . [Source: review in the *English Review*, December 1911–March 1912.]

An unsigned review showed that Conrad's considerable achievements were recognised by many discerning readers, even if they could not forget his Polish origins.

ANONYMOUS on *Under Western Eyes* (1911)

Keen and merciless in exposure and meticulously searching in analysis, *Under Western Eyes* is a psychologic study of remarkable penetration, and, as a novel, is entitled to rank with the best work that Mr Joseph Conrad has given us. We are revolted by Razumov's betrayal of his fellow-student (though Haldin's crime merited the swift and degrading execution that was its punishment), for Haldin had sought refuge in Razumov's rooms and had confessed to his crime under the conviction that his host was, like himself, a Nihilist. But by subtle strokes of art our sympathy – that is, at least, 'a sympathy of comprehension', to use De Quincey's striking phrase as applied to *Macbeth* – and perhaps something more, is enlisted with the betrayer. Except that by a quite arbitrary, and, it must be added, inartistic skipping of certain stages of his spiritual development and an equally arbitrary return to them, the narrative does not follow the sequence of events, we trace the various phases of his soul's disturbance from mere rage at being suspected by the police, through a tardy but ever-growing remorse, till, purified by love, he repents, and with high courage makes full confession to an inner circle of conspirators, to suffer at their cruel hands a punishment, horrible, brutal, and infinitely worse than death.

The book startles one by its amazing truth and by the intimate knowledge of the human heart that it reveals in its varied and masterly characterisation. Although, too, he still confuses the preterite with the perfect and often uses the wrong sign of the future, Mr Conrad's remarkable gifts as a writer of nervous and polished prose are as noteworthy here as always. Quite a masterpiece of writing, for instance, amid much that is excellent is the account of a convict's escape in Siberia. The muffled clanking of his chains, a sound he deadened with strips torn from his clothing lest it should betray his presence, is almost as unforgettable as the tapping of blind Pew's stick. [Source: unsigned review in the *Pall Mall Gazette*, 11 October 1911.]

*Under Western Eyes* did not solve Conrad's financial problems. Only with the publication of *Chance* in 1913 did he achieve a really popular success.

# PART TWO

# Modern Studies on Individual Novels

# I HEART OF DARKNESS

## Albert J. Guerard (1958)  The Journey Within

. . . *Heart of Darkness* is the most famous of these personal short novels [Guerard has been discussing *The Shadow Line* and *The Secret Sharer* – Ed.]: a *Pilgrim's Progress* for our pessimistic and psychologising age. 'Before the Congo I was just a mere animal.'[1] The living nightmare of 1890 seems to have affected Conrad quite as importantly as did Gide's Congo experience thirty years later. The autobiographical basis of the narrative is well known, and its introspective bias obvious; this is Conrad's journey into self. But it is well to remember that *Heart of Darkness* is also other if more superficial things: a sensitive and vivid travelogue, and a comment on 'the vilest scramble for loot that ever disfigured the history of human conscience and geographical exploration'.[2] The Congo was much in the public mind in 1889, when Henry Stanley's relief expedition found Emin Pasha (who like Kurtz did not want to be rescued), and it is interesting to note that Conrad was in Brussels during or immediately after Stanley's triumphant welcome there in April 1890.[3] This was just before he set out on his own Congo journey. We do not know how much the Georges Antoine Klein who died on board the *Roi des Belges* resembled the fictional Kurtz, but Stanley himself provided no mean example of a man who could gloss over the extermination of savages with pious moralisms which were very possibly 'sincere'.

*Heart of Darkness* thus has its important public side, as an angry document on absurd and brutal exploitation. Marlow is treated to the spectacle of a French man-of-war shelling an unseen 'enemy' village in the bush, and presently he will wander into the grove at the first company station where the starving and sick Negroes withdraw to die. It is one of the greatest of Conrad's many moments of compassionate rendering. The compassion extends even to the cannibal crew of the *Roi des Belges*. Deprived

of the rotten hippo meat they had brought along for food, and
paid three nine-inch pieces of brass wire a week, they appear to
subsist on 'lumps of some stuff like half-cooked dough, of a dirty
lavender colour' which they keep wrapped in leaves. Conrad
here operates through ambiguous suggestion (are the lumps
human flesh?) but elsewhere he wants, like Gide after him, to
make his complacent European reader *see*: see, for instance, the
drunken unkempt official met on the road and three miles farther
on the body of the Negro with a bullet hole in his forehead.[4] *Heart
of Darkness* is a record of things seen and done. But also Conrad
was reacting to the humanitarian pretences of some of the looters
precisely as the novelist today reacts to the moralisms of cold-war
propaganda. Then it was ivory that poured from the heart of
darkness; now it is uranium. Conrad shrewdly recognised – an
intuition amply developed in *Nostromo* – that deception is most
sinister when it becomes self-deception, and the propagandist
takes seriously his own fictions. Kurtz 'could get himself to
believe anything – anything'. The benevolent rhetoric of his
seventeen-page report for the International Society for the
Suppression of Savage Customs was meant sincerely enough. But
a deeper sincerity spoke through his scrawled postscript:
'Exterminate all the brutes!' The conservative Conrad (who
found Donkin fit to be a labour leader) speaks through the
journalist who says that 'Kurtz's proper sphere ought to have
been politics "on the popular side" '.

Conrad, again like many novelists today, was both drawn to
idealism and repelled by its hypocritical abuse. 'The conquest of
the earth, which mostly means the taking it away from those who
have a different complexion or slightly flatter noses than
ourselves, is not a pretty thing when you look into it too much.
What redeems it is the idea only. An idea at the back of it; not a
sentimental pretence but an idea; and an unselfish belief in the
idea . . . ' Marlow commits himself to the yet unseen agent
partly because Kurtz 'had come out equipped with moral ideas
of some sort'. Anything would seem preferable to the demoralised
greed and total cynicism of the others, 'the flabby devil' of the
Central Station. Later, when he discovers what has happened to
Kurtz's moral ideas, he remains faithful to the 'nightmare of my
choice'. In *Under Western Eyes* Sophia Antonovna makes a
distinction between those who burn and those who rot, and

remarks that it is sometimes preferable to burn. The Kurtz who had made himself literally one of the devils of the land, and who in solitude had kicked himself loose of the earth, burns while the others rot. Through violent not flabby evil he exists in the moral universe even before pronouncing judgement on himself with his dying breath. A little too much has been made, I think, of the redemptive value of those two words – 'The horror!' But none of the company 'pilgrims' could have uttered them.

The redemptive view is Catholic, of course, though no priest was in attendance; Kurtz can repent as the gunman of *The Power and the Glory* cannot. *Heart of Darkness* (still at this public and wholly conscious level) combines a Victorian ethic and late Victorian fear of the white man's deterioration with a distinctly Catholic psychology. We are protected from ourselves by society with its laws and its watchful neighbours, Marlow observes. And we are protected by work. 'You wonder I didn't go ashore for a howl and a dance? Well, no – I didn't. Fine sentiments, you say? Fine sentiments, be hanged! I had no time. I had to mess about with white-lead and strips of woollen blanket helping to put bandages on those leaky steam-pipes.' But when the external restraints of society and work are removed, we must meet the challenge and temptation of savage reversion with our 'own inborn strength. Principles won't do.' This inborn strength appears to include restraint – the restraint that Kurtz lacked and the cannibal crew of the *Roi des Belges* surprisingly possessed. The hollow man, whose evil is the evil of *vacancy*, succumbs. And in their different degrees the pilgrims and Kurtz share this hollowness. 'Perhaps there was nothing within' the manager of the Central Station. 'Such a suspicion made one pause – for out there there were no external checks.' And there was nothing inside the brick-maker, that papier-maché Mephistopheles, 'but a little loose dirt, maybe'.

As for Kurtz, the wilderness 'echoed loudly within him because he was hollow at the core'. Perhaps the chief contradiction of *Heart of Darkness* is that it suggests and dramatises evil as an active energy (Kurtz and his unspeakable lusts) but defines evil as vacancy. The primitive (and here the contradiction is only verbal) is compact of passion and apathy. 'I was struck by the fire of his eyes and the composed languor of his expression. . . . This shadow looked satiated and calm, as

though for the moment it had had its fill of all the emotions.' Of
the two menaces – the unspeakable desires and the apathy –
apathy surely seemed the greater to Conrad. Hence we cannot
quite believe the response of Marlow's heart to the beating of the
tom-toms. This is, I think, the story's minor but central flaw, and
the source of an unfruitful ambiguity: that it slightly overdoes the
kinship with the 'passionate uproar', slightly undervalues the
temptation of inertia.

In any event, it is time to recognise that the story is not
primarily about Kurtz or about the brutality of Belgian officials
but about Marlow its narrator. To what extent it also expresses
the Joseph Conrad a biographer might conceivably recover, who
in 1898 still felt a debt must be paid for his Congo journey and
who paid it by the writing of this story, is doubtless an insoluble
question. I suspect two facts (of a possible several hundred) are
important. First, that going to the Congo was the enactment of a
childhood wish associated with the disapproved childhood
ambition to go to sea, and that this belated enactment was itself
profoundly disapproved, in 1890, by the uncle and guardian.[5] It
was another gesture of a man bent on throwing his life away. But
even more important may be the guilt of complicity, just such a
guilt as many novelists of the Second World War have been
obliged to work off. What Conrad thought of the expedition of
the Katanga Company of 1890–1892 is accurately reflected in his
remarks on the 'Eldorado Exploring Expedition' of *Heart of
Darkness*: 'It was reckless without hardihood, greedy without
audacity, and cruel without courage . . . with no more moral
purpose at the back of it than there is in burglars breaking into a
safe.' Yet Conrad hoped to obtain command of the expedition's
ship even after he had returned from the initiatory voyage
dramatised in his novel. Thus the adventurous Conrad and
Conrad the moralist may have experienced collision. But the
collision, again as with so many novelists of the Second War,
could well have been deferred and retrospective, not felt
intensely at the time.

So much for the elusive Conrad of the biographers and of the
'Congo Diary'. Substantially and in its central emphasis *Heart of
Darkness* concerns Marlow (projection to whatever great or small
degree of a more irrecoverable Conrad) and his journey toward
and through certain facets or potentialities of self. F. R. Leavis

seems to regard him as a narrator only providing a 'specific and concretely realised point of view'.[6] But Marlow reiterates often enough that he is recounting a spiritual voyage of self-discovery. He remarks casually but crucially that he did not know himself before setting out, and that he likes work for the chance it provides to 'find yourself . . . what no other man can ever know'. The Inner Station 'was the farthest point of navigation and the culminating point of my experience'. At a material and rather superficial level, the journey is through the temptation of atavism. It is a record of 'remote kinship' with the 'wild and passionate uproar', of a 'trace of a response' to it, of a final rejection of the 'fascination of the abomination'. And why should there not be the trace of a response? 'The mind of man is capable of anything – because everything is in it, all the past as well as all the future'. Marlow's temptation is made concrete through his exposure to Kurtz, a white man and sometime idealist who had fully responded to the wilderness: a potential and fallen self. 'I had turned to the wilderness really, not to Mr Kurtz'. At the climax Marlow follows Kurtz ashore, confounds the beat of the drum with the beating of his heart, goes through the ordeal of looking into Kurtz's 'mad soul', and brings him back to the ship. He returns to Europe a changed and more knowing man. Ordinary people are now 'intruders whose knowledge of life was to me an irritating pretence, because I felt so sure they could not possibly know the things I knew'.

On this literal plane, and when the events are so abstracted from the dream-sensation conveying them, it is hard to take Marlow's plight very seriously. Will he, the busy captain and moralising narrator, also revert to savagery, go ashore for a howl and a dance, indulge unspeakable lusts? The late Victorian reader (and possibly Conrad himself) could take this more seriously than we; could literally believe not merely in a Kurtz's deterioration through months of solitude but also in the sudden reversions to the 'beast' of naturalistic fiction. In so far as Conrad does want us to take it seriously and literally, we must admit the nominal triumph of a currently accepted but false psychology over his own truer intuitions. But the triumph is only nominal. For the personal narrative is unmistakably authentic, which means that it explores something truer, more fundamental, and distinctly less material: the night journey into the unconscious,

and confrontation of an entity within the self. 'I flung one shoe
overboard, and became aware that that was exactly what I had
been looking forward to – a talk with Kurtz'. It little matters
what, in terms of psychological symbolism, we call this double or
say he represents: whether the Freudian id or the Jungian shadow
or more vaguely the outlaw. And I am afraid it is impossible to
say where Conrad's conscious understanding of his story began
and ended. The important thing is that the introspective plunge
and powerful dream seem true; and are therefore inevitably
moving.

Certain circumstances of Marlow's voyage, looked at in these
terms, take on a new importance. The true night journey can
occur (except during analysis) only in sleep or in the waking
dream of a profoundly intuitive mind. Marlow insists more than
is necessary on the dreamlike quality of his narrative. 'It seems to
me I am trying to tell you a dream – making a vain attempt,
because no relation of a dream can convey the dream-sensation,
that commingling of absurdity, surprise, and bewilderment in a
tremor of struggling revolt . . . ' Even before leaving Brussels
Marlow felt as though he 'were about to set off for the centre of
the earth', not the centre of a continent.[7] The introspective
voyager leaves his familiar rational world, is 'cut off from the
comprehension' of his surroundings; his steamer toils 'along
slowly on the edge of a black and incomprehensible frenzy'. As
the crisis approaches, the dreamer and his ship move through a
silence that 'seemed unnatural, like a state of trance'; then enter
(a few miles below the Inner Station) a deep fog. 'The approach
to this Kurtz grubbing for ivory in the wretched bush was beset
by as many dangers as though he had been an enchanted
princess sleeping in a fabulous castle.'[8] Later, Marlow's task is to
try 'to break the spell' of the wilderness that holds ' Kurtz
entranced.

The approach to the unconscious and primitive may be aided
by a savage or half-savage guide, and may require the token
removal of civilised trappings or aids; both conceptions are
beautifully dramatised in Faulkner's 'The Bear'. In *Heart of
Darkness* the token 'relinquishment' and the death of the half-
savage guide are connected. The helmsman falling at Marlow's
feet casts blood on his shoes, which he is 'morbidly anxious' to
change and in fact throws overboard.[9] (The rescue of Wait in *The*

*Nigger of the 'Narcissus'* shows a similar pattern.) Here we have presumably entered an area of unconscious creation; the dream is true but the teller may have no idea why it is. So too, possibly, a psychic need as well as literary tact compelled Conrad to defer the meeting between Marlow and Kurtz for some three thousand words after announcing that it took place. We think we are about to meet Kurtz at last. But instead Marlow leaps ahead to his meeting with the 'Intended'; comments on Kurtz's megalomania and assumption of his place among the devils of the land; reports on the seventeen-page pamphlet; relates his meeting and conversation with Kurtz's harlequin disciple – and only then tells of seeing through his binoculars the heads on the stakes surrounding Kurtz's house. This is the 'evasive' Conrad in full play, deferring what we most want to know and see; perhaps compelled to defer climax in this way. The tactic is dramatically effective, though possibly carried to excess: we are told on the authority of completed knowledge certain things we would have found hard to believe had they been presented through a slow consecutive realistic discovery. But also it can be argued that it was psychologically impossible for Marlow to go at once to Kurtz's house with the others. The double must be brought on board the ship, and the first confrontation must occur there. We are reminded of Leggatt in the narrator's cabin, of the trapped Wait on the *Narcissus*. The incorporation and alliance between the two becomes material, and the identification of 'selves'.

Hence the shock Marlow experiences when he discovers that Kurtz's cabin is empty and his secret sharer gone; a part of himself has vanished. 'What made this emotion so overpowering was – how shall I define it? – the moral shock I received, as if something altogether monstrous, intolerable to thought and odious to the soul, had been thrust upon me unexpectedly.' And now he must risk the ultimate confrontation in a true solitude and must do so on shore. 'I was anxious to deal with this shadow by myself alone – and to this day I don't know why I was so jealous of sharing with anyone the peculiar blackness of that experience.' He follows the crawling Kurtz through the grass; comes upon him 'long, pale, indistinct, like a vapour exhaled by the earth.' ('I had cut him off cleverly . . .') We are told very little of what Kurtz said in the moments that follow; and little of his incoherent discourses after he is brought back to the ship. 'His was an impenetrable darkness. I looked at him as you peer down at a man who is lying at the bottom of a precipice where the sun never shines' – a comment less vague and rhetorical, in terms of psychic geography, than it may seem at a first reading. And then Kurtz is dead, taken off the ship, his body buried in a 'muddy hole'. With the confrontation over, Marlow must still emerge from environing darkness, and does so through that other deep fog of sickness. The identification is not yet completely broken. 'And it is not my own extremity I remember best – a vision of grayness without form filled with physical pain, and a careless contempt for the evanescence of all things – even of this pain itself. No! It is his extremity that I seem to have lived through.' Only in the atonement of his lie to Kurtz's 'Intended', back in the sepulchral city, does the experience come truly to an end. 'I laid the ghost of his gifts at last with a lie . . .'

Such seems to be the content of the dream. If my summary has even a partial validity it should explain and to an extent justify some of the 'adjectival and worse than supererogatory insistence' to which F. R. Leavis (who sees only the travelogue and the portrait of Kurtz) objects. I am willing to grant that the unspeakable rites and unspeakable secrets become wearisome, but the fact – at once literary and psychological – is that they must remain *unspoken*. A confrontation with such a double and facet of the unconscious cannot be reported through realistic dialogue; the conversations must remain as shadowy as the narrator's conversations with Leggatt. So too when Marlow finds it hard to define the moral shock he received on seeing the empty cabin, or when he says he doesn't know why he was jealous of sharing his experience, I think we can take him literally . . . and in a sense even be thankful for his uncertainty. The greater tautness and economy of *The Secret Sharer* comes from its larger conscious awareness of the psychological process it describes; from its more deliberate use of the double as symbol. And of the two stories I happen to prefer it. But it may be the groping, fumbling *Heart of Darkness* takes us into a deeper region of the mind. If the story is not about this deeper region, and not about Marlow himself, its length is quite indefensible. But even if one were to allow that the final section is about Kurtz (which I think simply absurd), a vivid pictorial record of his unspeakable lusts and gratifications would surely have been ludicrous. I share Mr

Leavis's admiration for the heads on the stakes. But not even Kurtz could have supported many such particulars.[10]

'I listened on the watch for the sentence, for the word, that would give me the clue to the faint uneasiness inspired by this narrative that seemed to shape itself without human lips in the heavy night air of the river.' Thus one of Marlow's listeners, the original 'I' who frames the story, comments on its initial effect. He has dicovered how alert one must be to the ebb and flow of Marlow's narrative, and here warns the reader. But there is no single word; not even the word *trance* will do. For the shifting play of thought and feeling and image and event is very intricate. It is not vivid detail alone, the heads on stakes or the bloody shoes; nor only the dark mass of moralising abstraction; nor the dramatised psychological intuitions apart from their context that give *Heart of Darkness* its brooding weight. The impressionist method – one cannot leave this story without subscribing to the obvious – finds here one of its great triumphs of tone. The random movement of the nightmare is also the controlled movement of a poem, in which a quality of feeling may be stated or suggested and only much later justified. But it is justified at last.

The method is in important ways different from that of *Lord Jim*, though the short novel was written during an interval in the long one, and though Marlow speaks to us in both. For we do not have here the radical obfuscations and sudden wrenchings and violent chronological ambiguities of *Lord Jim*. Nor are we, as in *Nostromo*, at the mercy of a wayward flashlight moving rapidly in a cluttered room. *Heart of Darkness* is no such true example of spatial form. Instead the narrative advances and withdraws as in a succession of long dark waves borne by an incoming tide. The waves encroach fairly evenly on the shore, and presently a few more feet of sand have been won. But an occasional wave thrusts up unexpectedly, much farther than the others: even as far, say, as Kurtz and his Inner Station. Or, to take the other figure: the flashlight is held firmly; there are no whimsical jerkings from side to side. But now and then it is raised higher, and for a brief moment in a sudden clear light we discern enigmatic matters to be explored much later. Thus the movement of the story is sinuously progressive, with much incremental repetition. The

intent is not to subject the reader to multiple strains and
ambiguities, but rather to throw over him a brooding gloom,
such a warm pall as those two Fates in the home office might knit,
back in the sepulchral city.

Yet no figure can convey *Heart of Darkness* in all its resonance
and tenebrous atmosphere. The movement is not one of penetration and withdrawal only; it is also the tracing of a large grand
circle of awareness. It begins with the friends on the yacht under
the dark above Gravesend and at last returns to them, to the
tranquil waterway that 'leading to the uttermost ends of the earth
flowed sombre under an overcast sky – seemed to lead into the
heart of an immense darkness'. For this also 'has been one of the
dark places of the earth', and Marlow employs from the first his
methods of reflexive reference and casual foreshadowing. The
Romans were men enough to face this darkness of the Thames
running between savage shores. 'Here and there a military camp
lost in a wilderness, like a needle in a bundle of hay – cold, fog,
tempests, disease, exile, and death – death skulking in the air, in
the water, in the bush.' But these Romans were 'no colonists', no
more than the pilgrims of the Congo nineteen hundred years
later; 'their administration was merely a squeeze'. Thus early
Marlow establishes certain political values. The French gunboat
firing into a continent anticipates the blind firing of the pilgrims
into the jungle when the ship has been attacked. And Marlow
hears of Kurtz's first attempt to emerge from the wilderness long
before he meets Kurtz in the flesh, and wrestles with his
reluctance to leave. Marlow returns again and again, with
increasing irony, to Kurtz's benevolent pamphlet.

The travelogue as travelogue is not to be ignored; and one of
Roger Casement's consular successors in the Congo (to whom I
introduced *Heart of Darkness* in 1957) remarked at once that
Conrad certainly had a 'feel for the country'. The demoralisation
of the first company station is rendered by a boiler 'wallowing in
the grass', by a railway truck with its wheels in the air. Presently
Marlow will discover a scar in the hillside into which drainage
pipes for the settlement had been tumbled; then will walk into the
grove where the Negroes are free to die in a 'greenish gloom'. The
sharply visualised particulars suddenly intrude on the sombre
intellectual flow of Marlow's meditation: magnified, arresting.
The boilermaker who 'had to crawl in the mud under the bottom

of the steamboat . . . would tie up that beard of his in a kind of white serviette he brought for the purpose. It had loops to go over his ears.' The papier-maché Mephistopheles is as vivid, with his delicate hooked nose and glittering mica eyes. So too is Kurtz's harlequin companion and admirer, humbly dissociating himself from the master's lusts and gratifications. 'I! I! I am a simple man. I have no great thoughts.' And even Kurtz, shadow and symbol though he be, the man of eloquence who in this story is almost voiceless, and necessarily so – even Kurtz is sharply visualised, an 'animated image of death', a skull and body emerging as from a winding sheet, 'the cage of his ribs all astir, the bones of his arm waving'.

This is Africa and its flabby inhabitants; Conrad did indeed have a 'feel for the country'. Yet the dark tonalities and final brooding impression derive as much from rhythm and rhetoric as from such visual details: derive from the high aloof ironies and from a prose that itself advances and recedes in waves. 'This initiated wraith from the back of Nowhere honoured me with its amazing confidence before it vanished altogether.' Or, 'It is strange how I accepted this unforseen partnership, this choice of nightmares forced upon me in the tenebrous land invaded by these mean and greedy phantoms.' These are true Conradian rhythms, but they are also rhythms of thought. The immediate present can be rendered with great compactness and drama: the ship staggering within ten feet of the bank at the time of the attack, and Marlow's sudden glimpse of a face amongst the leaves, then of the bush 'swarming with human limbs'. But still more immediate and personal, it may be, are the meditative passages evoking vast tracts of time, and the 'first of men taking possession of an accursed inheritance'. The prose is varied, far more so than is usual in the early work, both in rhythm and in the movements from the general to the particular and back. But the shaped sentence collecting and fully expending its breath appears to be the norm. Some of the best passages begin and end with them:

Going up that river was like travelling back to the earliest beginnings of the world, when vegetation rioted on the earth and the big trees were kings. An empty stream, a great silence, an impenetrable forest. The air was warm, thick, heavy, sluggish. There was no joy in the brilliance of sunshine. The long stretches of the waterway ran on, deserted, into the gloom of overshadowed distances. On silvery sandbanks hippos and alligators sunned themselves side by side.

The insistence on darkness, finally, and quite apart from ethical or mythical overtone, seems a right one for this extremely personal statement. There is a darkness of passivity, paralysis, immobilisation; it is from the state of entranced languor rather than from the monstrous desires that the double Kurtz, this shadow, must be saved. In Freudian theory, we are told, such preoccupation may indicate fear of the feminine and passive. But may it not also be connected, through one of the spirit's multiple disguises, with a radical fear of death, that other darkness? 'I had turned to the wilderness really, not to Mr Kurtz, who, I was ready to admit, was as good as buried. And for a moment it seemed to me as if I also were buried in a vast grave full of unspeakable secrets. I felt an intolerable weight oppressing my breast, the smell of the damp earth, the unseen presence of victorious corruption, the darkness of an impenetrable night.'

It would be folly to try to limit the menace of vegetation in the restless life of Conradian image and symbol. But the passage reminds us again of the story's reflexive references, and its images of deathly immobilisation in grass. Most striking are the black shadows dying in the greenish gloom of the grove at the first station. But grass sprouts between the stones of the European city, a 'whited sepulchre', and on the same page Marlow anticipates coming upon the remains of his predecessor: 'the grass growing through his ribs was tall enough to hide his bones'. The critical meeting with Kurtz occurs on a trail through the grass. Is there not perhaps an intense horror behind the casualness with which Marlow reports his discoveries, say of the Negro with the bullet in his forehead? Or: 'Now and then a carrier dead in harness, at rest in the long grass near the path, with an empty water gourd and his long staff lying by his side.'

All this, one must acknowledge, does not make up an ordinary light travelogue. There is no little irony in the letter of 9 November 1891 which Conrad received from his guardian after returning from the Congo, and while physically disabled and seriously depressed: 'I am sure that with your melancholy temperament you ought to avoid all meditations which lead to pessimistic conclusions. I advise you to lead a more active life than ever and to cultivate cheerful habits.'[11] Uneven in language on certain pages, and lacking *The Secret Sharer*'s economy, *Heart of Darkness* nevertheless remains one of the great dark meditations in literature, and one of the purest expressions of a melancholy temperament.

*Heart of Darkness* and *The Secret Sharer* are both stories of insecure and morally isolated men who meet and commit themselves to men even more isolated. The most important moments of these intimate relationships could not be reported successfully: those whispered conversations with Leggatt in the narrator's cabin, Marlow's conversations with Kurtz at the edge of the jungle and on board the *Roi des Belges*. On the final level of psychological symbolism, communication is with a deepest self; a symbolic descent into the unconscious results in immobilisation and is followed by partial or full release. The double is exorcised, either to die or go free. But in the material terms of a relationship between flesh-and-blood men, these conversations are also important. Through them an act of communication has occurred, creating a bond of brotherhood and loyalty. In *Heart of Darkness* psychic needs most of all determine the loyalty to the 'nightmare' of Marlow's choice, but in *The Secret Sharer* we have both loyalty to the outcast double within the self and loyalty to the flesh-and-blood outsider: 'a free man, a proud swimmer striking out for a new destiny'. The success or failure of such attempted communications between individuals (and the ensuing acts of loyalty or betrayal) is the subject and central preoccupation of Conrad's greatest books, most obviously of *Lord Jim* and *Under Western Eyes*. But failure to communicate is more frequent than success, and men are driven back to their crippling solitude and normal human condition: to 'the tremendous fact of our isolation, of the loneliness impenetrable and transparent, elusive and everlasting; of the indestructible loneliness that surrounds, envelops, clothes every human soul from the cradle to the grave, and, perhaps, beyond'.[12]

SOURCE: extract from *Conrad the Novelist* (Cambridge, Mass., and London, 1958), pp. 33–48.

NOTES

[These have been reorganised from reference-notes and footnotes in the
original, with some abbreviations and deletions, and combined into a
single system of numbered items. – Ed.]

1. G.Jean–Aubry, *Life and Letters*, I, 141, and *The Sea Dreamer*, p. 175.
Reportedly said to Edward Garnett. In his *Joseph Conrad in the Congo*
(London, 1926), p. 73, Jean–Aubry gives a slightly different wording:
'Before the Congo I was only a simple animal.'

2. *Last Essays*, p. 17. In *Heart of Darkness* Conrad makes once his usual
distinction between British imperialism and the imperialism of other
nations. On the map in Brussels there 'was a vast amount of red – good
to see at any time, because one knows that some real work is done
in there.' His 1899 letters to E. L. Sanderson and to Mme Angèle
Zagorska on the Boer War express his position clearly. The conspiracy
to oust the Briton 'is ready to be hatched in other regions. It . . . is
everlastingly skulking in the Far East. A war there or anywhere but in S.
Africa would have been conclusive – would have been worth the
sacrifice' (Jean–Aubry, *Life and Letters*, I, 286). 'That they – the Boers –
are struggling in good faith for their independence cannot be doubted;
but it is also a fact that they have no idea of liberty, which can only be
found under the English flag all over the world' (ibid., I, 288).

3. Ibid., I, 121, 124; *The Sea Dreamer*, pp. 154–9.

4. Cf. 'The Congo Diary', *Last Essays*, p. 163. Conrad did not use the
skeleton tied to a post that he saw on Tuesday 29 July (p. 169). It might
have seemed too blatant or too 'literary' in a novel depending on
mortuary imagery from beginning to end.

5. *Life and Letters*, I, 137; *The Sea Dreamer*, p. 171.

6. F. R. Leavis, *The Great Tradition* (London, 1948), p. 183.

7. Lilian Feder finds a number of parallels with the sixth book of the
*Aeneid* in 'Marlow's Descent into Hell', *Nineteenth-Century Fiction*, IX
(March 1955), 280–92. Robert O. Evans finds chiefly the influence of
Dante's *Inferno* in 'Conrad's Underworld', *Modern Fiction Studies*, II
(May 1956), 56–62. My own views on literary influence differ from
those of Miss Feder and Mr Evans; but echoes and overtones may exist.
We may apply to *Heart of Darkness* Thomas Mann's word's on *Death in
Venice*: a little work of 'inexhaustible allusiveness'.

8. The analogy of unspeakable Kurtz and enchanted princess may
well be an intended irony; but there may be some significance in the fact
that here the double is imagined as an entranced feminine figure.

9. Like any obscure human act, this one invites several interpretations, beginning with the simple washing away of guilt. The fear of the

blood may be, however, a fear of the primitive toward which Marlow is moving. To throw the shoes overboard would then mean a token rejection of the savage, not the civilised-rational. In any event it seems plausible to have blood at this stage of a true initiation story.

10. The reader irritated by the hallucinated atmosphere and subjective preoccupation of *Heart of Darkness* should turn to R. L. Stevenson's short novel, *The Beach of Falesá* (1892). . . . [In which a new trader, Wiltshire, is worsted by Case, a long-established trader whose power over the natives is in great part due to the awe and fear aroused by the array of 'ju-ju' type figures outside his house. – Ed.] Had Conrad read *The Beach of Falesá* before writing the *Heart of Darkness?* The question is unimportant. The important thing is to recognise the immense distance from Case's carved figures to the skulls on Kurtz's palisade; from Case's pretended traffic with devils with Kurtz's role as one of the devils of the land; from Wiltshire's canny outwitting of a rival trader to Marlow's dark inward journey; from the inert jungle of Stevenson's South Pacific to the charged symbolic jungle of Conrad's Congo. . . . *The Beach of Falesá* is a good manly yarn totally bereft of psychological intuition.

11. *Life and Letters*, I, 148. *The Sea Dreamer*, p. 193, offers a slightly different translation of these lines.

12. Quoted from *An Outcast of the Islands*.

# *Lionel Trilling* (1965)    'Kurtz, Hero of the Spirit'

. . . Whether or not Joseph Conrad read either Blake or Nietzsche I do not know, but his *Heart of Darkness* follows in their line. This very great work has never lacked for the admiration it deserves, and it has been given a kind of canonical place in the legend of modern literature by Eliot's having it so clearly in mind when he wrote *The Waste Land* and his having taken from it the epigraph to 'The Hollow Men'. But no one, to my knowledge, has ever confronted in an explicit way its strange and terrible message of ambivalence toward the life of civilisation. Consider that its protagonist, Kurtz, is a progressive and a liberal and that he is the highly respected representative of a society which would have us believe it is benign, although in fact it is vicious. Consider too that he is a practitioner of several arts, a painter, a writer, a musician, and into the bargain a political orator. He is at once the most idealistic and the most practically successful of all the agents of the Belgian exploitation of the Congo. Everybody knows the truth about him which Marlow discovers – that Kurtz's success is the result of a terrible ascendancy he has gained over the natives of his distant station, an ascendancy which is derived from his presumed magical or divine powers, that he has exercised his rule with an extreme of cruelty, that he has given himself to unnamable acts of lust. This is the world of the darker pages of *The Golden Bough*. It is one of the great points of Conrad's story that Marlow speaks of the primitive life of the jungle not as being noble or charming or even free but as being base and sordid – and for *that* reason compelling: he himself feels quite overtly its dreadful attraction. It is to this devilish baseness that Kurtz has yielded himself, and yet Marlow, although he does indeed treat him with hostile irony, does not find it possible to suppose that Kurtz is anything but a hero of the spirit. For me it is still ambiguous whether Kurtz's famous deathbed cry, 'The horror! The horror!' refers to the approach of death or to his experience of savage life. Whichever it is, to Marlow the fact that Kurtz could utter this cry at the point of death, while Marlow himself, when death threatens him, can know it only as a weary grayness, marks the difference between the ordinary man and a hero of the spirit. Is this not the essence of the modern belief about the nature of the artist, the man who goes down into that hell which is the historical beginning of the human soul, a beginning not outgrown but established in humanity as we know it now, preferring the reality of this hell to the bland lies of the civilisation that has overlaid it?

SOURCE: extract from *Beyond Culture* (New York, 1965; London, 1966), pp. 19–32.

# *James Guetti* The Failure of the Imagination (1965)

*Heart of Darkness* is apparently an account of one man's moral and psychological degeneration and of another's spatial and intellectual journey to understand the essentials of the matter. A reader expects that such a story will follow certain rules: the journey will be difficult, but at its end will be a meaningful disclosure in which the 'degeneration' will be placed in a moral framework. I shall try to show in this discussion, however, that *Heart of Darkness* may be seen to deny, particularly, the relevance of such a moral framework and to question, generally, the possibilities of meaning for the journey itself – that as the narrative develops it is redefined so as to deny the basic assumptions upon which it appears to be constructed.

One of the two possible assertions of the title is this: the 'darkness' has a 'heart'; a reader penetrates the unknown and partially known to the known. Marlow suggests throughout the story that at the center of things there is meaning and that he is pursuing this meaning. And yet the intensity of Marlow's inquiries serves to emphasise the inconclusiveness of his findings. Again and again he seems about to declare the truth about Kurtz and the darkness, but his utterance most often takes the form of either a thunderous contradiction in terms or a hushed and introspective ambiguity. In this manner we are left with the second and dominant assertion of the title in particular and *Heart of Darkness* in general: it is the 'heart', above all, that is composed of 'darkness', there that the real darkness lies, and our progress must be through the apparently or partially known to the unknown.

The paradox implied in the title is nowhere more obvious than at what is usually taken to be the center of the story: Kurtz's death-bed cry, 'The horror! The horror!' These words seem a response to the most private nightmare, to the unknown itself, but Marlow insists that they are quite the reverse: a 'moment of complete knowledge'. He asserts that 'the horror' has to do not only with Kurtz's unspeakable history, but also with the world at large, 'wide enough to embrace the whole universe, piercing enough to penetrate all the hearts that beat in the darkness'. In attempting to resolve this apparent contradiction, we may inquire into what can be known of Kurtz's history.

He was, once, an idealist of a kind, a member of the 'new gang of virtue' of the trading company; according to Marlow, a man who apparently 'had come out equipped with moral ideas of some sort'. A complication of this view of Kurtz as a moral man is presented near the end of the story by a sometime journalist colleague: 'He electrified large meetings. He had faith – don't you see? – he had the faith.' From the journalist's account to this point, a reader might be inclined to accept the possible but over-simple view of Kurtz as a clear case of moral degeneration; the man once possessed 'the faith', which a reader may infer to be some high-minded and unambiguous creed, and then, in Africa, lost 'the faith'. Kurtz would have fallen, in these terms, within the framework of a traditional moral scheme, from a 'heaven' to a 'hell'. But as the journalist continues, his description turns upon itself:

' . . . the faith. He could get himself to believe anything – anything. He would have been a splendid leader of an extreme party.' 'What party?' I asked. 'Any party', answered the other. 'He was an – an – extremist.' Did I not think so? I assented.'                                        [p. 154][1]

Kurtz is characterised as a man who possessed all faiths, or any faith. Marlow, like a reader, momentarily does not understand this and asks, 'What party?' – implying that he too conceives 'the faith' as a single moral ideal to which Kurtz dedicated himself. But then the matter becomes clearer; 'the faith' is some quality or ability that enabled Kurtz to believe in any creed whatsoever. With this assessment Marlow agrees.

The problem of the connection between Kurtz's eloquent and unscrupulous moral facility and Kurtz himself – his essential being – concerns Marlow more than any other. On the last stage of the voyage up the river to the Inner Station, with the blood of his 'second-rate helmsman' in his shoes, he reflects this concern in a feeling of disappointment, as though the man he is seeking were 'something altogether without a substance'. Marlow imagines

Kurtz not 'as doing, you know, but as discoursing'; it is Kurtz's voice alone that is the man's 'real presence', 'his ability to talk, his words'. Even after the actual physical shock of Kurtz's appearance and, finally, of his death, Marlow insists: 'The voice was gone. What else had been there? But I am of course aware that next day the pilgrims buried something in a muddy hole'. The pilgrims buried an anonymous 'something', as if Kurtz's reality were completely detached from Kurtz as defined by his voice.

This separation between Kurtz's speech and Kurtz's unvoiced self is often described in relation to his 'degeneration'. As Marlow contemplates the human heads upon posts near Kurtz's station, he remarks:

> They only showed that Mr Kurtz lacked restraint in the gratification of his various lusts, that there was something wanting in him – some small matter which, when the pressing need arose, could not be found under his magnificent eloquence. [p. 131]

The 'whisper' of the wilderness 'echoed loudly within him because he was hollow at the core'. It is thus suggested that Kurtz found himself in a world which – in comparison to civilisation, with its externally imposed restraints of law, social morality, and public opinion – was a world of enticing and dangerous possibilities, where a man must depend upon his 'own innate strength', his 'power of devotion . . . to an obscure, back-breaking business'. Kurtz had no such devotion; his capacity for arbitrary eloquence and belief left him 'hollow at the core'. 'The faith', we may now suppose, was Kurtz's faith in himself, not as a moral being, but as a being who could use or discard morality: Kurtz lived as if what was most essential about him were wholly separate from what he professed to believe. But this, Marlow insists, is not simply hypocrisy:

> . . . . I had to deal with a being to whom I could not appeal in the name of anything high or low. I had, even like the niggers, to invoke him – himself – his own exalted and incredible degradation. There was nothing either above or below him, and I knew it. He had kicked himself loose of the earth. Confound the man! he had kicked the very earth to pieces. [p. 144]

Kurtz's 'degradation' is not the traditional result of a moral failure; it is 'exalted and incredible', perhaps god-like; it is the effect of his setting himself apart from the earth and the morality of the earth – apart, even, from the language of the earth with which he had such magnificent facility.

What Kurtz has done has general consequences. He has detached himself from the moral world, but in doing so he has, at least for Marlow, destroyed that world. Not simply has he 'kicked himself loose of the earth', but 'kicked the very earth to pieces'. Kurtz's personal amorality has public ramifications, and Marlow is shaken; he declares – looking ahead to Kurtz's 'The horror!' – that 'no eloquence could have been so withering to one's belief in mankind as his final burst of sincerity'. 'Belief in mankind', I think, implies the moral nature of mankind, the very business in which Kurtz could be so adept, and in releasing himself from this general morality, Kurtz has illustrated not only the possibility of such a release but also, as Marlow suggests, the possible inadequacy and irrelevance of morality to all men. Kurtz's 'failure' thus becomes his achievement, and if it remains partially a failure, the adequacy of morality in general is nonetheless questioned.

This problem, in part, is a familiar one to readers of Conrad. The imaginative, moral man enters a world of danger and enticement; he struggles, alone, to retain his morality. Often he fails. But in *Heart of Darkness* the matter is more complicated, for here the possible moralities, the means of restraint, may be seen to be less available – as alternatives, unreal. I have attempted to show something of the manner in which morality may be seen to fail Kurtz in *Heart of Darkness*; what follows is an account of the failure of morality in more pervasive terms.

Throughout the story a reader is confronted with various kinds of 'restraint' that are clearly unsatisfactory. The chief accountant 'accomplishes something' with his fastidious dress, for example, and the manager masks his envious and continual deceit with a hypocritical concern for saying and doing the 'right thing'. The most obvious case of this false kind of discipline is Marlow's native helmsman; he

. . . thought all the world of himself. He was the most unstable kind of fool I had ever seen. He steered with no end of a swagger while you were by; but if he lost sight of you, he became instantly the prey of an abject funk, and would let that cripple of a steamboat get the upper hand of him in a minute [p. 109]

In addition to these pseudo-moralities, there are men for whom restraint is unnecessary:

. . . . you may be too much of fool to go wrong – too dull even to know you are being assaulted by the powers of darkness. . . . Or you may be such a thunderingly exalted creature as to be altogether deaf and blind to anything but heavenly sights and sounds. [pp. 116–17]

None of these responses to the wilderness is possible for Marlow, nor, to Marlow's mind, for Kurtz. Both are men to whom the simpler falsehoods of appearance as morality do not appeal, and each, of course, possesses sufficient imagination to render him dangerously vulnerable to the 'darkness'.

Marlow declares that in confronting the wilderness, the 'truth' of it, a man must

. . . meet that truth with his own true stuff – with his own inborn strength. Principles won't do. Acquisitions, clothes, pretty rags – rags that would fly off at the first good shake. No; you want a deliberate belief. [p. 97]

At this point Marlow's conception of restraint sounds fine indeed. He continues, asserting that when the wilderness appealed to him – as it must to every man – he had a 'voice' of his own. Immediately following his testimonial to his own 'voice', however, he admits that what prevented him from going 'ashore for a howl and a dance' was only that he was too busy keeping his steamboat in one piece: 'I had to mess about with white-lead . . . watch the steering, and circumvent those snags. . . . There was surface-truth enough in these things to save a wiser man.' Marlow's idea, as the kind of 'truth' that a man may use to defend himself against the 'truth' of the wilderness, is only a practical concern; it is founded upon keeping oneself busy, upon attending to matters of the surface.

Marlow says at one moment [p. 85] that it is in 'work' that a man may 'find' himself, his own 'reality'; later, however, he appears to contradict himself, and remarks:

When you have to attend to things of that sort, to the mere incidents of the surface, the reality – the reality, I tell you – fades. The inner truth is hidden – luckily, luckily. But I felt it all the same. . . .          [p. 93]

As these quotations indicate, Marlow uses the term 'reality' in two ways: the primary reality is the suggested essence of the wilderness, the darkness that must remain hidden if a man is to survive morally, while the secondary reality is a figurative reality like work, an artificial reality by which the truly real is concealed or even replaced. And Marlow admits that this reality of the second sort is simply a deluding activity, a fictitious play over the surface of things.

Marlow's account of his own restraint as a fiction reflects his nature as a 'wanderer'; he is as morally rootless, perhaps, as Kurtz himself. In speaking of the 'droll thing life is', Marlow describes his difficulties in a way that is suggestive in terms of Kurtz's experience:

I have wrestled with death. It is the most unexciting contest you can imagine. It takes place in an impalpable grayness, with nothing underfoot, with nothing around, without spectators, without clamour, without glory, without the great desire of victory, without the great fear of defeat, in a sickly atmosphere of tepid scepticism, without much belief in your own right, and still less in that of your adversary. If such is the form of ultimate wisdom, then life is a greater riddle than some of us think it to be.          [p. 150–1]

Marlow suggests that at certain moments – in struggling with death or, perhaps, with a wilderness – it is most difficult for a man to see any reality in a connection between moral 'rights' and his experience; a man's most severe challenges are necessarily encountered in an 'atmosphere of tepid scepticism'. When Marlow himself struggles to keep the steamer afloat, struggles for his life, he replaces his own 'tepid scepticism' with work; he is forced to do so by his physical danger. Kurtz's situation has by no means been so simple. Like Marlow, he had no dominating or saving 'idea', but neither did he have Marlow's physical danger with its consequent activity – the work that luckily hides the reality.

In this manner Kurtz appears even more vulnerable that Marlow. For him the 'tepid scepticism' was more intense; he viewed the disparity between his moral fictions and an amoral reality more starkly. Why he necessarily did so, I have considered only in part, but if we are to rely at all upon Marlow's insistence that Kurtz's experience corresponds to his own, then we may conclude for the moment that Kurtz's act of 'kicking himself loose of the earth' was caused by his inability to save himself with fictions; when Kurtz's vision – the vision which Marlow assumes to be so similar to his own – destroyed the truth of morality and restraint, it also destroyed their availability.

It is on this account that Marlow refuses to condemn Kurtz in a moral way. The manager of the company remarks that Kurtz's 'method' is 'unsound', but Marlow denies this, asserting that it is 'no method at all'. The manager conceives that Kurtz *was* once a 'remarkable man' when his method was sound, perhaps, but that since then he has gone wrong. Talk of 'sound' or 'unsound' is irrelevant for Marlow, however, and Kurtz *is* a 'remarkable man' exactly because he has escaped the world of sound and unsound, because he has shown that these terms are inadequate as a measure of his experience. Kurtz's crime or achievement, then, is not that he has managed things badly for the company or, more generally, that he has sinned in a uniquely horrifying way, but that by means of an act of vision he has cut himself off from the possibility of sin. At the moment of this conversation with the manager, Marlow formally declares his sympathy with Kurtz.

Throughout *Heart of Darkness*, again, it is not simply the codes of the minor characters that are shown to be ignoble, nor is it only Marlow's code that is proved a tenuous fiction. Discipline in general is defined in the story not only as restraint, but also as a singleness of idea or intention – in contrast, of course, to something like Kurtz's multiple faith or to the infinite possibilities of the wilderness. This kind of spiritual rigidity is the important quality of the book which Marlow finds on his way to the Inner Station – *An Inquiry into some Points of Seamanship*:

Not a very enthralling book; but at the first glance you could see there a singleness of intention, an honest concern for the right way of going to work. . . . The simple old sailor, with his talk of chains and purchases, made me forget the jungle and the pilgrims in a delicious sensation of having come upon something unmistakably real. [p. 99]

The 'reality' of the book, its single-minded concern with work, is clearly the artificial or secondary reality that I have remarked, but it is more interesting to note here that when such reality seems possible, it seems so only in terms that are anomalous in the wilderness. It is apparent that this book is totally out of place in the jungle, that despite Marlow's desperate grasp on the book as a symbol of moral reality, this reality is rendered false and unreal by means of the very quality by which he declares it established: its irrelevance to the wilderness surrounding it.

In a similar manner, the wilderness may be seen elsewhere to deny singleness of purpose or its equivalents, restraint and morality. As Marlow proceeds down the coast at the beginning of his journey, he encounters a French gun-boat firing into the jungle:

There wasn't even a shed there, and she was shelling the bush. It appears the French had one of their wars going on thereabouts. Her ensign dropped limp like a rag; the muzzles of the long six-inch guns stuck out all over the low hull; the greasy, slimy swell swung her up lazily and let her down, swaying her thin masts. In the empty immensity of earth, sky, and water, there she was, incomprehensible, firing into a continent. Pop, would go one of the six-inch guns; a small flame would dart and vanish, a little white smoke would disappear, a tiny projectile would give a feeble screech – and nothing happened. Nothing could happen.                                                            [pp. 61–2]

War, with its polarities of life and death, victory and defeat, enemy and enemy, may be seen generally as a straightforward matter. Guns, too, are traditionally and rigidly purposeful, and when they are fired something ought to happen. Here nothing happens: the guns 'pop'; the projectiles are 'feeble'; there is no enemy and no effect. In a parallel description, explosives are used at the first station to remove a cliff: 'The cliff was not in the way or anything; but this objectless blasting was all the work going on.' The blasting is not only 'objectless', but also without result, for 'no change appeared on the face of the rock'. A moment later Marlow sees six natives – 'criminals' – in chains, hears another explosion, and then synthesises these phenomena with his recollection of the gun-boat:

Another report from the cliff made me think suddenly of that ship of war I had seen firing into a continent. It was the same kind of ominous voice;

but these men could by no stretch of imagination be called enemies. They were called criminals, and the outraged law, like the bursting shells, had come to them, an insoluble mystery from the sea.  [p. 64]

The law – with its apparent, straightforward purpose – like the shells and the blasting has been negated; it has become a mystery, incomprehensible, and has no effect as law, but merely renders the savages indifferent and unhappy. Here the law, the blasting, and the warfare, then, are characterised as having no disciplined purpose or effect, and the disparity between these devices of civilisation and the wilderness which they attempt corresponds to the disparity between morality and the wilderness described previously. The scope of this disparity between human schemes and the wilderness is ever widening.

It has been remarked here that Marlow's own capacity for restraint in Africa depends upon his busy thoughtlessness; and he has said that this restraint reflects a concern only with the incidents of the surface, as opposed to the 'reality'. The narrator who begins *Heart of Darkness* defines Marlow's manner of story-telling in a way that is puzzling, yet clearly analogous to Marlow's own characterisations of his moral attitude:

The yarns of seamen have a direct simplicity, the whole meaning of which lies within the shell of a cracked nut. But Marlow was not typical . . . and to him the meaning of an episode was not inside like a kernel but outside, enveloping the tale which brought it out only as a glow brings out a haze, in the likeness of one of these misty halos that sometimes are made visible by the spectral illumination of moonshine.
[p. 48]

In *Heart of Darkness* we observe Marlow moving along the coast of the wilderness or over the surface of the river, and here we encounter the idea of his language moving over the outside of an 'episode', surrounding the episode but never penetrating it. Marlow's attempts at meaning in general, then, take the same form as his attempts at morality in particular. Both meaning and morality are seen to be matters of the surface or exterior, while the reality – not Marlow's artificial reality but the reality beyond surfaces – is something deep within, something at the center that is not approached. There is an important difference, however, between Marlow's moral attitudes and his more generally meaningful attitudes: in the first instance he continually suggests that it would be imprudent to look beneath the surface; in the second he just as frequently admits that it is impossible to do so.

The emphasis of the passage quoted above is affirmative; the narrator implies that the search for meaning can be satisfied, somehow, in a concern with the exterior. And yet the very structure of *Heart of Darkness* – with the journey to the Inner Station, toward the man who constitutes the end of the search, and, certainly, toward some meaning in terms of the pervasive metaphor of 'meaning at the heart' – seems to assert that there is a more significant reality within; the fact of the search for Kurtz and for some disclosure of meaning implies that matters of the surface are not enough.

Previously I have suggested that Kurtz remained a voice for Marlow, even after Marlow had confronted him at the Inner Station, and that, even upon Kurtz's death, Marlow evidences his uncertainty as to whether there was ever anything else to the man but a voice, admitting only that the pilgrims buried 'something'. This attitude toward Kurtz – and it is never modified – implies a failure by Marlow, for although he struggles into the heart of darkness, declares his sympathetic allegiance to Kurtz, watches the man die, and journeys out again, he ends where he began. Marlow remarks his failure more than once:

. . . arguing with myself whether or no I would talk openly with Kurtz; but before I could come to any conclusion it occurred to me that my speech or my silence, indeed any action of mine, would be a mere futility. . . . The essentials of this affair lay deep under the surface, beyond my reach, and beyond my power of meddling.          [p. 100]

Marlow's attitude toward the reality of the wilderness remains as bemused as his idea of the meaning of Kurtz's experience. Although he constantly suggests that at the center of the wilderness lies 'the amazing reality of its concealed life', and although he often asserts that he is penetrating 'deeper and deeper into the heart of darkness', in his insistence upon the vague and the paradoxical the 'purpose' of the wilderness remains always 'inscrutable'. It escapes definition except in terms of its awesome, passive magnitude: ' . . . the silent wilderness surrounding this cleared speck on the earth struck me as something great and invincible, like evil or truth'. Marlow is no nearer a central reality at the geographical heart of the darkness than he was when, proceeding down the coast, he was aware of a 'general sense of vague and oppressive wonder'.

It thus seems generally impossible to move beyond the surface in any meaningful way. Reality in this story exists not in the positive but in the negative, for it is all that human disciplines cannot reach, all that lies beyond these disciplines within the center of a man, of a wilderness, and, as Marlow implies, of experience itself. Language too, like all other resources of the human imagination, fails in attempting to discover the meaning of Kurtz and of experience:

> He was just a word for me. I did not see the man in the name any more than you do. Do you see him? Do you see the story? Do you see anything? . . . No, it is impossible; it is imposible to convey the life-sensation of any given epoch of one's existence – that which makes its truth, its meaning – its subtle and penetrating essence. It is impossible. We live, as we dream – alone. . . .                              [p. 82]

Kurtz was a word and remained a word, even when he and Marlow were face to face: attempts to discover a meaning beyond the word failed. And Marlow is not speaking only of Kurtz. He begins with his inability to convey some meaning in terms of Kurtz in Africa, but he continues, characteristically, with the insistence that this inability is universal, that by focussing on Kurtz's particular 'aloneness' or remoteness from the world of meanings there is revealed a general condition of human experience.

Language has meaning, in *Heart of Darkness*, in terms of the exteriors of experience – the coast of a wilderness, the surface of a river, a man's appearance and his voice – and this meaning can exist as a reality so long as one remains ignorant, deliberately or otherwise, of all that lies beyond these exteriors, of what language cannot penetrate. For with the intimation that there is something beyond the verbal and, indeed, the intellectual capacities, comes the realisation that language is fiction. And if we desire to discover a reality greater than that of words, we are confronted not with the truth within, but with the real disparity between the

gimmickry of the human mind and this truth. Because Marlow
wishes to know more than surfaces, the reality of surfaces is
destroyed. His knowledge of reality may now exist only as his
knowledge of the unbridgeable separation between the world of
man's disciplined imagination and that something or nothing to
which this world is assumed to relate.

Thus, whereas Marlow uses the term 'reality' in two ways, the
reality which he – and a reader – discovers is of a third sort. It is a
reality which exists in the realisation that 'surface' and 'heart' are
inevitably separate matters, and that mind can have ordered
awareness only of the former. Marlow's final reality is a state of
suspension between the disciplined world of mind and language
and the world of essences at the center of experience – whatever
these may be – which mind attempts to apprehend but cannot, a
dream-state of suggestions and futilities. Marlow is finally aware
of both sorts of 'reality', certain of neither.

It is for these reasons that Marlow does not view Kurtz's last
utterance only as a cry of selfish despair, but declares that Kurtz
had 'summed up'. And as a summation of the literary experience
of *Heart of Darkness*, 'The horror!' can have but one meaning: all
hearts are in darkness; the morality and meaning with which
man surrounds himself and his experience is unreal; the reality of
experience lies beyond language and the processes of the human
imagination.[2] In revealing this knowledge to Marlow, Kurtz has
taken a step that Marlow would not take explicitly: ' . . . he had
made that last stride, he had stepped over the edge, while I had
been permitted to draw back my hesitating foot'. Because he has
relinquished his hold upon his ideals and his eloquence, because
he has wholly detached himself from matters of the surface, Kurtz
is able at last to define that about which Marlow himself – in his
preoccupation with both the reality of the surface and the reality
of the 'heart' – has been so reluctant and so ambiguous. Marlow
is torn, throughout the story, between the desire to achieve a
realisation as final as Kurtz's and the conviction that he must
deny such a realisation if his life is to have meaning. Kurtz is
destroyed in his movement toward and final confrontation of
what Marlow views as the ultimate truth: that the essentials of
experience remain amoral and, even, alinguistic.

*Heart of Darkness*, then, as the account of a journey into the
center of things – of Africa, of Kurtz, of Marlow, and of human

existence – poses itself as the refutation of such a journey and as the refutation of the general metaphorical conception that meaning may be found within, beneath, at the center. At the end of the search we encounter a darkness, and it is no more defined than at the beginning of the journey and the narrative; it continues to exist only as something unapproachable. The stages of such a journey and such a discourse, the struggle with vagueness and paradox, accompanied always with the sense that one is not yet at the heart of the matter, must suffice. Once again amid the disciplines and meanings of civilisation that are so easily and carelessly assumed to be real, Marlow calls to mind his experience beyond these meanings and declares that anxious ministrations to his weakened body are beside the point: ' . . . it was my imagination that wanted soothing'. . . .

SOURCE: extract from '*Heart of Darkness* and the Failure of the Imagination', *Sewanee Review* LXXIII, No. 3 (Summer 1965), pp. 488–502. The substance of this essay was embodied in its author's *The Limits of Metaphor* (Ithaca, N. Y.,1967).

NOTES

1. [Ed.–Page references in square brackets inserted after major quotations relate to the text of the novel published in volume VI of the 20-volume edition of *The Works of Joseph Conrad* (London and Edinburgh, 1925).]

2. [Ed.–In *The Limits of Metaphor* (p. 61), Guetti observes: 'What Kurtz actually sees, of course, cannot be known, but in relating his vision to the rest of the story we must place it in the scheme of meaning which Marlow has constructed for it. Here it has meaning in the way that I have suggested, although we may well be uncertain regarding Marlow's reliability. This uncertainty is of such proportions, however, that we must ignore its larger implications, for if we do not then *Heart of Darkness* becomes a psychological case history of Marlow's prejudicial concerns and distorted perceptions, and there is, I think, little point or consistency in such an assessment of the story. Even in ignoring these implications, our uncertainty in accepting Marlow's remarks remains a powerful factor in relation to the schematic separation between mind and 'reality' that I have discussed. We can never be sure whether Marlow is right about Kurtz's experience, or if Marlow *could* be right.']

## K. K. Ruthven        The Savage God (1968)

. . .The story of *Heart of Darkness* is told by Marlow, who once had
the job of taking a rickety steam-boat up the Congo to bring back
from a distant trading-post an ivory-trader called Kurtz. Marlow
and Kurtz are Europeans who react differently to the primitive
lure of Africa: the narrator holds on to his European values even
when in the very heart of darkness, but Kurtz surrenders his
European heritage, exploits the natives by making them think
him a god, and abandons the moral values in which he has been
educated by participating in certain unspecified but 'unspeakable rites' [p. 118].[1] On the journey back down the Congo Kurtz
dies, and on his death-bed cries, enigmatically, 'The horror! The
horror!' [p. 149]. Everything turns on the interpretation of this
cry, with its 'strange and terrible message of ambivalence toward
the life of civilisation':[2] is it a deathbed renunciation of an evil
life, as the narrator and some critics would like to believe, or is it
(as Marlow suspects) simply exultant, a confirmation of the
unspeakable and an unrepenting rejection of the European
values Marlow cherishes? It is possible to regard Kurtz as the
hero of this story because he not only has the courage to reject the
obsolete values of a dying civilisation, but risks destruction by
facing the unknown and tackling it on its own terms; and if Kurtz
is the hero, *Heart of Darkness* is implicitly an attack on the values of
western society and an annunciation of the Savage God. The clue
to all this is the way in which Conrad describes Europe and
Africa, for the choice Kurtz is required to make is not between a
good Europe and a bad Africa but between two different kinds of
badness: Kurtz must choose between the mausoleum of Europe
and the wilderness of Africa. Europe is presented persistently as a
place of death, a 'whited sepulchre' [p. 55] which is by
implication a museum of dead values. Africa, on the other hand,
is an alien world, Europe's antitype, a place at once horrific and
vital, evoking complex responses in the European. Its landscape
is hostile and un-Wordsworthian, with dense vegetation 'like a
rioting invasion of soundless life, a rolling wave of plants, piled

up, crested, ready to . . . sweep every little man of us out of his little existence' [p. 86] – as it is in Altdorfer's *St George*. Pullulating with 'hidden evil', the jungle is also a present reminder of our own prehistory, for sailing up the Congo is 'like travelling back to the earliest beginnings of the world' [p. 92], with the result that Marlow and his crew feel like 'wanderers on prehistoric earth' [p. 95]. This Frazerian-anthropological element is developed in a manner that curiously anticipates Freud or Jung when Conrad treats the experience as an act of penetration to the most ancient core of the European mind, a stirring of racial memories: hearing the incomprehensible yells of the savages Marlow remarks that 'if you were man enough you would admit to yourself that there was in you just the faintest trace of a response to the terrible frankness of that noise, a dim suspicion of there being a meaning in it which you – you so remote from the night of first ages – could comprehend' [p. 96]. Many others have experienced the same shock of recognition: Rupert Brooke, for example, 'felt strange ancient jungle cries awaking within' him when he saw his first *siva-siva*: the revelations of travel are never simply geographical. Certainly, the journey up the Congo as Conrad describes it is something in the nature of a psychic voyage into the innermost recesses of the mind, to a point at which European morality has not even begun to operate. All this and more is evoked by Conrad's enigmatic and evocative title, which is a truly dark conceit, 'mysterious, significant, full of obscure meaning' (*Tales of Unrest*, p. 139). Stanley's *Through the Dark Continent* had popularised the association of Africa with darkness so thoroughly that Booth's study of working-class conditions appeared with the title *In Darkest England and the Way Out* in 1890, the year in which Stanley's *In Darkest Africa* was published (England, too, was one of the dark places of the earth). The phrase 'heart of darkness' compels attention but resists analysis, as symbols should, and in this way Conrad is able to penetrate our bias against the primitive, enabling us to experience the African darkness without feeling that we are simply reverting to barbarism.

Marlow, like all fugitives from the European graveyard, the 'world of straightforward facts' [p. 61], has to decide whether to surrender to the primitive lure of Africa or resist it – whether, in the words of one of Lawrence's poems, to let go or to hold on. Looking at the jungle Marlow asks, 'Could we handle that dumb

thing, or would it handle us?' [p. 81]. Marlow is solidly and
naïvely Victorian in his moral outlook, believing that hard work
is a great exorciser of spiritual doubts (the same mentality
prescribed cold baths as a solution to the problem of sexual
desire); so Marlow resists the call of the jungle by tinkering on
with his steam-boat. In the Chief Accountant we have an almost
comic example of the man who resists, for the Chief Accountant
has held out against 'the great demoralisation of the land' [p. 68]
by wearing starched collars and keeping his books in apple-pie
order: he is Marlow's hero, not ours. Kurtz, on the other hand,
submits to the 'heavy, mute spell of the wilderness' which attracts
Europeans 'by the awakening of forgotten and brutal instincts,
by the memory of gratified and monstrous passions' [p. 144]. In
Marlow's opinion he lacks the innate strength of the Chief
Accountant; he is 'hollow at the core' [p. 131], the original
Hollow Man. The experience of Africa is for Marlow simply a
test of European integrity: we must all 'face the darkness' [p. 49]
and resist it as the Chief Accountant does, not succumb to it like
Kurtz. But what we know of Conrad makes it impossible for us to
accept this as his point of view. For Conrad, surely, it is enough
simply to face the darkness and 'live in the midst of the
incomprehensible' [p. 50]. Conrad's heroes are people who
immerse themselves in the destructive element (Conrad was busy
with *Lord Jim* at the time of writing *Heart of Darkness*) and Kurtz
is Conrad's hero: he destroys himself in the act of total submission
to the new and destructive element of Africa.

Kurtz releases his *id* from the restraints of his European *ego*
when he allows his forgotten and brutal instincts to revive and stir
the memory of gratified and monstrous passions. Marlow sees
Kurtz as a Faustian figure whose 'unlawful soul' has been
beguiled 'beyond the bounds of permitted aspirations' [p. 144],
but we are nevertheless meant to feel that in relaxing his
European habits Kurtz has achieved a sort of moral emancipation: 'He had kicked himself loose of the earth . . . he had
kicked the very earth to pieces' [p. 144], as even Marlow can see.
Kurtz felt that in doing what he did he was 'on the threshold of
great things' [p. 143], an ambiguous statement Marlow would
interpret as referring to Kurtz's greed as an ivory-collector, but
that we are tempted to interpret as a reference to Kurtz's courage
as a pioneer in the psychic wilderness of Africa. Marlow

disapproves of Kurtz too strongly to be a reliable commentator on him, and for a closer approximation to the truth we have the testimony of the young Russian who, as a disciple of Kurtz, is similarly by no means an impartial witness. Even so, the Russian tells us about qualities in Kurtz that Marlow never mentions. 'This man has enlarged my mind', says the Russian [pp. 125, 140]: 'You can't judge Mr Kurtz as you would an ordinary man' [p. 128]. We need not doubt either of these statements: Kurtz has somehow entered a realm of experience which is beyond the conventional scope of good and evil, and this is something that Marlow, a mere tourist in the dark side of the mind, can barely understand.

Conrad complicates the business of Kurtz's secession from western values by hinting at an ambivalence in Kurtz's attitude. This is difficult to pin down because Marlow is such an unreliable narrator and only too ready to interpret facts in the light of his own prejudices. It is the Russian, however, who tells us that Kurtz 'hated all this, and somehow he couldn't get away' [p. 129]; and Marlow would have us believe that Kurtz experienced 'both the diabolic love and the unearthly hate of the mysteries [he] had penetrated' [p. 147]. The truth seems to be that Kurtz died before his emancipation from European values was complete. Part of him is still European and belongs to the world of the International Society for the Suppression of Savage Customs, a world represented by Marlow's altruistic aunt who would like to turn Africa into a sort of black Europe, and it is for this world that Kurtz's altruistic pamphlet is written; but the other part of Kurtz is as ferocious as the wilderness itself, and answers the question of how to treat Africans with the terse advice: 'Exterminate all the brutes' [p. 118]. This is why Kurtz's apocalyptic last words, 'The horror! The horror!' are so ambiguous. The suggestion that they represent a confirmation of the unspeakable comes surprisingly from Marlow, who in the course of telling the story begins at last to grasp the tremendous implications of Kurtz's decision to go native: 'No eloquence', says Marlow, 'could have been so withering to one's belief in mankind as [Kurtz's] final burst of sincerity' [p. 145]. Even Marlow is beginning to understand that the truth is not always comforting and that the cry of the Savage God, however horrific, is nevertheless authentic. Kurtz's cry had 'the appalling face of a glimpsed truth' – it was 'an affirmation, a

moral victory paid for by innumerable defeats, by abominable
terrors, by abominable satisfactions. But it was a victory!' [p.
151]. Remove those disapproving adjectives (tokens of an
obsolete morality) and you have the key to Conrad's assessment
of Kurtz's achievement. It was an excellent strategy to have
Marlow change his mind about Kurtz. It not only makes the
function of the narrator more dramatic, but also engages our
sympathies for Kurtz: when a solidly respectable man like
Marlow can be made to change his mind, it is not easy for the rest
of us to dismiss Kurtz as a moral weakling who simply went to
pieces in Africa. That such a strategy was necessary is obvious
when one considers how the general public would have reacted to
a straightforward exposition of the ideas embodied in *Heart of
Darkness*. Had Conrad spoken openly in favour of Kurtz's lapse
into barbarism he would have been grouped in the popular mind
with Wagner, Verlaine, Ibsen, Nietzsche, Zola and other
distinguished degenerates. Max Nordau found the symptoms of
mental illness in all modern art, and would have regarded
Conrad's treatment of Kurtz as further evidence in support of his
general thesis. 'The filth of Zola's art and of his disciples in
literary canal-dredging has been got over', he wrote in
*Degeneration* (1895), 'and nothing remains for it but to turn to
submerged peoples and social strata': *après Zola le déluge*.

For an insight into contemporary attitudes towards empire and
barbarism it is helpful to compare *Heart of Darkness* with Alan
Boisragon's *The Benin Massacre* (1897), a book about an incident
that brought the savagery of the Dark Continent before the
newspaper-reading public and kept it there for several weeks. It
was an incident that must have stirred in Conrad memories of his
own voyage up the Congo of 1890, and may have been a catalyst
in the process that led to the writing of *Heart of Darkness*.
Boisragon was one of two Englishmen who managed to escape
from an ambush in which nine other Englishmen, all unarmed,
were shot down by native tribesmen while on a mission to the
king of Benin, in southern Nigeria. Benin was the capital of a
theocracy of priests who practised ritual killings, and the annual
ceremonies were in progress when the massacre occurred. A
punitive expedition was organised by the British and Benin was

taken in February 1897. R. H. Bacon's *Benin the City of Blood*
(1897) gives a strictly military account of this brilliantly
organised reprisal in which Maxim machine-guns reasserted the
White Queen's supremacy, and condemns the atrocities of Benin
as 'the result of centuries of stagnant brutality'. Some of the
horrors Bacon thought it pointless to describe are listed in the
'Diary of a Surgeon with the Benin Punitive Expedition' by F. N.
Roth, reprinted by his brother H. Ling Roth in *Great Benin: Its
Customs, Art and Horrors* (1903). Roth had talked to Boisragon who
assured him that 'all the white men who were massacred behaved
well'. Benin city was like a concentration camp:

All about the houses and streets are dead natives, some crucified and
sacrificed on trees, others on stage erections, some on the ground, some
in pits, and amongst the latter we found several half-dead ones. I
suppose there is not another place on the face of the globe so near
civilisation where such butcheries are carried on with such impunity.

Bound and gagged female slaves had been disembowelled and
left to die and the main thoroughfare to the king's palace was
'strewn with dead, crucified and beheaded bodies in all states of
decomposition'. Fire broke out and in no time at all the whole
place was razed; only then did the stench of putrefaction clear
from the air.

Boisragon was a man of very great courage. Badly wounded,
he walked three days in the bush without food or water, equipped
only with a compass, watch and pocket-knife, and was disappointed when a doctor declared him unfit to go on the punitive
expedition. The attitude he takes in his book towards Africa is
orthodoxly colonial. In many respects a polo-playing Marlow,
Boisragon displays no misgivings about what he's doing in Africa:
the British are all nobly engaged in 'the glorious work of rescuing
the native races in West Africa from the horrors of human
sacrifice'.[3] Africans look 'very like monkeys' and practise 'such
gentle customs as human sacrifices, cannibalism, twin-killing,
and others'. But the bad old days are now gone, he believes,
thanks largely to 'the sterling work of Miss Slessor of the Scotch
Mission'. Nowadays, 'every river has its cricket and tennis club';
every Saturday there is a cricket match, tea is served by the
ladies, and a brass band plays selections from *The Gaiety Girl*;

meanwhile, a few miles away, Benin tribesmen are crucifying and disembowelling their slaves. It all gives point to Conrad's repeated opinion that the intrusion of Europeans into Africa is a 'fantastic invasion': Boisragon's naive juxtaposition of village cricket and ritual murder epitomises the fantastic nature of the invasion Conrad tries to evoke in images like that of the French gun-boat firing shells 'into a continent', or of the piles of rivets strewn along the edges of the essentially unrivetable jungle, or of the two Europeans whose shadows 'trailed behind them slowly over the tall grass without bending a single blade'. To read *The Benin Massacre* in connection with *Heart of Darkness* is to perceive how far Conrad had emancipated himself from the received ideas of his time, and to understand why it was necessary for him to be so cautious and evasive when making out a case for Kurtz: little imagination is needed to realise what Boisragon would have thought of Conrad's hero. And in the end, of course, the caution and the evasiveness paid dividends: the subtlety of Conrad's narrative is both determined and nourished by the need to conceal a proposition that would have scandalised the majority of his readers; in veiling the idea, he transformed a polemical issue into a work of art. . . .

Source: extract from 'The Savage God: Conrad and Lawrence', *Critical Quarterly*, x, nos 1 & 2 (Spring & Summer 1968), pp. 41–6.

#### NOTES

1. Page references, in square brackets, relate to the 1946 reprint (in Dent's Uniform Collected Edition) of the novel's first publication in book form in the composite volume *Youth, A Narrative, and Two Other Stories* (1902).
2. Lionel Trilling, 'On the Modern Element in Modern Literature', *Partisan Review*, xxviii (1961). [Subsequently included in *Beyond Culture*; the relevant portion of this essay is given above – Ed.]
3. For this and subsequent references, see pp. 189, 83, 29, 33, 34, 39 ff., 92, 131, 61 ff., 83 and 92 of Alan Boisragon's *The Benin Massacre* (1897).

## Avrom Fleishman    Class Struggle as Tragedy (1967)

The narrative achievements of *Nostromo* have been amply praised – its complex characterisation, its rich texture of social life, its tragic view of man in the modern world – but not yet for the political maturity from which they proceed. The novel marks the fulfilment of Conrad's political imagination; it represents the history of a society as a living organism. Indeed, the complex narrative structure of the novel reflects this sense of history's unfolding processes. Men of varied classes and nationalities are shown caught up in a situation that their acts transform into history, that gives shape to their lives, and – what is rarer still in fiction – that is seen to continue beyond them. This personally created history gives meaning to individual destinies: it acts as a tragic nexus which, in the absence of organic community, is the only order that transcends the limits of personal life. 'Where freedom is absent', Irving Howe has observed, 'politics is fate.' So, in a Latin American nation in which the forces of imperialism and capitalism, nationalism and socialism are brought into play, politics impinges on every point of individual and social life. But if politics is fate, history is freedom, and through Conrad's organic unfolding of Costaguana's past and future, the drama that is played out in *Nostromo* is given its meaning, as the past and future give meaning to the present.

Conrad himself conceived of the writing of *Nostromo* as an act of historical imagination. He describes it in *A Personal Record*, in a tragicomic anecdote [pp. 98–100] about the intrusion of a neighbor while he was struggling with the novel:

I had, like the prophet of old, 'wrestled with the Lord' for my creation, for the headlands of the coast, for the darkness of the Placid Gulf, the

light on the snows, the clouds on the sky, and for the breath of life that
had to be blown into the shapes of men and women, of Latin and Saxon,
of Jew and Gentile. . . .

'How do you do?'

. . . The whole world of Costaguana (the country, you may remember, of my seaboard tale), men, women, headlands, houses,
mountains, town, *campo* (there was not a single brick, stone, or grain of
sand of its soil I had not placed in position with my own hands); all the
history, geography, politics, finance; the wealth of Charles Gould's
silver-mine, and the splendour of the magnificent Capataz de
Cargadores . . . all that had come crashing down about my ears. I felt I
could never pick up the pieces – and in that very moment I was saying,
'Won't you sit down?'

The language here subtly modifies the traditional metaphor of
the artist as a creator in the image of God, and makes him
specifically the creator of a *historical* world. The artist's vocation
becomes not merely to be faithful to the forms of things but to give
an account of them in their total unity. It is this quality of organic
fullness that makes *Nostromo* a major novel, in the tradition of
those nineteenth-century fictions that endow themselves with the
status of histories – from the local scale of *Middlemarch* to the
international one of *War and Peace*.

What makes such novels histories (as distinguished from
historical novels, which usually select authentic details as
background to a plot) is their density, their approach in
complexity to the actual condition of historical life. They
dramatise the 'history, geography, politics, finance' which are
off-stage presences in lesser works. As Conrad himself put it in his
Author's Note: 'the few historical allusions are never dragged in
for the sake of parading my unique erudition, but . . . each of
them is closely related to actuality; either throwing a light on the
nature of current events or affecting directly the fortunes of the
people of whom I speak' (pp. xx–xxi).

Despite its advances over his earlier work, it is important to see
*Nostromo* as an integral part of Conrad's achievement and to
estimate its political meaning in the context of his developing
social attitudes. The limits of such an undertaking must be borne
in mind: the characters in the novel are unique beings and the
situation depicted is a fictional creation, not a historical fact. We
may nevertheless proceed with some confidence because of the

consistency not only of Conrad's opinions of certain forces like imperialism, but also of his imaginative techniques for representing certain types of political actors: conquerors and colonists, aristocrats both real and ideal, alienated and integrated men. In addition, a new character form emerges in the novel and goes on to become the predominant heroic type in his political fiction.

Nostromo and Martin Decoud are the first in a series of young men in Conrad who bear a family resemblance to their ancestors in the Waverley novels. Such figures as the naïve Waverley and Morton, of *Old Mortality*, have been defined in a recent study of Scott:

The hero can best be described by the words of Nigel Olifaunt – 'a thing never acting but perpetually acted upon'. But he is nevertheless the protagonist. He stands at the center of the struggle. He may not move, but his chances, his fortunes, are at stake. He is a victim, at the mercy of good and bad forces alike. He never aspires to property, nor actively courts the heroine. But he does not remain a victim, and he receives the heroine and property at the end.[1]

This is not the place to examine the full relationship of Conrad to Scott and the Scott tradition of historical fiction, but we can isolate a few of the factors which account for the striking similarities between their characteristic heroes. We have seen [in Fleishman's earlier discussion of *Romance* – Ed.] the advantages Conrad gained, as Hueffer described them, from the peculiar position of John Kemp as a naïve outsider in a colonial society: from his perspective, and measured against his normality, *colons*, rebels, and English are shown to deviate from moral and political ideals. Kemp is squarely in the Scott tradition, and *Romance* is inspired by the same adventurousness, shifting background, and swashbuckling action as the most popular Waverleys.

Yet between *Romance* and *Nostromo* there is a difference that centers in Conrad's new conception of the hero. The point may best be made by looking at the Waverley hero again:

The hero is not precisely Everyman, but every gentleman – not in some supercilious social sense, but in the profound conviction that society is a compact of independent owners of property. He is a passive hero because, in the words of Edmund Burke, a member of civil society surrenders the right 'to judge for himself, and to assert his own cause. He abdicates all right to be his own governor. He inclusively, in a great measure, abandons the right of self-defense, the first law of Nature.'[2]

In Scott, then, the hero emerges as the embodiment and protagonist of society itself. But in Conrad, the Waverley hero is made to represent the unpropertied classes which are exploited by and revolt against the social order, and he often is an intellectual, claiming the right to judge for himself. He remains, however, a waverer; his vigorous activity is still a shifting response to forces impinging upon him from without. Yet his career affirms not the stable order of civil society but its need to become an organic community that will no longer require the destruction of its most heroic members.

Nostromo has often been assumed to be a pathetic failure, rather than a tragic hero, because the critics have not identified him with the social movements in which he becomes engaged. By the same token, the final chapters of the novel, which depict Nostromo's melodramatic love and death, have been taken to be irrelevant because of a failure to see them within the symbolic pattern of the entire novel. In this pattern, Nostromo's career represents the history of an entire class, the proletariàt – its enlistment and exploitation in the industrialisation of the country, its entry into the separatist revolution (fighting for class interests not directly its own), its growth of self-consciousness and discovery of an independent political role, its temptation by the materialistic drives of capitalism, and its purgation by traditional idealists in its own camp.

The pattern is a tragic one, as we shall see, because it is founded on contradictions within the hero and his class, rather than on circumstance. As in classical tragedy, the hero is bounded by forces larger than himself, yet what happens to him is the expression of his own nature. Like classical drama, too, the novel connects the individual hero with a social group – which he represents not only symbolically but dramatically – in historical action. Conrad's special version of tragedy is that this very social rootedness of the individualist hero contains the contradictions which destroy him. The career and development of Nostromo follow a dialectic as incisive and ironic as one of the character studies of Hegel's *Phenomenology of Mind*.

Nostromo is to be understood as the symbol of a class. At the same time, and without avoiding the contradiction, he is an individual, a vigorous egoist, whose drives to maintain his gilded reputation and at the same time to become integrated in the making of a community cause him to oscillate between vigorous social action and almost total estrangement. Totally lacking in political sensibility, Nostromo joins the Waverley heroes in running the full gamut of political commitment. The climax of his career, in which he benefits society and establishes his highest honor, only leads to his deepest isolation.

Another form of this tragic pattern is presented by Decoud, whose intellectual aloofness from his comic-opera nation and simultaneous awareness of its precise historical needs lead to an oscillation similar to Nostromo's – and to eventual self-destruction. In political terms, however, Decoud's plan, the separation of the province of Sulaco from the state-of-nature anarchy of Costaguana, is a design for social integration, an attempt to render the province, as he puts it, 'habitable' – that is, to make it a city of men, a civilisation. But separatism brings with it the prospect of further revolutionary ferment and eventful fragmentation through class struggle, as well as the possibility of reintegration in new political forms.

*Nostromo*, prodigal of favors, has seen another of its characters considered as its hero. But Charles Gould is a hero in the Lingard (or Kurtz) tradition, a composite of the colonist and the conqueror – the former by virtue of his native birth and dedication to his property as a sacred trust, the latter by his placing of foreign material interests before those of the country. The mine, revived in an effort to vindicate his abused father, becomes an end in itself, leading to the estrangement of his excellent wife. The mining operation is repeatedly compared to the original slave mines of the Spanish conquerors (much as the Belgian conquest of the Congo is compared to the Roman conquest of Britain in *Heart of Darkness*). Gould's American backer, Holroyd, is portrayed in familiar terms as the imperialist man dominated by money hunger, with an admixture of the white-man's-burden missionary zeal characteristic of the period. These associations sharply limit Gould's role as hero, and make him instead Conrad's deepest probing of the captain of industry's soul.

The problem of interpreting *Nostromo* is often complicated by the interpreter's own sense of history, not to speak of his political sympathies. The most rewarding commentator on the novel, Albert Guerard, confesses as much when he writes, 'the novel's own view of history is sceptical and disillusioned, which for us today must mean true'.[3] Guerard goes on to describe the shortcomings of the society which emerges from the victory of 'material interests' and identifies them with the present crisis in Latin America and other underdeveloped areas: 'In my interpretation [the grim predictions by Monygham and Mrs Gould] look forward to a period when – as in Guatemala yesterday, as in the Middle East today – the conflicts induced by capitalist exploitation outweigh the benefits accrued.'[4]

Guerard is arguing against the view of Robert Penn Warren that, for all its human losses, the new state of affairs in the Occidental Republic (i.e., Sulaco, after separation from Costaguana) is preferable to the chaotic and unjust old order, with its succession of bandit governments and bloody coups. Warren finds his text in the novel's epigraph, 'So foul a sky clears not without a storm' – presumably connecting the storm with the separatist revolution depicted in the novel.[5] It is one of the minor ironies of literary history that Warren, like other New Critics, has been critical of the values of modern industrial society, yet when a judgement of society is to be made he bases it on typically capitalist norms: political stability, the security of life and property, expanding production and trade. There is nothing to quarrel with in such values, but they are not the only results of the victory of 'material interests.'

A third party to the dispute on Conrad's judgement of Costaguana's future is Irving Howe, who attempts to reconcile both of the opposed views with the Marxist theory of the successive stages of social change. The bourgeois separatist revolution is a necessary one, but it breeds new, capitalist evils in its turn, which generate a proletarian revolution, the final stage of progress. Not bound by the Marxist theory, Howe interprets this prospect as an undesirable one: 'Both critics seem to me right: the civil war brings capitalism and capitalism will bring civil war, progress *has* come out of chaos but it is the kind of progress that is likely to end in chaos.[6]

If there were no indication of Conrad's views on the future of

Latin America, it would be impossible to evaluate the condition of society at the end of *Nostromo*. But in 'Autocracy and War', written in the year after the novel was published, Conrad indicates fairly clearly how he envisaged the outcome of the dominance of 'material interests' (as capitalism is referred to in *Nostromo*):

A swift disenchantment overtook the incredible infatuation which could put its trust in the peaceful nature of industrial and commercial competition. . . . democracy, which has elected to pin its faith to the supremacy of material interests, will have to fight their battles to the bitter end, on a mere pittance. . . . The true peace of the world . . . will be built on less perishable foundations than those of material interests.[7]

Conrad does not stop with this prediction of capitalism's issue in imperialist war. There are narrative situations in *Nostromo* which support the view that he looked forward to the proletarian stage of the Latin American revolution not only with resignation but with a certain warmth toward the rising populace. A generally neglected but, to my mind, climactic and spectacular chapter of *Nostromo* (the third of Part Three) brings Gould together with an emissary of Hernandez, the leader of the insurgent peasantry. The peasants have yet to throw their weight into the battle between the capitalist mine owner, who is supported by the aristocratic Blanco party, and the Caesarist dictator Montero, who is supported by the *Lazarones*, or *Lumpenproletariat* of the city slums. As they were to do in the then-imminent Mexican Revolution, the peasantry (under leaders like Zapata, whom Hernandez resembles) hold the balance of power but because of their traditional estrangement from the urban proletariat are inclined to join the aristocratic-capitalist forces.

The peasants recognise their own power, manifesting it even in the humility of their emissary's proposal for a *rapprochement* with Gould:

'Has not the master of the mine any message to send to Hernandez, the master of the Campo?'
. . . .
'You are a just man', urged the emissary of Hernandez. 'Look at those people [the aristocrats] who made my compadre a general and have turned us all into soldiers. Look at those oligarchs fleeing for life, with

only the clothes on their backs. . . . We need ask no man for anything;
but soldiers must have their pay to live honestly when the wars are over.
It is believed that your soul is so just that a prayer from you would cure
the sickness of every beast, like the orison of the upright judge. Let me
have some words from your lips that would act like a charm upon the
doubts of our *partida*, where all are men.'

. . .Charles Gould, with only a short hesitation, pronounced the
required pledge. He was like a man who had ventured on a precipitous
path with no room to turn, where the only chance of safety is to press
forward.                                                      [pp. 360–1][8]

The passage prefigures the future power of Hernandez as
Minister of War of the new republic and the proletarisation of his
peasant band as workers in the mine. It is also revealing because
it expresses Gould's diminishing control of the course of the
revolution, in which he must continue to participate even though
it is inimical to his interests. The metaphor of the 'precipitous
path' is a perfect figure for the absoluteness of the historical
process. Though Gould's moral imagination is outraged by an
alliance with what he considers another of the anarchic and
criminal forces in the country (it is clear that Conrad does not
depict the peasant band in the same light), he must sacrifice
principle to maintain his position. Indeed, he must become a
party to the future proletarian revolution in the very process of
securing the capitalist-backed separatist revolution.

If the internal and external evidence in Conrad's own words were
not sufficient to indicate his view of Latin American history, the
historical sources on which he drew would do so. It has recently
been shown that he used South American travelogues by
Masterman and Eastwick, and it becomes possible to deduce his
own position by seeing his distance from them. Masterman
exhibits a typical attitude: 'The history of South America, like
that of Mexico, has hitherto been written in blood and tears, and
I fear will continue to be so written until Anglo-Saxons or
Teutons shall there outnumber the Indo-Spanish race.'[9]
Conrad is equally far removed from the opinions of Eastwick,
who subtitled his account of life in a republic 'How To Make
the Scum Rise to the Top', found the Creoles lazy and lacking
the Yankee's entrepreneurial spirit, and proposed imperialist

annexation if a country failed to pay its foreign debts.[10]

Conrad did, however, use many names and incidents from the history of Venezuela and Paraguay cited in these accounts. (It was in Venezuela that he had his own brief experience of South America.) But his creation of Costaguana's past tallies not as closely with the history of these nations as with that of Colombia.[11] The precise background of *Nostromo* needs to be determined not merely for historical accuracy but for literary interpretation, for in the history of Colombia are to be found some of the central concerns of the novel, concerns which might otherwise remain baffling.

Like Costaguana, Colombia emerged from its war of independence under Bolivar as an unmanageable confederation which included the provinces that were soon to become Venezuela and Ecuador. After the latter had broken away, the centrifugal tendencies continued (in both the historical and fictional countries) because of the virtual isolation of the provinces by the Cordillera – the mountain range in both Costaguana and Colombia. Colombia's history throughout the nineteenth and much of the twentieth century is one of extended civil war between Liberals and Conservatives, divided largely on the issue of federal or centralised government. It is a history of unstable constitutionalism with interludes of dictatorial sclerosis – much like the history of Costaguana, with its regime of terror under Guzman Bento and its subsequent reversion to a succession of weak or criminal governments.

The main political issue in both the fictional and the historical realm is the same: the centralist party in Colombia, like the Unionists under Guzman Bento, was opposed to the federalist party – which in Costaguana is made up of the aristocratic Blancos. Federalism of this kind is a separatist tendency that expresses the desire of the aristocrats to be free of the exactions of the central government, which they can rarely control. Defeated by Guzman Bento, the Blancos are satisfied to remain subservient to the political rule of the capital while economic masters in their own province, until the intervention of an outside force raises again the issue of provincial separation.

Such an outside force existed in both Colombia and Costaguana, and even the form of its intervention is somewhat similar. In the former, it was the European and United States'

interest in building a mid-hemisphere canal which, with the
encouragement and the active support of the nationalists by the
United States government, led to the separation of the Province
of Panama from Colombia. The creation of an independent
Panama was deemed necessary in order to have a more tractable
lessor of the canal route than Colombia, and to get a better
bargain on the rental fees. In the fictional country, the outside
force is the Gould concession, backed by European and
American capital and the naval presence of the United States,
which also seeks a better deal by manufacturing a new state.
Here, too, the result is the independence of a province which is
tractable and will, it is hoped, be stable in its dealings with
foreign enterprises. The connection between the historical and
the fictional events lies not only in their parallelism; the United
States intervention in Panama culminated in 1904, during the
writing of the novel, and must be considered an active influence
upon its creation.

Despite the popularity of Anglo-Saxon racist political theories
during this period, which backed the United States as the natural
ally of England, Conrad was hostile to the growth of United
States power and its deployment in Panama. Earlier, during the
Spanish-American War he had professed support of Spain
because of his sympathy with the Latin race and fear for its future
(1 May 1898). Subsequent references to 'Yankee Conquistadores
in Panama' (26 December 1903) equate American expansion
with that of Belgium in the Congo.[12] In the same letter, Conrad
tells of an invitation to visit Colombia from that country's
ambassador in Spain and England, S. Pérez Triana; he may have
heard the Colombian case against the United States from him, as
well as receiving praise from the son of the former Liberal (!)
President for his account of the Colombian civil war.

As for Theodore Roosevelt, Conrad vented on him the full
measure of his scorn (dragging him into a review of a travel
book):

That peripatetic guide, philosopher and friend of all nations, Mr
Roosevelt, would promptly excommunicate [the author] with a big
stick. The truth is that the ex-autocrat of all the States does not like
rebels against the sullen order of our universe. Make the best of it or
perish – he cries.[13]

Conrad's exposure, in *Nostromo*, of Roosevelt's moralistic and providential rationalisations of imperialism takes the form of a satire of the American financier Holroyd's missionary Christianity.[14] Given Conrad's political judgement of the United States, Holroyd's prophecy of its dominance not only over Latin America but over all the world – and not only economically but culturally – has the sound of a trump of doom [p. 77].

The history of Costaguana is to be judged in the light of Conrad's consistent attitudes toward imperialism. In his terms, the ascendancy of foreign 'material interests' is a form of conquest. The separatist revolution, which is supported by these interests, must be read as a mixed blessing. It marks the triumph of imperialism but, as it is formulated by its theoretician, Decoud, it is also the beginning of a nationalist revolution that will intervene and liberate the other portion of Costaguana. Further, as we have seen, it will inevitably turn against the foreign elements which fostered it. Decoud emerges as the prophet of the nationalist movements of our time, in his understanding of imperialism:

'Now the whole land is like a treasure-house, and all these people are breaking into it, whilst we are cutting each other's throats. The only thing that keeps them out is mutual jealousy. But they'll come to an agreement some day – and by the time we've settled our quarrels and become decent and honourable, there'll be nothing left for us. It has always been the same. We are a wonderful people, but it has always been our fate to be' – he did not say 'robbed', but added, after a pause – 'exploited!'                                                                 [p. 174]

Decoud's historical perspective on the new imperialism is borne out in the dénouement of the novel. The war between the newly independent Occidental Republic and its parent nation, Costaguana, is brought to a close through a show of force by ships of the imperialist powers, led by the 'U.S.S. Powhattan' [p. 487]. The United States is the first great power to recognise the new republic [p. 485]. The visiting entrepreneur has a choice of the Amarilla Club of the Blancos or the Anglo-American Club – 'Mining engineers and businessmen, don't you know', Captain Mitchell explains [p. 474] – or one may stop at one of the two American bars – 'New Yorkers mostly frequent that one' [p. 479].

Given the intimate connection of the novel's themes with the history of imperialism in Latin America, it is possible to read (though by no means to exhaust) *Nostromo* as a record of the transition from precapitalist to capitalist – and, prospectively, to postcapitalist – society. To do so, it is necessary to analyse these stages of society by their component classes, and at the same time to consider the main characters in the novel as representatives of those classes.

## The People

The title of *Nostromo* has been found wanting by many who take seriously its grand historical theme, but Conrad's choice of the name has something to tell us about his larger intentions. The hero who bears this name is not only a romantic individual but acquires dramatically the status of a complex symbol. On the meaning of this symbol, Conrad is more explicit than is elsewhere his practice:

Nostromo does not aspire to be a leader in a personal game. He does not want to raise himself above the mass. He is content to feel himself a power – within the People. . . . He is a man with the weight of countless generations behind him and no parentage to boast of. . . . . Like the People.

In his firm grip on the earth he inherits, in his improvidence and generosity, in his lavishness with his gifts, in his manly vanity, in the obscure sense of his greatness and in his faithful devotion with something despairing as well as desperate in its impulses, he is a Man of the People, their very own unenvious force, disdaining to lead but ruling from within. Years afterwards . . . listening in unmoved silence to anarchist speeches at the meeting, the enigmatical patron of the new revolutionary agitation, the trusted, the wealthy comrade Fidanza with the knowledge of his moral ruin locked up in his breast, he remains essentially a man of the People.

. . . Antonia the Aristocrat and Nostromo the Man of the People are the artisans of the New Era, the true creators of the New State. . . .[15]

[pp. xxi–xxiii]

It is thus the collective sense of his nickname – 'our man' (like Lord Jim, 'one of us') – and not its Italian meaning, 'boatswain', that is emphasised in the title of the novel.

Nostromo's career, as outlined here, represents the exploitation of the proletariat on behalf of the various political forces that contend for the country without reference to the interests of its masses. He ultimately tries to emancipate himself and materially supports the proletarian revolution, but he does so through crime – the concealment of and slow theft from the silver hoard. Nostromo's corruption by silver, which is, in part, a complex symbol of 'material interests,' evokes the moral danger of taking on the values of the propertied classes that yawns before revolutionary movements.

Nostromo is, however, not only the dramatic representative of the people but an individual – indeed, an individualist, a stern foreman, a would-be popular hero. His existence is a more complex affair than its primary symbolic function; it involves the relation of the individual ego to the collective identity of the people. It is the unwillingness to see the hero in this double aesthetic role that has obscured for most critics his tragic stature.

The focus of *Nostromo* is not 'material interests' and their representative, Gould, but the people and their representative, Nostromo. Permeating the novel, densely filling the interstices between characters, providing motive and meaning to their actions, are the people. Costaguana is the most palpable presence in *Nostromo* by virtue of the gross human fact of popular suffering. It is 'a great land of plain and mountain and people, suffering and mute, waiting for the future in a pathetic immobility of patience. . . . on all the lips she found a weary desire for peace, the dread of officialdom with its nightmarish parody of administration without law, without security, and without justice' [p. 88]. The vision is Mrs Gould's, and, despite her limited perspective (she finds, for example, that all Costaguanans look alike), she is able to perceive it because 'having acquired in Southern Europe a knowledge of true peasantry, she was able to appreciate the great worth of the people' [p. 89].

The people stand in danger of that primary evil of industrialism: dehumanisation. In the days before the revolution ('nobody had ever heard of labour troubles then') the naïve human spirit of the European-born Cargadores led them to strike every bullfight day. Nostromo's role as foreman, master of labor, is to roust out the men on the mornings after from their 'black, lightless cluster of huts, like cow-byres, like dog-kennels' [p. 95].

When he later rebels against his own exploitation, he becomes at the same time conscious of the proletariat over whom he has been boss: 'What he had heard Giorgio Viola say once was very true. Kings, ministers, aristocrats, the rich in general, kept the people in poverty and subjection; they kept them as they kept dogs, to fight and hunt for their service' [p. 415].

Nostromo's career is, then, a record of growing class consciousness. His offended egoism first leads to withdrawal: 'What did he care about their politics? Nothing at all' [p. 417]. But egoism also turns him against his former employer; the mine 'appeared to him hateful and immense, lording it by its vast wealth over the valour, the toil, the fidelity of the poor, over war and peace, over the labours of the town, the sea, and the Campo' [p. 503]. Finally, he reasserts his origins and his ties to his mentor, recognising himself 'a republican like old Giorgio, and a revolutionist at heart (but in another manner)' [p. 525].

The 'other manner' is his acquisition of silver. It is not mere rationalisation by which Nostromo explains it to himself: 'The rich lived on wealth stolen from the people, but he had taken from the rich nothing – nothing that was not lost to them already by their folly and their betrayal' [p. 541]. The point is supported by the plot of the novel, for what provokes Nostromo to steal is the businesslike complacency of his employers towards their loss. To them it is only money, well lost for political gains. To him it is labor, courage (facing the dangers he encounters), and pride – in short, the values of the work ethic and their just reward.

Nostromo takes up the silver, which Conrad has carefully designated as a symbol of capitalism by making it the mine's actual product, and acquires a secret taint on his erstwhile 'incorruptible' character. The taint of wealth goes further: when the revolutionary party leader visits Nostromo at his deathbed in search of the bequest of his fortune to the movement, he claims it because 'the rich must be fought with their own weapons' [p. 562]. It is, then, a mark of his dedication to the revolution that Nostromo does not answer, does not allow the curse to be passed on to the people.

And yet, for all his developing class consciousness, Nostromo remains bedevilled by the contradictions of his own character. An egoist whose pride has been hurt, he tries to identify himself with the people, but just when his egoistic desire for reputation is satisfied in the fullest measure, he is isolated by his guilty conscience and by his hidden crime. He then tries to take on another identity along with the old – that of Captain Fidanza, seaman-merchant and respectable patron of the radical party. How are we to regard this ironic mixture of alienation and integration, of individualism and social responsibility, of self-transcendence and self-destruction?

Nostromo's political career centers on four acts: the rescue of the escaping President Ribiera and the suppression of the rioting *Lumpenproletariat*; the 'off-stage' secret mission to Hernandez; the removal of the silver from Sulaco to save it from the invading Monterist forces; and the summoning of General Barrios' army to defeat the Monterists and establish an independent Occidental Republic. In the first case, Nostromo's act is along strict class lines, favoring the aristocratic Blancos against the demagogic popular party. In the second, he is the emissary of Father Corbelàn, serving the efforts of the aristocracy (Corbelàn is of the Avellanos family) to put itself in league with its own peasantry, despite their 'bandit' status. In the third, the interests of the mine – of the new capitalist order – are uppermost, but here Nostromo breaks with his role of upper-class factotum when he discovers his exploitation. In the last action, his guiding principle is the separatism of Decoud and is in the popular interest: to protect the community of Sulaco from the depredations of a ruthless military regime.

It is at this point that Nostromo identifies himself with the community most fully and most altruistically – at precisely the time of his greatest egoism, when he is already absorbed in his own plans to become rich. Individualism here fosters social action, but later, his social integration is eroded by personal preoccupations. This ironic relationship of communal identity and inveterate isolation is what gives Nostromo's career, like the larger historical action of the novel, its tragic character. Community and individual are found to be both interdependent and mutually exclusive: they create and they destroy each other – at least at this imperfect level of social development.

We are now in a position to justify the otherwise intolerably melodramatic conclusion of the novel, in which Nostromo, drawing off silver in order to 'become rich slowly', is shot by his revolutionary mentor, Giorgio Viola, who takes him for the

young worker, Ramirez, the unwelcome suitor of his daughter.
Given the class conflicts and symbolic suggestions of the novel,
the dénouement reads like a myth of radical politics: Viola, the
old-guard Garibaldino, rejects Ramirez because he is a native of
Sulaco and therefore lacking in traditional class consciousness.
(It is the European element that forms the working-class elite and
the native half-breeds who constitute the tools of the demagogues
Gamacho and Fuentes [p. 529].) The idealist Viola fails to
recognise Nostromo because of his both literal and symbolic poor
vision. The faded radical is out of touch with the new proletariat
and is himself ridden by class prejudices (e.g., those of the
European workers against the natives).

Nostromo is, even without Viola's myopia, directly destroyed
by the contradictions between self-seeking and class consciousness. He uses the silver, at least in part, for the support of the
radical movement, but he keeps his secret so well that he becomes
totally isolated. He is killed by that isolation, through Viola's
ignorance of his identity and designs. As in *Lord Jim* and other
Conrad fables of the individual's relation to the social organism,
there is in *Nostromo* a residual resistance to complete assimilation
with the people, and this heroic individualism accounts both for
the hero's demise and for his stature.

Like every tragic figure, Nostromo cannot be held by the world
any longer – cannot be contained, at least within its usual
morality. Like every tragic figure, he takes on himself the burden
of guilt (or at least the illusion of it): the guilt of failing to bring a
priest for the dying wife of Viola, the guilt of leaving Decoud
behind to die. Nostromo is the sacrifice that societies make in
order to live, and thereby he is made awesome. His very self-
sacrifice leads him to rid himself of the conventional social
bonds – to be, with the aged Oedipus, beyond society. Like every
tragic hero, he achieves freedom, a certain recklessness born of
the infinity of possibilities which opens before him when he
acquires the treasure and becomes alienated from all classes and
all men. He becomes the benefactor of the people, but the new
order he has brought about is repressive in its turn. He joins the
revolutionary party, but he never becomes ideologically committed to social or political action.

He is now free of everything but the treasure, the very
instrument of his flight to freedom. There remains only to rid

himself of that bond and he will be free, so free that there remains for him only to die. 'In the exulting consciousness of his strength, and the triumphant excitement of his mind, he struck a blow for his freedom.' He tells his beloved, Giselle Viola, of the treasure and when she asks how he got it, 'He wrestled with the spell of captivity. It was as if striking a heroic blow that he burst out: "Like a thief!" ' [p. 540]. In judging his own crime, Nostromo frees himself from 'captivity', strikes a 'heroic blow', fulfills himself as tragic hero. He points the way toward an ideal social hero who achieves full integration with his nation or his class. But he himself does not fulfill that ideal. He is, rather, another kind of hero, the tragic figure torn apart by the contradictions involved in his effort to transcend his historical situation and his own ego. This dialectical negation is as far as Conrad will go in leading our imagination toward the ideal of community.

## The Intellectual

The parallel between Nostromo and Decoud is suggested by the latter himself: 'I am no patriot. I am no more of a patriot than the Capataz of the Sulaco Cargadores, this Genoese who has done such great things for this harbour – this active usher-in [sic] of the material implements for our progress' [p. 191]. The two characters are twin studies of the relationship between personal and social motives, between egoism and the urge for community. 'A victim of the disillusioned weariness which is the retribution meted out to intellectual audacity' – so Conrad describes Decoud; a 'victim of the disenchanted vanity which is the reward of audacious action' – so he describes Nostromo [p. 501]. The man of action and the man of intellect are in the vanguard of the nation's progress, but they are no patriots, never ridding themselves of their skepticism or their selfishness.

Although Decoud claims that his motives are not patriotic, his patriotism is not merely an invention to win his beloved, Antonia Avellanos, whose enthusiasm requires similar sentiments of him. He often speaks as though this were the case, and has succeeded in convincing some readers, but Conrad betrays Decoud's psychic need to do so: 'He soothed himself by saying he was not a patriot, but a lover' [p. 176]. Perversely, to the woman herself,

Decoud insists on his lack of idealism: 'he seized every opportunity to tell her that though she had managed to make a Blanco
journalist of him, he was no patriot' [p. 186]. He goes on to
explain: 'First of all, the word had no sense for cultured minds, to
whom the narrowness of every belief is odious; and secondly, in
connection with the everlasting troubles of this unhappy country
it was hopelessly besmirched; it had been the cry of dark
barbarism, the cloak of lawlessness, of crimes, of rapacity, of
simple thieving.' Yet despite his wish to dissociate himself from
his country's history, Decoud becomes the author of his
province's declaration of independence and the father of its
development into a community.

What are we to make of this lover of contradictions, this skeptic
who becomes a national hero almost against his will? It is easy to
identify him with Conrad in his ambivalence toward his Polish
tradition, as Morf has done: the words 'Pro Patria!' which he
utters ironically are those with which Conrad bitterly describes
his grand-uncle's wasted dedication to Polish independence (*A
Personal Record*, p. 35). Conrad carried his Polishness ironically,
yet in the time of crisis he finally returned to the fold. Decoud is
subjected to Father Corbelàn's Dostoevskian anathemas, but he
defends himself as Conrad might have done: 'I believe I am a true
*hijo del pays*, a true son of the country, whatever Father Corbelàn
may say. . . . A Sulaco revolution. . . . The Great Cause may be
served here' [pp. 213–14]. Decoud's nationalism, then, partakes
of the larger visions of Conrad's political imagination, the 'Great
Cause' or 'idea' of community which may be served by national
liberation.

If Decoud, for all his irony, does affirm his identity with the
nation and with some larger community through his theory and
practice of revolution, it is his separation from the revolution and
from other men that brings about his suicide. Conrad is unusually
explicit in his authorial comment: 'the truth was that he died
from solitude, the enemy known but to few on this earth, and
whom only the simplest of us are fit to withstand. The brilliant
Costaguanero of the boulevards had died from solitude and want
of faith in himself and others' [p. 496]. The meaning of this
solitude may readily be found in the metaphysics of individuality
and community. In a crucial passage, Conrad sets out in
metaphysical terms Decoud's inability 'to grapple with himself

single-handed'. Separated from 'others', the self does not find its pure essence but on the contrary loses its identity:

After three days of waiting for the sight of some human face, Decoud caught himself entertaining a doubt of his own individuality. It had merged into the world of cloud and water, of natural forces and forms of nature. In our activity alone do we find the sustaining illusion of an independent existence as against the whole scheme of things of which we form a helpless part. Decoud lost all belief in the reality of his action past and to come. [p. 497]

Individuality is an illusion, then, but it is a 'sustaining illusion' necessary to life. Reality consists of natural forces and historical action, joined in an oppressive web of circumstance. Belief in the reality of one's actions, faith in oneself and others (with its complementary skepticism) are predicated on political engagement in history, for all its brute awesomeness. Without that involvement, the individual returns to primal nothingness: 'He beheld the universe as a succession of incomprehensible images . . . the solitude appeared like a great void' [p. 498] .

In the absence of social connection, the self's only link is to nature, but it is an empty nature and a hollow link. Wishing to sever this umbilical cord as well, Decoud has nowhere to go but into the abyss: 'The cord of silence . . . must let him fall and sink into the sea, he thought' [p. 499]. He can do nothing but die.

There is this difference between nature and society as bases of human existence: Decoud sinks into the bay and disappears 'without a trace, swallowed up in the immense indifference of things' [p. 501], while society's loss of him is remembered and he becomes part of history, a national hero. For society, unlike nature, cares – or can care when it moves towards community. His suicide and its aftermath are an enactment of the philosophy which holds that man's life is social – or it is nothing.

Decoud's career dramatises Conrad's view of the relation of the intellectual and his class, the intelligentsia, to the political world. One indication of Conrad's intention, which must be qualified by the low reliability of the source, is Retinger's account of his collaboration with Conrad in 1914 on plans for a play based on *Nostromo*:

There was to be a South-American intellectual, artist, and patriot leading the revolt in the name of the people against a ruthless dictator, who dies exclaiming: 'Je meurs honteusement, mais glorieusement, pour des principes que je méprise', because in his heart he was an aristocrat, and here it came to him to lead the masses. . . . When years later I went to Mexico and there witnessed fighting and revolutions, and made friends with fat generals and visionary dreamers – all the time, while history was enacted in front of me, I was thinking: 'Here they are staging Conrad's play for me alone.' The dreamer, artistic patriot, was Diego Rivera, with his flamboyance, his readiness for action, and his complete scepticism as far as social or political problems were concerned.[16]

This transmogrification of Decoud into a kind of intellectual Gaspar Ruiz is consistent with the Conrad myth; the 'intellectual, artist, and patriot' becomes a popular leader but remains a tragic figure separated from the community. Decoud, like Nostromo, gives direction to a whole society but resists the assimilation of his precarious identity in the community, to his ultimate downfall. Decoud and Nostromo are the sacrifices that revolutions exact in order to succeed; they are the leaders, like those described by the narrator of *Under Western Eyes*, who begin revolutions but do not survive to guide them.

*The Capitalist*

The characterisation of Gould can be read as a parable of the sociology of capitalism, in its classical formulation by Weber, Sombart, and Veblen. Gould is a technician, trained in mining engineering in the course of his preparation to redeem the wrongs done to his father; a speculator, investing little capital of his own but engaging the confidence of international financiers; and a puritan: although his wife indulges a taste for carriages drawn by white mules, Gould's abstemiousness keeps him in frequent residence at the mining camp – the dominant image one is left with has him in the saddle. His ideology is chiefly distinguished by its absence, so that it is not possible to describe him in the terms applied to his backer, Holroyd . . ., the very type of *The Protestant Ethic and the Spirit of Capitalism*, who wants to spread Protestantism in Catholic countries and with it the culture and politics favorable to economic expansion.

Yet even more than Holroyd, Gould epitomises the capitalist spirit of economic activity. He is an egoist seeking victory over obstacles natural, economic, and political, a victory which is in itself more to him than the material benefit either to himself or to others – investors, workers, or the nation at large. Benefit there is, of course, but (to use a technological metaphor) it is a by-product of the mining operation rather than its real product, which is silver, i.e., money, or its international standard. The silver underscores his peculiarly capitalist behavior, as Marx described it: it is wealth without value, money as a mere abstraction, an end without an aim. Silver thus becomes an ironic symbol of Gould's distortion of the work ethic. Economic activity comes to dominate his entire behavior; his politics imply the support of any government at all which will allow that activity to continue. The ultimate failure of Gould's original policy of reliance on 'material interests' is dramatised by his wife's discovery that what were means for her husband have become all-absorbing ends in themselves.

Gould is also an imperialist, a composite of Conrad's two fictional types, the conqueror and the colonist. He is anxious to affirm his third-generation roots in the land and his commitment to its fortunes; he justifies his reopening of the mine with foreign capital 'because the security which it demands must be shared with an oppressed people. A better justice will come afterwards' [p. 84]: he does not realise the historical irony of his last remark. Nevertheless, Gould remains unassimilated, not only because of the English cut of his clothes, but because of the temperament and values that go with them.

His own self-consciousness tells him as much, but it also tells us more:

After all, with his English parentage and English upbringing, he perceived that he was an adventurer in Costaguana, the descendant of adventurers enlisted in a foreign legion, of men who had sought fortune in a revolutionary war, who had planned revolutions, who had believed in revolutions. For all the uprightness of his character, he had something of an adventurer's easy morality which takes count of personal risk in the ethical appraising of his action. He was prepared, if need be, to blow up the whole San Tomé mountain sky high out of the territory of the Republic. This resolution expressed the tenacity of his character, the remorse of that subtle conjugal infidelity through which his wife was no longer the sole mistress of his thoughts, something of his father's imaginative weakness, and something, too, of the spirit of a buccaneer throwing a lighted match into the magazine rather than surrender his ship.                                              [pp. 365–6]

This remarkable passage suggests not only the image of the conqueror, the alien who wishes to take spoil from the country rather than to identify himself with it, but also the image of the nihilist, like the Professor of *The Secret Agent* or Jörgenson of *The Rescue*, who would rather bring everything down with him than accept partial or temporary defeat. Conrad's expressed view, we recall, was that the capitalist is the greatest anarchist, and Gould's terrorism connects him with the subjects of the anarchist tales. The connection is made when he reveals his preparations to blow up the mine, in rejecting Hirsch's offer to sell him dynamite; the chief engineer of the railroad remarks that his policy is 'radical. . . . I mean going to the roots, you know', and Gould replies: 'Why, yes. . . . The Gould Concession has struck such deep roots in this country, in this province, in that gorge of the mountains, that nothing but dynamite shall be allowed to dislodge it from there' [pp. 205–6].

Above all other connections of Gould with the Conrad canon, he must be seen as an ironic version of the [Rajah] Brooke myth, the story of the man who goes alone into a disturbed area and establishes personal order over it, for good or ill. Like many of the exemplars of this pattern, the 'King of Sulaco', as he is called, is destroyed by his undertaking – his 'Imperium in Imperio'. He discovers, in the course of the revolution, that he cannot remain an *éminence grise* in the arena of history but must openly support the Separatist forces; he must agree to reconciliation with Hernandez, although he feels the moral taint of dealing with a bandit; he must sacrifice the stuffy idealism of which Decoud accuses him: 'He could not believe his own motives if he did not make them first a part of some fairy tale. The earth is not quite good enough for him, I fear' [p. 215].

When, through Gould's support, the popular cause is victorious, he begins the process of his own destruction, first, by his absorption in the mine, which alienates him from his wife, and then by his creation of an industrial proletariat which will eventually drive him out. Monygham predicts that 'the time approaches when all that the Gould Concession stands for shall weigh as heavily upon the people as the barbarism, cruelty, and misrule of a few years back' [p. 511]; and Mrs Gould has a similar vision of her husband's enterprise:

She saw the San Tomé mountain hanging over the Campo, over the whole land, feared, hated, wealthy; more soulless than any tyrant, more pitiless and autocratic than the worst Government; ready to crush innumerable lives in the expansion of its greatness. He did not see it. He could not see it.                                                                                [p. 521]

It is this failure to know himself (except in brief moments like the one quoted earlier), his failure to judge his own moral and political condition, that distinguishes Gould from his blood-brother, Kurtz. Lacking even that negative heroism that rises to acknowledge the horror within the self, Gould falls somewhere between the poles of heroism and villainy.

## The Aristocrat

The sympathy with which Conrad portrays the old aristocratic leader Avellanos has rubbed off on his politics, but it is the sentiment felt toward an amiable anachronism – a softened version of the irony with which Conrad regards the aristocracy throughout his political writings. Avellanos earns this sympathy on two accounts, his long and honorable career and his present effeteness. He is an active leader in the artificial creation of the progressive Ribiera regime and energetically aids in its defense against the Monterist coup. But the dominant image of him is set in the council chamber of the Blanco party, after his cronies have gone out to welcome the conquering enemy, where Decoud finds him slumped over the table at which he had presided. What Decoud later writes of him could be said of the best of his class:

as I looked at him, it seemed to me that I could have blown him away with my breath, he looked so frail, so weak, so worn out. . . . hasn't he seen the sheets of 'Fifty Years of Misrule', which we have begun printing on the presses of the *Porvenir*, littering the Plaza, floating in the gutters, fired out as wads for trabucos loaded with handfuls of type, blown in the wind, trampled in the mud? . . . It would be unreasonable to expect him to survive. It would be cruel.                                                     [p. 235]

For the rest of the novel he is an invalid, and he dies during the evacuation to the interior.

If there is melancholy at the passing of the noble vestiges of the aristocratic tradition, there is only contempt for the present aristocracy. Decimated by years of struggle with the central government – in which their original program of federalism was an attempt to achieve local autonomy and, through it, their own dominance in the provinces – they have contented themselves with resisting further attempts to bring their hereditary fiefs into contact with the rest of the nation or with the outside world. Sir John, the visiting head of the railroad company (whose intrusion the Blancos resist until the Ribiera government convinces them it is in their interest), remarks of their provincial realm: 'But I had no notion that a place on a sea-coast could remain so isolated from the world. If it had been a thousand miles inland now – most remarkable! Has anything ever happened here for a hundred years before to-day?' [p. 36].

Sir John is narrow-minded, of course, in his belief that only his railroad and other modern advances constitute history, but the static insulation of the aristocratic estates from the modern world under the rule of the Blancos gives point to the demagogic slogans which call them 'Feudalists! Goths!' After the visit of Ribiera and Sir John they accept the coming of the railroad, as they later accept the reopening of the mine, but at the impending invasion of the Monterist forces they are ready to cringe before the conqueror. It is the contemptible speeches they make to rationalise their cowardice that prod their last active spirit, Decoud, to develop his plan for separation.

Decoud's separatism is in origin an aristocratic plan, closely resembling the federalism of the Blancos' original program. But it does not imitate the insularity aimed at by the latter. The new separatism is based on popular sovereignty, on exposure to the modern world – for better or worse – and on continued efforts to liberate and annex the remaining portion of Costaguana. That Decoud's plan is a genuinely popular one is evidenced by the league of forces that defeats the Caesarist generals and establishes the Occidental Republic. These forces include the peasantry, led by Hernandez; the proletarians, represented by the mine workers; and the military force under General Barrios, a disreputable 'Indio' with a rough, native's manner. Decoud's genius lies in discovering not only the geographical rationale for the existence of a separate nation but the political coalition that represents, at least temporarily, the genuine interests of the people.

With the success of his plans and the establishment of the republic, the idea of separation becomes an end in itself – a florid statue is even erected to it [p. 482] – and Decoud's newspaper, the *Porvenir*, becomes merely 'Conservative, or, rather, I should say, Parliamentary', according to Captain Mitchell [p. 478]. The new state is headed by Don Juste Lopez, one of the most timorous of the aristocrats. This figurehead is sufficient indication of its debased character. It can be seen only as a transitional stage to some fuller realisation of the interests of the people, of which the first stage will be the extension of the revolution to Costaguana.

There is one other member of the aristocracy who sees the decline of his own class and the emergence of the new, and who puts himself in touch with the new. That this role should be assigned to Father Corbelàn, later Cardinal-Archbishop Corbelàn, is somewhat surprising in view of his conservative stand on other matters, particularly on preserving the Church's economic and political power. Upon reflection, Corbelàn's politics can be seen to contain a mixture of aristocratic contempt for the rising capitalist class and a patronising but deep-rooted affection for the peasantry. Both these attitudes emerge when Corbelàn replies to Monygham's prediction that 'material interests' will not support the planned revolution in Costaguana: 'We have worked for them; we have made them, these material interests of the foreigners. . . . Let them beware, then, lest the people, prevented from their aspirations, should rise and claim their share of the wealth and their share of the power' [p. 510].

Corbelàn's political activity throughout the novel shows a consistent responsiveness to the needs of the lower classes. It is he, through Nostromo, who establishes contact with Hernandez's band and brings the peasantry to support the first revolution; it is he who plots the coming revolution with Antonia Avellanos and the political refugees from Costaguana. The final irony of aristocratic politics enters here: 'And do you know where they [Antonia and Corbelàn] go for strength, for the necessary force?' Monygham asks Mrs Gould. 'To the secret societies amongst immigrants and natives, where Nostromo – I should say Captain

Fidanza – is the great man' [p. 511]. It is in alliance with the people that 'the last of the Avellanos and the last of the Corbelàns' find their political future.

SOURCE: chapter VI in *Conrad's Politics* (Baltimore, Md, and London, 1967), pp. 161–84.

NOTES

[These have been reorganised and renumbered from the original – Ed.]

1. Alexander Welsh, *The Hero of the Waverley Novels* (New Haven, Conn., and London, 1963), p. 41.

2. Ibid., p. 57.

3. A. J. Guerard, *Conrad the Novelist* (Cambridge, Mass., and London, 1958), p. 177.

4. Ibid., p. 198.

5. R. Penn Warren, Introduction to *Nostromo* (New York, 1951), pp. xxix ff.

6. I. Howe, *Politics and the Novel* (New York, 1957), p. 106. Howe cites Trotsky's theory of the permanent revolution, in which the proletariat takes over the function of the inept bourgeoisie in bringing an undeveloped country out of feudal stagnation, but this does not quite fit Costaguana, which will have a two-stage revolution.

7. Conrad, *Notes on Life and Letters* (1921; reprinted in Dent's Uniform Collected Edition), pp. 106–7.

8. [Ed. – Page references in square brackets relate to the text of the novel as published in the Dent Uniform Collected edition (London, 1946–55).

9. G. F. Masterman, *Seven Eventful Years in Paraguay: A Narrative of Personal Experience among the Paraguayans* (1869; reprinted London 1870), p. iv. Another recently discovered source is Ramon Paez, *Wild Scenes in South America: Or, Life in the Llanos of Venezuela*, discussed in C. T. Watts, 'A Minor Source for *Nostromo*', *Review of English Studies*, XVI (1965), 182–4.

10. E. B. Eastwick, *Venezuela: Or, Sketches of Life in a South American Republic* (2nd edn, London, 1868); cf. Jocelyn Baines's belief in Conrad's affinity to Eastwick, in his *Joseph Conrad: A Critical Biography* (London and New York, 1960), p. 296.

11. Jerry Allen (*The Sea Years*, p. 22 ff.) has provided excellent materials for studying Conrad's treatment of historical data, although

she does not pursue this study herself. Colombia was the only South American nation in revolt when Conrad visited its sister republic of Venezuela, and there are good grounds for believing that he was engaged in smuggling arms to the Conservative revolutionaries: arms which were being provided by the same ultras for whom he had engaged in gun-running in the Second Carlist War. The evidence for identifying Costaguana and Colombia geographically has been assembled in E. M. W. Tillyard, *The Epic Strain in the English Novel* (London, 1958), pp. 199–203, although Tillyard is moved by one inconsistency to reject the identification.

Despite the structural similarity of Colombia and Costaguana in what follows, it is well to remember the differences. The immediate cause of the Colombian Conservatives' revolt was the secular education program of the Liberals. But in *Nostromo* the issues are purely economic: control of the mine. While the aristocratic Blanco party of the novel includes dedicated Church supremacists (e.g., Father Corbelàn, who seeks the return of confiscated Church property), its main impulse is the progressive one traditionally animating liberal parties: it is the Blancos who invite foreign capital under the Ribiera regime, and who try to create the rúle of law under which it can flourish. Despite their forward-looking tendencies, the Blancos are treated as moribund anachronisms, incapable of controlling the industrial and popular forces at work in the land.

Although Conrad took this subtly critical position on the aristocratic party, having outgrown his youthful ultramontanism, he retained his original contempt of the *Lumpenproletariat* and of any party which appeals to it. In *Nostromo* the latter is described as Liberal, but it is not clear whether this is an inaccurate imputation by the rival Blancos. Conrad's main animus is against the militarist *caudillo* which harnesses this anarchic force (the same relationships are observable in most fascist revolutions in South America, as well as in Europe). The old socialist and nationalist revolutionary Giorgio Viola, who represents the real proletariat of the port and the mine, has nothing but contempt for the demagogic orators and their mobs.

12. G. Jean-Aubry (ed.), *Life and Letters*, I, 236 and 325–6 respectively.

13. *Notes on Life and Letters*, op. cit., p. 62.

14. In the early history of attempts to build a Panama Canal, there is a remarkably similar figure, the 'mystical and imaginary New York capitalist' Frederick M. Kelley, who declared: 'Seven years ago my thoughts were directed to this field of honorable enterprise and investigation by HIM who directs the minds of men to what does good or confers distinction; and I have labored ever since, in an earnest and

reverent spirit, to accomplish what seemed to be quite in accordance with the arrangement of providence'; quoted in J. Fred Rippy, *The Capitalists and Colombia* (New York, 1931), p. 46.

15. Conrad wrote in the same vein to Cunninghame Graham that *Nostromo* is 'a romantic mouthpiece of the "people" which (I mean "the people") frequently experience the very feelings to which he gives utterance': letter of 31 October 1904, *Life and Letters*, 1, 338. Here and in the novel the term 'people' connotes a specific class – the peasant and working class – and not the community of all members of the nation which it elsewhere suggests.

16. Retinger, *Conrad and His Contemporaries*, pp. 122–3.


## *Bruce E. Johnson*    The Psychology of Self-Image (1971)

*Nostromo* is a study of identity and self-image as a source of value, and as such the novel has deliberately been made pseudo-political. Political manoeuvres and ideals, so apparently the source of value for many men, are here seen as masks consciously and unconsciously used to disguise and reveal simultaneously the true source of value; and this is true for everyone in the novel (with the possible exception of Don José Avellanos), from Pedrito Montero with his poetic vision of Second Empire decadence to Charles Gould and his rule of law.

While it seems harmless to regard *Nostromo* as a political novel, doing so may obscure the manner in which various conceptions of self are brought into elegant parallels and contrasts. A political awareness ought not confuse us about Conrad's use of the political drama in Costaguana as a kind of wood stain necessary to bring out the grain of intricately compared self-conceptions. Political belief and action may be an aspect of the 'formal cause' of *Nostromo*, but it is wrong to consider it part of what Aristotle would have called the final cause of that novel. Politics, like love, has always been one of the witches' brews in which the self feels it can grow to recognisable form. Especially the young mind has often sought to define itself by some confusion of love and politics, as did Conrad himself with 'Rita' in Marseilles. What I shall try to make clear in the course of this argument is that politics in *Nostromo* is distinctly an aesthetic means to an end, and that despite its surface the novel has little to contribute to Conrad's nearly compulsive interest in human solidarity except in a negative way. For at least this novel I am inclined to take the side of Irving Howe against that of Eloise Knapp Hay.[1]

Charles Gould is essentially apolitical. We are told he broods about the silver mine as thought it were a powerful personality that had killed his father only because it had not been properly disciplined. So long as Don Carlos must pay blackmail to chaotic local authority, the mine is likely to find an unexpected and destructive way of expressing its power. To discipline the mine is, for Charles, a means of relating himself to the father he had known mostly through long letters describing his defeat by the mine and by a government which had punished him with it. Don Carlos can transcend the pathos of his father's death and perhaps achieve a victory that has been honored throughout centuries as a way of achieving identity: one continues the role of the father but kills the dragon he could not master, not through indignation or for revenge but as a self-defining gesture. I do not mean to sound either psychoanalytical or to pursue archetypes, but the early pages of *Nostromo* insist on this relationship between father, son, and mine.

Thus Charles initially does not want the silver or a stable government in themselves, for any intrinsic reasons. Without political stability he cannot succeed where his father has failed; and without the stream of silver there is of course no power and no overt measure of success. Conrad suggests that the mine becomes a demanding mistress: Emilia Gould will bear no children, and Charles is insistently described as riding off to spend the night at the mine. For reshaping his father's dilemma, Charles has what Conrad regards as the Northern, even English talent for idealising 'material interest', for making material success mean more than measurable quantities of silver and power and for justifying the pursuit of that success by some 'idea'. The American capitalist Holroyd will, he says, abandon Gould should the mine get into fairly deep trouble and cease to be a good investment; he will see Gould through the kind of difficulties that can reasonably be expected to have a silver lining, but his immediate motives are severely practical. He has, however, that same Northern talent for idealising material interests and so actually believes that his ultimate purpose is to introduce a form of Protestantism into Catholic Costaguana and to extend the moral rights of North American empire. One of the comic ironies of the novel springs from the fact that the old priest Father Roman, having been shown how to blow up the mine should anything happen to Gould and Don Pépé, thereby helps save Costaguana for the militant Protestantism of Holroyd [pp. 566–7].[2]

Conrad is far from despising the idealised materialism of Gould. At first, Emilia is able to take her sense of purpose almost entirely from her husband's: 'And at once her delight in him, lingering with half-open wings like those birds that cannot rise easily from a flat level, found a pinnacle from which to soar up into the skies' [p. 65]. The project of the mine becomes indistinguishable from their new love: 'It was as if they had been morally bound to make good their vigorous view of life against the unnatural error of weariness and despair [meaning, of course, Charles's father]' [p. 82]. The skeptic, Decoud, likes to imagine that he is precisely opposite to Charles Gould, but even Decoud acknowledges that Gould's 'sentimentalism' ('The sentimentalism of the people that will never do anything for the sake of their passionate desire, unless it comes to them clothed in the fair robes of an idea') constitutes illusions which 'somehow or other help them to get a firm hold of substance' [p. 265]. Ironically, the men most successful with the material things of this world (Holroyd and Gould) are never called 'materialistic' by Conrad: that adjective is reserved for Nostromo, whose identity is contrasted with Gould's: 'It was not the cold, ferocious, and idealistic self-conceit of a man of some northern race; it was materialistic and imaginative. It was an unpractical and warm sentiment, a picturesque development of his character, the growth of an unsophisticated sense of his individuality' [p. 461].

This is not to say that Nostromo depends upon material wealth; on the contrary he gives or gambles away most of his money and silver buttons until, imagining himself exploited, he turns with a vengeance to the treasure of silver bars. The point is that the idealistic Gould disdains the merely material as even the reputation-mad Nostromo never would, yet perhaps because of this disdain is able literally to move mountains while Nostromo gets himself killed trying to move a relatively few silver bars. As *Lord Jim* suggests, Conrad is amazed at the power of the idea over the material world and perhaps over the organic pulse of the material that might be called nature.

Gould changes the face of nature, transforms the paradise of snakes so often alluded to in the novel (and the subject of a sketch by Emilia Gould) into the scarred gorge of the Sam Tomé mine. Perhaps it is not stretching an idea too far to remember that the color of the mine, the color of hope, is also the green of nature and especially of the paradisical gorge before it is transformed by Charles's instruments of hope. The phrase 'paradise of snakes' of course invites symbolic readings. Although it is suggestive of the Fall, it seems to me we are invited primarily to speculate about the inevitability of what Charles has done to that state of nature in the gorge and to that paradise of snakes Sulaco had been before the great victory: nature innocent of power and sophistication beyond the direct danger of passionate self-interest. When Emilia Gould looks at the sketch of the virgin gorge late in the novel, she may simply wish it had never been disturbed. Yet as I read *Nostromo* it is easy to believe not in the Fortunate Fall, but in a necessary one. The great victory will lead, as Dr Monygham suggests, to new conflicts inherent in the 'democratic' spirit so welcome to Nostromo and his Italian compatriots, and in the intensified, idealised materialism of the foreign interests. What Gould has done to Sulaco, however, is no more nor less evolutionary than what Europe has done to Kurtz; yet just as Kurtz can become more vicious than his savages, so presumably can future conflicts in Sulaco surpass the anarchy which opens the novel and even the battles which establish the independent state. Charles insists, however, there is no turning back:

And Mrs Gould gazing at the last [her watercolour sketch of the San Tomé gorge] in its black wooden frame, sighed out:

'Ah, if we had left it alone, Charles!'

'No', Charles Gould said, moodily; 'it was impossible to leave it alone.'

'Perhaps it was impossible', Mrs Gould admitted slowly. Her lips quivered a little, but she smiled with an air of dainty bravado. 'We have disturbed a good many snakes in that paradise, Charley, haven't we?'

'Yes; I remember', said Charles Gould, 'It was Don Pépé who called the gorge the paradise of snakes. No doubt we have disturbed a great many. But remember, my dear, that it is not now as it was when you made that sketch.' He waved his hand toward the small water-colour hanging alone upon the great bare wall. 'It is no longer a paradise of snakes. We have brought mankind into it, and we cannot turn our backs upon them to go and begin a new life elsewhere.'                [pp. 231–2]

This conversation occurs late at night, just before Decoud is to give Mrs Gould the rumor that a battle has been fought near Santa Marta and the Ribierists defeated. As she leaves her husband and walks down the hall toward Decoud and the news that will finally commit Charles and all his energies to the independence of Sulaco, she is described in a brilliantly visualised paragraph as though moving through 'patches of sun that chequer the gloom of open glades in the woods'; she would like to be a creature of that paradise, wandering still in the innocence she and Charles once shared. Yet paradise was full of snakes to begin with, and man was born to fall: this is perhaps Conrad's emendation of the Christian story.

Charles's and presumably Conrad's main point lies, however, in the paradox of the phrase itself, 'paradise of snakes'. There is no paradise once the consciousness of man is introduced. The gorge may well have been a paradise *for* snakes, but with the introduction of man it becomes a Garden of Eden with not one serpent but many working for the fall of man. The idea of there being many snakes underlines Conrad's new metaphor for the creation of self and the description of consciousness. Each man will discover his own serpent, will see his fall in a different light and with different metaphors for its understanding. The idea of 'passion' scarcely applies at all to Charles's and Nostromo's falls; neither of these losses of innocence has any meaning at all outside the unique self-image or project each man has chosen for himself. The only common denominator lies in something like Sartre's description of the way all men have their freedom about the unconscious world – about, in the case of both these men, the silver. Sartre argues that 'doing' is really a form of having or appropriation, and that the self in having things really tries to make them part of itself according to the archetypal pattern of self trying to found itself, trying to become God. Something of the sort is clear in Gould's later behavior and self-conception. Of Nostromo we learn that he wants to 'clasp [the silver], embrace, absorb, subjugate in unquestioned possession . . .' [p. 590]. Something like Sartre's model will provide a convenient generalisation about many of the self-images in *Nostromo*, largely because Conrad perceived some of the same qualities in human consciousness. The keynote of this novel, however, is nonetheless a kind of relativity. In *An Outcast*, 'Karain', 'The Lagoon', and so forth, there was one serpent. Now there are many; indeed, one man's fall is another's salvation.

Although Conrad had always spoken of the problems involved in creating self, nowhere before *Nostromo*, not even in *Lord Jim*, does he employ so direct a vocabulary for the discussion. The novel is full of phrases such as 'self-discovery', 'sense of individuality', 'conscious and subconscious intentions', 'betrayed individuality', 'thinking, acting individuality', 'lost personality', 'doubt of his own individuality' and so on and on. Of course Marlow could not have used the vocabulary appropriate to an omniscient author. Nevertheless, the existence of such a vocabulary suggests Conrad's preoccupation with pursuing value behind politics and beyond even the subtlest conception of man as a political animal. Mrs Hay's excellent chapter on *Nostromo* rests finally on the claim that Conrad wants to denounce a political theory which is devoid of genuine moral principle but insists that whatever is good for material interests is good for the nation. No doubt Conrad hated the implication that a capitalistic wave of the future had made it unnecessary for a nation and its citizens painfully to discover moral relationships between the individual and society. Material interests, as we can all agree, bring with them peculiarly cold forms of inhumanity, in which the individual can no longer locate his authentic self among the proffered economic identities. What begins with the desirable outfitting of Gould's miners in protectively green and hopeful uniforms ends in the leviathan impersonality of economic process. One has the feeling that Gould's growing silence and stolidity are the inevitable result of his dedication to the mine, and that his single principle is an unconscious attempt to put man in some kind of grotesque sympathy with the earth itself.

Despite Conrad's distaste for the arrogance of this 'progressive' capitalism – suggested to him most directly by the rationalisations of American imperialism in Cuba and the Philippines – he subordinates the political issue to a more resonant and ultimately more important objection to Gould. These material interests – especially the mine – have a metaphysical as well as political importance. (We cannot pursue here their origins in religious doctrine, in issues discussed by Tawney and Max Weber as inherent in the rise of capitalism.) Such interests represent, in effect, the seduction of human nature by the nonhuman in-itself (to use Sartre's word); and this seduction usually involves treating the 'material' as though it lived a superior, clean life of its own, above – in the case of the mine, literally above – the tangle of human moral error. Thus Gould gives a personality to the mine and thinks of his father as a man who did not 'understand' it.

We cannot then say that the silver, symbolising these material interests and their progressive capitalism, kills Nostromo; and, in fact, the entire sense of the contrast Conrad meant to suggest between Charles Gould and Nostromo must be reexamined as a problem in forms of identity. Gould has lost himself by idealising an economic function, as many men are able to in an age when economic romance perhaps appears superior to that between a man and a woman or a man and his country. It is to Conrad's credit as a sympathetic artist that he can summon at least a cool understanding of the mine's appeal. But what Conrad sees in Gould's attitude toward the silver is not what he sees in Nostromo's after his return from the Isabels. As with the doubloon in *Moby Dick*, we must here describe a paradigm of meaning for the silver ('I look, you look, they look') rather than argue that simple Nostromo joins Monygham, Mrs Gould, and Conrad in appreciating the destructiveness of material interests. There can be no doubt that the silver is meant as a symbolic axis; but we need not assume that its meaning will be largely or ultimately political to a sensitive reader watching the characters revolve about its influence.

To Nostromo the shipment of silver at first seems to offer a capstone for his vanity. Rescuing the ingots will secure a reputation already approaching legend. This expectation is of course undercut ironically by the 'builder of railways' who suggests that since no one could have run off with such a load of silver, 'Gould, Decoud, and myself judged that it didn't matter in the least who went'. 'He took a slightly different view', says Monygham in partial sympathy with Nostromo's own grand estimate of the affair [p. 356]. It does not at the outset matter to Nostromo where the silver comes from or what it symbolises to his employers, so long as they obviously value it.

The silver and the idea of the mine induce in Gould a loss of moral sensitivity; in Nostromo, on the contrary, the treasure causes the very birth of moral awareness in a man who has always found his identity in vain reputation. Gould depends on the absolute will of the inanimate, on the irrational demands of the earth; Nostromo listens only to the voice of others, of his people and of the ruling Europeans. I suggest that Conrad meant to show two opposite directions both leading to a form of inhumanity, two apparently opposite means of achieving a sense of self which end nearly in the destruction of individual identity.

When Nostromo swims ashore and falls asleep in the fort, he has completed the first step in his loss of identity. In a famous passage he arises from his 'lair in the long grass', as 'natural and free from evil in the moment of waking as a magnificent and unconscious wild beast'; but then 'in the suddenly steadied glance fixed upon nothing from under a forced frown, appeared the man' [p. 458]. In his passion to enhance a reputation, Nostromo, 'our man', has gotten into a situation where he cannot even show himself in Sulaco. Secrecy is imperative, and secrecy is one of the demands that will erode Nostromo's sense of identity. This man who has fed upon the regard of even the lowest Indian must go sneaking about the waterfront avoiding the contacts so necessary to his psychic well-being. Before meeting Dr Monygham he believes that the arrival of Sotillo had decided the fate of Sulaco, and that no one except Decoud 'cared whether he fell into the hands of the Monterists or not. . . . And that merely would be an anxiety for his [Decoud's] own sake' [p. 463]. Nostromo's position would not be so difficult for a man taking his identity from something other than vain reputation; but Nostromo, suddenly deprived of adulation, childishly feels victimised, betrayed into a scheme which seems after all to have been an insignificant part of the complex crisis. He refuses to leave Sulaco without something to show for his career there, something material which cannot, as his popular role does, suddenly disappear like mist over the harbor. Conrad tells us at this moment that Nostromo has 'no intellectual existence or moral strain to carry on his individuality, unscathed, over the abyss left by the collapse of his vanity' [p. 466]. Except for his anger at the fine gentlemen who have exploited him (a sentiment he borrows to fit the occasion from old Viola), Nostromo shares none of Conrad's disgust at the subtle corruption spread by material interests. Nor is the reader encouraged to see Nostromo's plight as the result of material interests working their merciless logic upon human frailty.

If we are to suggest that Nostromo's destruction is, along with everything else in the novel, in the service of Conrad's attack on the mystique of progressive capitalism, then surely his possession of the silver must be our principal evidence. His first reaction to the débâcle is that he has simply been 'betrayed' out of his old identity, and must now, in all his unintelligent simplicity, create a new basis for an identity: 'The word [*betrayed*] had fixed itself tenaciously in his unintelligence. His imagination had seized upon the clear and simple notion of betrayal to account for the dazed feeling of enlightenment as to being done for, of having inadvertently gone out of his existence on an issue in which his personality had not been taken into account' [pp. 469–70]. Later he is extraordinarily ready to feel guilty for Decoud's death. But we may be sure that had he been able to retain faith in his old identity neither event would have affected him morally. The loss of that self has created a moral sensibility or allowed a weak, innate one to grow sizably. His mind – 'the popular mind is incapable of scepticism' [p. 470] – must believe in something; and, after all, he is surrounded with the insistent argument that the universe is run according to 'power, punishment, pardon', quite apart from whether or not one accepted the priests' claims of earthly power. Thus the silver which has clouded and finally obliterated a true moral sense in Charles Gould has ironically developed one in Nostromo. The silver may kill 'our man' who has become his own man, but it cannot easily be said to have corrupted him. He is no longer reliable and – according to Captain Mitchell's sort of definition – incorruptible; but he is morally awake as he never has been before. Who other than Nostromo himself is to say this is a loss? If we are to condemn material interests for contributing to such changes in Nostromo, we shall lose our case. What kills Nostromo is not the taint of silver, symbolising progressive capitalism; the silver might have had the same effect on him had it been melted down from the trinkets of the ladies of Sulaco by Don José Avellanos personally. Nor is he destroyed through moralising the amoral, a sin which would indeed connect his death with the corruption of Charles Gould and of progressive capitalism in general. He feels, rather, that there must be compensation for the betrayal which has forced him 'out of his existence'. The escape with the silver has irrevocably shown him how easily his identity could be dissolved, a basic truth which the fame of his subsequent ride to Cayta cannot erase. He demonically wants from the silver a rudimentary sense of recompense; had he lost his identity in another way, his method of seeking restitution might easily have been different.

What connects the story of Nostromo with that of Charles Gould is thus not the objection to progressive capitalism but the drama of identity – cohering, dissolving, finding new form, always producing a sense of value or its equally powerful absence, destroying and creating. As a rule the attempts of various characters to take identity from abstractions, especially from one kind or another of political idealism, fail. Neither Viola nor Don José Avellanos fails in the attempt (though Avellanos is sorely tested when the sheets of his history of Costaguana are used for gun wadding), and Captain Mitchell seems able to identify himself with 'historic events'. But on the whole one wonders whether dedication to even the most enlightened political morality and idealism would not dehumanise its champion; if we are to take Dr Monygham as in significant part the voice of Conrad, then, as he says, there is 'something inherent in the necessities of successful action which carried with it the moral degradation of the idea' [p. 582]. Though Conrad is amazingly farsighted, even prophetic in his criticism of the pseudo ethic of material interests, he is even wiser in the above observation. A man must take his identity not only from ideas but from the painful commitment to other human individuals so conspicuously absent from Nostromo's final state of mind and – as he becomes absorbed in the mine – from Charles Gould's.

Concerned always with his reputation, with the verdict of the many, Nostromo is remarkably distant from even those closest to him, from old Viola and, as Conrad makes brilliantly clear in her death scenes, from Teresa. In one of the many structural ironies which create the unity of this sprawling novel, Nostromo is deeply moved by another human soul – for all its weakness and naïvety – only just before he dies. Concerned that recompense be made for his lost identity, 'the only thing lost in that desperate affair' [p. 485], he is shot by Viola before Giselle can affect him permanently. As Gould grows further from all intimate human contact, so Nostromo dies essentially alone, both men destroyed by modes of identity that make no room for the dependence on another single human being which sustains Monygham, Teresa, and Mrs Gould, to name only conspicuous examples. Faith in another fallible human may ultimately be no more secure a source of identity than a faith in ideas that will be corrupted by their very enactment or in a reputation established by the impersonal crowd; but at least such intimate dependence defines one's humanity as Gould's and Nostromo's never can be.

There is in this novel an intricate playing on the name Nostromo, and it is probably for this reason rather than for any centrality in the plot that 'our man' gives his name to the whole performance. As long as he depends on being their man (his European employers' and the crowd's) he cannot really be his own. After sinking the lighter and abandoning Decoud on the Isabels, Nostromo says that the 'captain' is no more. All along, Teresa has objected to the name given him by the fine gentleman, *Nostromo*, as no *name* at all – that is, no indication of independent individuality. But when he realises that his own name – Giovanni Battista Fidanza – must supplant the other names and titles, Nostromo reserves none of his energy for the love which might genuinely confirm a new identity. His visits to Viola and the girls become – until the moment he is captivated by Giselle – only an excuse to accumulate a silver recompense for the loss of his most ominous and perhaps most accurate name, Nostromo.

Nonetheless the man who cannot even entertain seriously the abstract ideal, political or otherwise, is destroyed as surely as Nostromo and Gould. So much has been written about Decoud's skepticism that it is unnecessary to rehearse its failure in detail. Obviously, however, Conrad meant us to compare it not only with Nostromo and Gould but with Emilia Gould, whose life also pivots on love for another human being. What, then, are the differences between these two, or between Monygham and Decoud? Monygham, tortured like some Sartrean hero until he finds himself capable of anything, exists only in the light of Emilia Gould's regard. He has, however, a peculiar ability to idealise the distinguishing feature of his life: 'For Dr Monygham has made for himself an ideal conception of his disgrace' [p. 418]. He has, as Conrad says, exaggerated a correct feeling, failing to explain at least partially his fantastic confessions under torture by 'physiological facts or reasonable arguments'. Partly guilty, he is also partly innocent, but shapes his life to the contour of that guilt. He denies the perfectibility of man even while worshiping the nearly perfect Emilia Gould, and offers himself in sacrifice not to the new state of Sulaco or to Emilia's love for her husband (and hence to Charles's success), but to the idealised guilt that in his own eyes makes him the man for such dirty and deadly work as the deception of Sotillo.

Mrs Gould, sustained by love for her husband, is also for a time capable of idealising the mine and even material interests. When that idealism fades with the slow corruption of her husband, she is after all surrounded by people in whom she can readily believe: Antonia, Monygham, even for a time Decoud himself. Furthermore, neither Monygham nor Emilia is primarily an intellectual creature, though Monygham has a quasi-intellectual farsightedness that enables him to see the long-run oppressiveness of the San Tomé mine. Monygham is also both intellectually and emotionally aware of the threat that Decoud, because of his unsupported intellect and his inability to idealise more than his fragile love for Antonia, cannot tolerate. The identities Conrad imagines here demanded a sense of *individual* existence; but as Monygham has reason to know, the element common to all physical dangers is 'the crushing, paralysing sense of human littleness, which is what really defeats a man struggling with natural forces alone, far from the eyes of his fellows. He was eminently fit to appreciate the mental image he made for himself of the capataz, after hours of tension and anxiety precipitated suddenly into an abyss of waters and darkness, without earth or sky, and confronting it not only with an undismayed mind but with sensible success' [pp. 484–5]. Of course the danger facing

Decoud when he is isolated with the treasure is not physical. Yet Decoud and Nostromo would seem to react in opposite ways to such physical and psychological isolation. Monygham in the above passage sees that there are times when the sense of identity is so fragile that one feels oneself absorbed as just another part of the physical universe. And it is this threat, this terrifying sublimation, which awaits the man who cannot idealise his actions and is denied the presence of a human love that might have continued to define him. Decoud is very nearly the kind of skeptic whom Stein had suggested tries to climb out of the destructive element of dreams and ideals and to deny that they are a necessary part of our humanity. Decoud drowns and dies, as Stein said he would, because he tries to be the natural man, avoiding that 'unnatural' fervor of idealism except as a formal exercise.

Once again it is easy to see how a great many of Conrad's characters are placed by their relation to nature, by the degree to which they accept, deny, distort, or are simply unaware of the seemingly unnatural position Victorian science had created for human consciousness. Decoud's isolation on the island reminds us how that situation was used in the eighteenth century as a means of expressing not only theories of nature but maps of the human mind as well. Robinson Crusoe bends nature zestfully to his middle-class economic will; and we can imagine an American transcendentalist isolated as Decoud was and mystically penetrating even the dispiriting nature of the placid gulf. Far from discovering in nature a profound symbolic revelation of the God-given stuff of economic and spiritual success, Decoud (like Marlow in *Heart of Darkness*, unable to read his environment) 'beheld his universe as a succession of incomprehensible images'. He does not even feel, as Ishmael in *Moby Dick* does, that there *is* a meaning though man will never penetrate the symbolic masks to its presence. The nature which absorbs Decoud is an impersonal process, the ghostly and amoral analogue, on the metaphysical level, of material interests.

Decoud cannot finally resist the temptation to merge with unconscious nature; he cannot even distinguish himself from it. Yet – appearances to the contrary – is not the same or a very similar attraction characteristic of the ultimate projects of both Nostromo and Charles, and is not the silver symbolic of this?

Though, as I have said, Nostromo initially defies absorption by the placid gulf (in a scene that is meant on a very accessible level as a contrast to Decoud's later suicide in those same waters), both men are finally carried to their deaths literally and figuratively weighted with silver. In desiring to 'clasp, embrace, absorb' the silver, Nostromo has also lost the sense of boundaries between the human and unconscious matter. Indeed Conrad focuses here as in *Lord Jim* on man's various attempts to be self-caused and self-founded, to become in-itself (to 'absorb' the silver or be absorbed by it). Such a project, the archetypal project for Sartre, is, however, futile and destructive. We can well understand the different motives in all three men (Charles, Nostromo, and Decoud) that bring them to the same grotesque imitation of matter. It is especially clear why 'our man', having grounded his identity in the opinion of others, should now turn to what seems to him most permanent and unlike that ephemeral acclaim. He will later continue his life in the public eye, but only because he can simultaneously hoard the true foundation of his being.

What happens to Decoud is the most conspicuous example of the pattern I am suggesting. When he weights his pockets with silver before shooting himself and plunging into the placid gulf, an important symbolic connection is made between men who otherwise seem unlike one another. After all, Decoud unlike Nostromo has cared nothing about public opinion, though the two share an inability to idealise their desires. Charles, on the contrary, is expert at idealising his passions and epitomises the spiritualised material interests for which Decoud can summon no real enthusiasm. Nonetheless, when Decoud reaches his extremity, it is the silver that comes to symbolise the metaphysics of his disappearance into the plenitude of an indifferent nature:

After three days of waiting for the sight of some human face, Decoud caught himself entertaining a doubt of his own individuality. It had merged into the world of cloud and water, of natural forces and forms of nature. In our activity alone do we find the sustaining illusion of an independent existence as against the whole scheme of things of which we form a helpless part. [p. 556]

The bars of San Tomé silver are chosen to speed and perfect his entry into this world: 'Don Martin Decoud, weighted by the bars of San Tomé silver, disappeared without a trace, swallowed up in the immense indifference of things' [p. 560]. The intimation is that the silver satisfies a related project on the part of Charles and Nostromo. The language surrounding Charles's hopes for the mine echoes, as I have said, with the idea of permanence, incorruptibility, stability, purity, and, in short, with the infinite density of in-itself. Although his talent for the idealisation of material interests would seem to lift the silver out of its existence as in-itself by the sheer energy of human significance, the movement of his character away from all forms of human contingency (even from his wife's love, which is barely contingent at all) uncovers the true nature of his project. Claire Rosenfield senses his similarity to Lord Jim:

As Thomas Moser suggests, Conrad found the subject of love uncongenial; but in Charles Gould he reveals the successful characterization of a man unable to love for reasons which were congenial to Conrad. He is attempting to be faithful to an image of himself; he is a romantic like Lord Jim. Like Lord Jim he allows his egoism to isolate him completely from other human beings. The man who attempts to sentimentalise his actions is simply another portrait of a type which Conrad successfully created again and again – the self-deluded idealist.[3]

But we ought to be suspicious of any claim that such a figure was simply congenial to Conrad. Gould's increasing isolation is intuitively seen by the man himself – and by many others – as god like. Gould sees Holroyd as a kind of god (as Miss Rosenfield observes), and he himself is Holroyd's chosen one in Sulaco. The evidence that Charles projects a godlike role for himself and the mine is too numerous to mention here. It is his mode of establishing this godhead that really reminds one of Lord Jim. Like Jim, he very subtly desires to be like the unconscious natural world, specifically like the silver, but also to be entirely conscious of – and in that sense also to have founded – his own immutability. The familiar paradox and futility of Lord Jim is repeated. Needless to say, Conrad is far from simply 'congenial' to the idea that man may be lost so that God can be born. Conrad knows that in the sense of founding values man must be godlike, but not at the expense of losing his humanity. The abandoned Jewel and

Emilia Gould are the most conspicuous signs of this betrayal, although there are much broader trails of such indication left behind both men. I suspect that although Conrad appreciated the importance of any such project to become God, he would have insisted on several perspectives. First, that although it is difficult to say how aware either Gould or Jim is of the true nature of his project, both have consciously chosen it and yet are unwilling to take the responsibility for having done so. Their projects continually dodge the one quality that Conrad would have insisted on as godly: responsibility. It is precisely at this point that Kurtz becomes important in Conrad's contemplation of the man-god, for though Kurtz's path to divinity has been more direct and in pattern somewhat unlike Jim's and Charles's, he alone has had the courage to assume responsibility for his divine prerogatives. Compare his 'The horror!' with Jim's hand placed carefully over his mouth at the moment of death.

Charles, Nostromo and Decoud have all failed in the fundamental necessity of consciousness to distinguish itself from the dumb world. That sounds like a strange way of describing what is wrong with them, but it seems to me the most basic way. Although Decoud and Nostromo are not striking examples of the man-god in either the Lord Jim or Kurtz pattern, both are seduced by in-itself and both strive to be continually aware of the immutability they can never really establish.

The San Tomé silver, then, whatever political implications it may have, serves primarily as a symbol of the most primitive and yet perhaps most difficult task confronting consciousness: to know what it is not, to appreciate its own unique mode of being. The implication of *Nostromo* for Conrad's psychological models is enormous but not essentially different from *Lord Jim*. *Nostromo*, however, suggests that Conrad had become more nearly aware that Kurtz's hollowness was not so much the failure of consciousness as its permanent condition of radical freedom, continual becoming, and total contingency. In *Nostromo* he was never further from resembling Freudian or depth-psychology models, nor from the rubrics of will and passion or ego and sympathy. Decoud on the Isabels is much like Roquentin in the park, both men threatened by the plenitude of being to the point where neither feels capable of that fundamental, self-defining act of consciousness: negation, the secretion of nothingness which is the

nature of consciousness. Though Roquentin sees and feels the
threat everywhere (in the very roots of the tree he watches),
Conrad has made it much more difficult to see the ultimate threat
in the silver. There are, after all, subtle temptations for Conrad to
use more conventional language. We are told, for instance, what
terms to use for understanding Decoud's suicide:

He had recognised no other virtue than intelligence, and had erected
passions into duties. Both his intelligence and his passion were
swallowed up easily in this great unbroken solitude of waiting without
faith. Sleeplessness had robbed his will of all energy, for he had not slept
seven hours in seven days.                                       [p. 557]

The review of categories is hastily made: intelligence, passions,
duties, faith, will; and the very breakneck pace of the list
indicates how little it interests Conrad except in its suggestion of
the way Decoud, in contrast to Steinian idealists, creates his
imitation of ideals. But see what has happened to will: from the
ostensibly principal subject of enquiry it had been in the early
work we now find it checked off almost as an afterthought and
weakened by so mundane (though admittedly devastating) a
thing as lack of sleep. The truth is that the conception of will has
little bearing on any of the characters in this novel. For Gould
and Nostromo, passion and will – in so far as we can use these
categories at all – are one, subsumed by the more viable conception of identity and self-image. The very language of the novel
shows how the drama of identity has replaced the vocabulary of
classical psychology. If there is any place in *Nostromo* where the
struggle between will and passion might have been adduced,
surely it is the moment when Nostromo decides to possess the
treasure. Yet, as I think most readers will agree, no such frame is
suggested for that decision. We can imagine how in an earlier
novel, nonetheless, there might have been a rhetoric of classical
psychology seriously designed to universalise the particular in a
distressing and occasionally dishonest way.

*Nostromo* still demonstrates, to be sure, Conrad's tendency to
doubt the power of intellect. Nor is the idea of conscience entirely
absent. But on the whole the old conceptions (intellect, conscience, passion, duty, will, sympathy, ego) are all reshaped by
approaching a character through his own sense of identity, as of

course they were in a small way in even his first novel. Since the classical categories appear to hinder Conrad's appreciation of human behavior that simply escapes or eludes them, it becomes vital that he consider the birth of value without the dubious aid of these models. Granted, he had produced great art with their powerful economies of thought and emotion, but he could not have written either *Lord Jim* or *Heart of Darkness* while strongly under their influence. When any one of them preoccupied Conrad – as, say, Schopenhauerian will did in 'Falk' – the true subject of his story was often submerged and lost in the more easily managed expectations of the model. Thus the threat from absurdity that seems to have been the real importance of his experience in Bangkok never emerges in 'Falk', as it most certainly does in *Heart of Darkness*, where the conception of unbridled ego very soon proves inadequate to adduce Kurtz's significance.

For reasons that are not entirely clear, Conrad's increasing interest in self-image as the arbiter of value parallels the development in Europe and the United States of what has been called the psychology of personality. British behaviorism and the study of 'mind in general' gave way in the work of Freud and of the Gestalt psychologists in the first two or three decades of the century to a concern with unique personality (even if only eventually to return to mind in general with a vengeance). In the thirties the United States added the work of Gordon Allport, Henry Murray, and Kurt Lewin – among others – to advances in Freudian and German Gestalt psychology until, as one contemporary psychologist summarises the matter, 'Concern with the self and self-image is one of the most striking features of recent theoretical developments.' 'The self, which perished as a psychological entity some time before the turn of the century, has been rediscovered as a vital and necessary conceptual referrant. I predict that it will not soon be lost again.'[4] Of course in art the self did not 'perish as a psychological entity some time before the turn of the century'; on the contrary, so-called Impressionism and the Romantic influence of Schopenhauerian solipsism had given it a vogue. But there is undeniably a strong taste in much of Conrad's work for displaying mind in general, a taste which has, by the way, enabled an occasional student to underline all Conrad's comments on conscience, intellect, will, passion, and so on, and offer the sum as Conrad's 'psychology'. Though it is an absurd critical method, the fact that it can be done at all shows Conrad's often rather slavish enthusiasm for a Victorian pastime so much at odds with his avowed impressionism and with the surpassing power of his imagination.

While it is undeniable that my analysis of *Lord Jim*, *Heart of Darkness*, and *Nostromo* also depends to some extent on a sense of mind in general, it must be clear that none of the Conradian insights that may be compared with Sartre are given labels in the novels, nor are they manipulated as categories and faculties. The only fundamental categories necessary in this model are consciousness and what it is not. The individual choice of project is as various and unique as the fundamental fact that everything is either conscious or not will allow. The fresh existential insights of these three novels are perfectly and unavoidably dependent on what I have called Conrad's metaphor or model of self-image. The cliché is, after all, no cliché at all.

SOURCE: chapter 6 of *Conrad's Models of Mind* (Minneapolis, 1971), pp. 106–25.

NOTES

[These have been slightly revised and renumbered from the original – Ed.]

1. I. Howe, *Politics and the Novel* (New York, 1957), pp. 76–113; E. Knapp Hay, *Political Novels of Joseph Conrad* (Chicago and London, 1963), ch. 5.

2. [Ed. – Page references in square brackets relate to the text of the novel as published in the Modern Library edition (New York, 1951).]

3. Claire Rosenfield, *Paradise of Snakes: An Archetypal Analysis of Conrad's Political Novels* (Chicago, 1967), p. 58.

4. R. H. Knapp, 'The Psychology of Personality', in B. Berelson (ed.), *The Behavioral Sciences Today* (New York, 1963), pp. 158, 164.

*Royal Roussel* The Ironic Vision (1971)

The landscape of *Nostromo* is a revelation of the darkness. For all its size, it does not give the impression of massive solidity, of a world of 'matter . . . as vulgarly understood'.¹ Dominated by 'boundless' plains [p. 87]² which pass into 'the opal mystery of great distances' [p. 8] and by the peaks of the Cordillera which appear as if they 'had dissolved . . . into great piles of grey and black vapours' [p. 6], this landscape suggests instead the infinite substance of 'inconceivable tenuity' from which creation has sprung. At the center of the geography of *Nostromo* lies the darkness of the Golfo Placido. Like the night 'without limit in space and time' [p. 241] which Edith Travers encounters, it negates the forms of creation and confounds the objects of everyday life into one homogeneous obscurity: 'Sky, land, and sea disappear together out of the world when the Placido – as the saying is – goes to sleep under its black poncho' [p. 6]. In the 'vastness' of the gulf at night, 'your ship floats unseen under your feet, her sails flutter invisible above your head' [p. 7]. All things are 'merged into the uniform texture of the night' [p. 302].

The darkness of the Golfo Placido not only transcends the physical structures of creation. It transcends, and negates, all levels of consciousness – both rational and emotional – as well. It is the source and end of both the empty, formal eloquence of Don Juste and Avellanos and the more primitive irrationality and barbarism of the Monteros. When Decoud voyages into the Placido, he finds that 'no intelligence could penetrate the darkness of the Placid Gulf' [p. 275] and that he was robbed of his power of analysis. He finds that his one emotional hold on the world, his love for Antonia, evaporates too and that, like Edith Travers, he is reduced to a state of enervated languor in which his appearance is like 'that of a somnambulist' [p. 499].

In *Nostromo* the landscape does not exhibit toward men the active hostility of the jungle in *Heart of Darkness*. As the name Placido suggests, its chief characteristic is its imperturbability. It has about it a sense of 'universal repose' [p. 494] which reflects the stability of being that the darkness possesses. Outside of time and space, the matter of the 'eternal something'[3] cannot decay or die, and for Conrad, as we have seen, all material objects share in this stability in so far as they are in their essence material. The silver of the mine is, by virtue of this fact, incorruptible; although its form can be changed from ore to ingot it remains in some sense unaltered, and for this reason it can be trusted to 'keep its value for ever' [p. 300].

It is the intuition of matter's self-contained being which the characters of the novel find so destructive. Perhaps in no other work by Conrad does one find such a sense of the 'immense indifference of things' [p. 501] toward man; denied an equivalent stability by the fact that mind is not in essence material, consciousness sees this indifference as a constant reminder of its own insubstantiality. When Nostromo descends into the 'shadowy immobility' of the plain of Sulaco after his unsuccessful attempt to save the treasure, he finds that 'its spaciousness, extended indefinitely by an effect of obscurity, rendered more sensible his profound isolation' [p. 422]. And Nostromo's sense of isolation here, flowing from the felt tension between the infinity and eternality of matter and the vulnerability of his own personality, marks the change which overtakes the Capataz after his failure. It measures precisely the distance between the permanence of things and the corruptibility of human identity.

We are introduced to Costaguana through the narrator's description of its geography in the opening chapter, and throughout the novel the landscape exists as a constant, detached presence of which the reader is always aware. Like the white dome of the Higuerota, 'a colossal embodiment of silence' [p. 27] whose 'cool purity seemed to hold itself aloof from a hot earth' [p. 26], the landscape envelops the human world, yet stands apart from it. In his Author's Note, Conrad describes his first, imaginative glimpse of this landscape as a 'vision of a twilight country . . . with its high shadowy Sierra and its misty Campo for mute witnesses of events flowing from the passions of men' [p. ix]. While reading the novel, we are continually made conscious of such a perspective which measures the temporality of man's existence from the vantage point of the eternality of things.

In its symbolic role, the physical setting of the novel does more than provide an area of action; it defines a level of awareness which views men against the darkness, a view permeated by 'the crushing, paralysing sense of human littleness' [p. 433]. This level of awareness characterises the narrator of *Nostromo*. The narrating consciousness of this novel is typified by its air of cool dispassionate analysis. The narrator rarely involves himself in the world of his story and then only parenthetically. He recalls, for example, that 'those of us whom business or curiosity took to Sulaco . . . can remember the steadying effect of the San Tomé mine' [p. 95], or again remarks that to Decoud 'as to all of us, the compromises with his conscience appeared uglier . . . in the light of failure' [p. 364]. To compare the occasional quality of these instances of the narrator's assertiveness with the involvement of Marlow in his story of Jim is to measure in some degree the distance which exists between the narrator of *Nostromo* and his creation.

We should not allow this distance, however, to mislead us into thinking that *Nostromo* is written from some objective point of view by a consciousness which passively reflects the world before it. Conrad has given us, in his Author's Note, an insight into the conditions which governed his writing of the novel. Paradoxically, this was not for him a time of placid disengagement but rather of deep involvement with his characters and their world when Costaguana became as real for Conrad as England. He speaks of his two-year 'sojourn' there and remarks that 'on my return I found (speaking somewhat in the style of Captain Gulliver) my family all well, my wife heartily glad that the fuss was all over, and our small boy considerably grown during my absence' [p. x]. It is clear, moreover, that his sense of being involved in the reality of Costaguana extended to its inhabitants. As to their histories, he continues, 'I have tried to set them down, Aristocracy and People, men and women, Latin and Anglo-Saxon, bandit and politician, with as cool a hand as was possible in the heat and clash of my own conflicting emotions. . . . I confess that, for me, that time is the time of firm friendships and unforgotten hospitalities' [p. xi].

In this context the narrator's reserve seems the result less of an intrinsic impersonality than of a studied restraint, less of the absence of emotion than of the deliberate negation of it. If there is a distance between himself and his world, it is a distance which the narrator has imposed, and in this sense the writing of *Nostromo* involves again a twofold movement. It demands initially the creation of a realistic world, of the visible surface of life inhabited by men and women with whom one can establish 'firm friendships'. This positive act of creation, an act in which the consciousness of the artist journeys outward to involve itself with things and men in what is for Conrad one version of the adventure, is implicit in the existence of the novel. But as in *Heart of Darkness* and *Lord Jim*, although in a much more thoroughgoing way, this positive act is deliberately framed in a vision which negates it just as Marlow's voyage to Kurtz is framed in the vision of his nameless listener. The world of Costaguana is created only so that it may be imposed against the darkness of the Golfo Placido, the narrator's ties to this world are invoked only so that they can be dismissed as irrelevant.

The anonymity of the narrator is thus the deliberately chosen stance of a consciousness which has abandoned the adventure and, with it, any hope for a positive self. He sees that to attempt to win such an identity from the darkness is, in fact, like 'attacking immensity itself' [p. 87] and it is against the vision of this immensity, imaged in the Sierras and Campos of Costaguana, that he frames the stories of the two principal adventurers in the novel, Charles Gould and Nostromo.

The origins of both Charles Gould's and Nostromo's adventures lie in similar experiences of the vulnerability and transience of the self. For Gould, this experience comes when, as he learns of his father's death, the recognition that 'by no effort of will, would he be able to think of his father in the same way' fills him with a 'vague and poignant discomfort of mind . . . closely affecting his own identity' [p. 65–6]. For Nostromo it comes much later in the narrative when he awakens, on the morning after his attempt to save the treasure, with the strange sense that he had somehow 'gone out of existence' [p. 419]. In both cases, their discovery flows from the recognition by consciousness of its own nature and position in the world. Their sense of mortality reflects mind's ironic realisation that it has no positive ground, that it lacks the same stable existence which the silver of the San Tomé possesses, and this realisation by consciousness of the void at its center is emphasised by the quality of the expressions of Gould and Nostromo at this crucial moment. Nostromo's glance on awakening, a glance 'fixed upon nothing from under a thoughtful frown' [p. 412] echoes Charles Gould's expression when, on learning of his father's death, he had stared past Emma's head 'at nothing' [p. 63]. And the parallel here suggests how, for Conrad, their new awareness of death is founded in a profound sense of the insubstantiality of consciousness itself.

The lives of Stein and Jim in *Lord Jim* are a statement of the impossibility of consciousness's escaping from the threat of this void by retreating to a self-enclosed world of its own creation. If man is to avoid abandoning himself to the anonymity and detachment of the narrators of *Heart of Darkness* and *Lord Jim* and win for himself a positive identity, then he must do so by facing the darkness directly. He must subjugate the tenuous materiality of the eternal something to the rule of consciousness, and, by doing so, assimilate to consciousness this matter's completeness of being.

For both Gould and Nostromo, the adventure has as its object just such a conquest. The silver which is the center of both their lives is an image of the lower levels of creation from which consciousness has sprung. In one aspect it suggests in its power to evoke the irrationality of men like Sotillo and Montero, the level of emotion which has given birth to rational consciousness, but beyond this, in its repose, it evidences the stability of being which is denied man. Both Gould and Nostromo in their dealings with the silver suggest that the ultimate end of their quest is to possess just this quality.[4] Both accept the fact that they cannot avoid what Conrad referred to, in a letter to Garnett, as 'the contest of man interlocked with matter – the mortal in alliance with the immortal to make utility in the gross'.[5] At that critical point for Conrad's characters where mind and world meet, where the imagination seizes on some aspect of the material world and attempts to give it form, to control matter and make it subservient to spirit, they do not turn away. In this same letter, Conrad had spoken of 'material . . . gripped, moulded . . . by man',[6] and the relations of Gould and Nostromo to the silver are described in terms which suggest just such a contest. Nostromo yearns 'to clasp, embrace, absorb, subjugate in unquestioned possession this treasure' [p. 529]. In the same manner, Gould feels his father had not 'grappled' with the San Tomé mine in the proper way and tells his wife 'I shall know how to grapple with this' [pp. 62, 63].

At first this would seem an impossible task. The experience of Kurtz has already demonstrated the inability of reason alone to control the darkness. It has not the power. In the opening pages of *Nostromo*, the narrator describes the financier and the chief engineer of the railway surveying its route:

This was not the first undertaking in which their gifts . . . had worked in conjunction. From the contact of these two personalities, who had not the same vision of the world, there was generated a power for the world's service – a subtle force that could set in motion mighty machines, men's muscles, and awaken also in human breasts an unbounded devotion to the task. Of the young fellows at the table . . . more than one would be called to meet death before the work was done. But the work would be done; the force would be almost as strong as a faith. Not quite, however.                                    [p. 41]

The relationship of the two men is an image of all men's attempts to translate, through their own strength, vision into fact. It would seem, too, that it is a final pronouncement on the failure of this attempt, an assurance that the force of mind will never be equal to its faith.

Perhaps there is another way. Even if man's innate strength is not enough to triumph over the darkness there is still an alternative possibility. If he cannot defeat the darkness in a face to face confrontation then perhaps there is some way he can use the darkness against itself. It may be possible, in other words, that he can harness the darkness in the same way that men harness other natural forces.

It is this strategy which governs Gould's attitude toward the San Tomé mine. His father, he thinks, was wrong in 'wasting his strength and making himself ill by his efforts to get rid of the Concession' [p. 60]. The inevitability of his involvement with the mine and the force it symbolises is a fact which he accepts. The younger Gould, however, sees latent possibilities in this situation. Mines, he thinks, 'might have been worthless, but also they might have been misunderstood' [p. 59]. Using a different approach, he implies, the mind might itself become the means of achieving a rational end, and Gould defends his interest in the silver as just such an employment of the darkness to realise a spiritual vision:

I pin my faith to material interests. Only let the material interests once get a firm footing, and they are bound to impose the conditions on which alone they can continue to exist. That's how your money-making is justified here in the face of lawlessness and disorder. It is justified because the security which it demands must be shared with an oppressed people. A better justice will come afterward.      [p. 84]

Gould is, in this sense, an idealist and, like Kurtz, he represents himself as an emissary of light in a land of darkness. As Decoud remarks, Charles Gould 'cannot act or exist without idealising every simple feeling, desire, or achievement' [pp. 214–15]. He is, however, an idealist with a difference. As his aversion to Avellanos's 'claptrap' [p. 83] rhetoric shows, he sees the useless-ness of opposing the darkness with the unaided power of idealism. In his argument with Antonia, Decoud clearly draws the distinction between Gould and the traditional liberalism of her father. 'You write all the papers', he tells her, 'all those State papers that are inspired here, in this room, in blind deference to a theory of political purity. Hadn't you Charles Gould before your eyes? . . . He and his mine are the practical demonstration of what could have been done. Do you think he succeeded by his fidelity to a theory of virtue?' [pp. 182–3]. Unlike his father, then, Gould does not attempt to suppress the corruption of Costaguana. He faces it and attempts to use it so that he can employ the power of the silver to establish rational justice in his country. 'Charles Gould', the narrator observes, 'was competent because he had no illusions. The Gould concession had to fight for life with such weapons as could be found at once in the mire of a corruption that was so universal as almost to lose its signifi-cance. He was prepared to stoop for his weapons' [p. 85].

Is it really possible to use the darkness in this way? Initially the answer seems to be yes. Through his directorship of the San Tomé mine, Gould becomes the controlling force in the province. His control is based on the advantage which the silver gives him in the game of bribery which is politics in Costaguana, but it is an advantage which he uses not to enrich himself but to bring about the rule of order. In this way, Gould transforms the silver, initially the center of the country's irrationality and corruption, into 'a rallying point for everything . . . that needed order and stability to live' [p. 110]. Gould's success in mastering the political chaos of Costaguana is indicative of a more fundamental conquest of the alien materiality of the darkness. By using the silver to realise his dream of security in Costaguana, Gould seems in fact to have achieved the act of incarnation which marks the successful assimilation by consciousness of its source. The Concession no longer appears to him, as it did to his father, as something alien and hostile. Instead it has become imbued with a spiritual quality which allies it to the nature of consciousness itself. It is surrounded by 'the marvellousness of an accomplished fact fulfilling an audacious desire' [p. 105]. Uniting vision and fact in this way, the mine would seem to be the realisation of Emma's hopes when, laying her hands on the first bar of silver, she 'by her imaginative estimate of its power . . . endowed that lump of metal with a justificative conception, as though it were not a mere fact, but something far-reaching and impalpable, like the true expression of an emotion or the emergence of a principle' [p. 107].

Because Gould completes the act of incarnation he is allowed to exist for a time with the freedom which comes when the self achieves an independent being. Although he lives in Costaguana, Gould remains untouched by the darkness of the land. His mind, unlike Kurtz's, 'preserved its steady poise as if sheltered in the passionless stability of private and public decencies at home in Europe' [p. 49], and this independence of consciousness appears most clearly in the political stance which he initially takes in Costaguana. Although he uses the power of the mine to assure that the circle of order he has drawn around Sulaco remains unbroken, he maintains a certain distance from the political situation. He does not back one government over another, but accepts each as an inevitable manifestation of the 'persistent barbarism' [p. 231] of Costaguana and maintains an 'offensively independent' [p. 92] attitude toward those he must bribe. Gould uses the force of the silver rather than Avellanos's abstract appeal to rational political principle, but he uses it with the 'cold, fearless scorn' [p. 143] of a man who is sure of his control of it and of the stability of his own existence.

The complete history of the Gould Concession, however,

reveals that Gould's power and his sense of stable existence is only transitory. Gould's initial sophistication protects him from Lord Jim's sudden and destructive discovery of the darkness beneath his dreams. But although Gould does win an early victory, he does not escape the fundamental process of Conrad's world in which the source of life continually negates and reabsorbs its own creation. In Gould's case, this process of reabsorption manifests itself not in a sudden onslaught of the darkness but rather in the slow transformation of his rational dream into more and more primitive levels of awareness.

The first step in his transformation is marked by the appearance of an undertone of irrationality in Gould's idealism, and Conrad is careful to emphasise that this irrationality does not emerge independently of Gould's initial vision but is a mutation of this vision. 'Charles Gould's fits of abstraction', observes the narrator, 'depicted the energetic concentration of a will haunted by a fixed idea. A man haunted by a fixed idea is insane. He is dangerous even if that idea is an idea of justice' [p. 379]. It is this same 'picturesque extreme of wrong-headedness into which an honest, almost sacred, conviction may drive a man' that also attracts Decoud's attention. 'It is like madness', he thinks, 'it must be – because it's self-destructive. . . . It seemed to [Decoud] that every conviction, as soon as it became effective, turned into that form of dementia the gods send upon those they wish to destroy' [p. 200].

The practical effect of this emerging madness is to make Gould increasingly concerned with the physical safety of the Concession. From an ideal conception of political order which was to be implemented through the mine, Gould's vision gradually contracts to an obsession with the security of the mine itself. The ideal of rational justice ceases to exist 'on its only real, on its immaterial side' [p. 75] and becomes identified with the material agency through which it was to be realised. No longer the means to an end, the mine becomes the end itself, whose preservation and well-being are, in Gould's eyes, equivalent to the successful achievement of his dream.

The gradual transformation of reason into madness marks the destruction of the feeling of independence and freedom which had characterised the early period of Gould's success. Under increasing pressure to assure the safety of the Concession, Gould abandons his stance of a distanced manipulation of local politics and intervenes directly. 'The extraordinary development of the mine', the narrator observes, 'had put a great power into his hands. To feel that prosperity always at the mercy of unintelligent greed had grown irksome to him. . . . It was dangerous' [p. 143]. As a result, Gould comes to feel that 'there must be an end now of this silent reserve. . . . The material interests required from him the sacrifice of his aloofness' [p. 378]. Yet with his surrender to material interests, Gould, instead of controlling the darkness, becomes controlled by it. The founding of the Occidental Republic which is the eventual result of Gould's decision to give his direct and open support to Ribera, represents consequently not the triumph of light but only another manifestation of the persistent tyranny which has always characterised Costaguana. This is the meaning of Dr Monygham's prophecy: 'the time approaches when all that the Gould Concession stands for shall weigh as heavily upon the people as the barbarism, cruelty, and misrule of a few years back' [p. 511].

In *Nostromo*, the slow decay of idealism into irrationality is imaged as a process of petrification in which spirit is gradually materialised. Such a transformation is suggested not only by the allusions to the growing weight of the mine's autocracy or its increasing power to 'crush innumerable lives in the expansion of its greatness' [p. 521], but is also implied in the references to the history of the financier Holroyd. Like Gould, Holroyd begins as an imaginative materialist who attempts to use material interests to establish his vision of a 'pure form of Christianity' [p. 317]. In a way which suggests the ultimate end of Gould's venture, however, fact has come to rule spirit in Holroyd's empire. His 'religion of iron and silver' has decayed into a 'sort of idolatry' [p. 71] and manifests itself in 'the great Holroyd building (an enormous pile of iron, glass and blocks of stone . . .)' [p. 80]. In a similar manner, the only evidences of the Spanish attempt to civilise and Christianise the country are ruins–'heavy stonework of bridges and churches' – which 'proclaimed the disregard of human labour' [p. 89] in the same way Holroyd's business has destroyed his employees and 'devoured their best years' [p. 81].

The absorption of mind by matter appears most clearly, however, in the novel's description of the slow solidification of Gould's consciousness. As the material interests of the Concession increasingly come to dominate his attention, Gould sinks beneath the level of irrationality to a point at which all awareness seems to disappear in an almost total identification with the physical fact of the mine. Mrs Gould herself is both witness to and unwilling participant in this process. 'The fate of the San Tomé mine was lying heavy on her heart', we are told; '. . . It had been an idea. She had watched it with misgiving turning into a fetish, and now the fetish had grown into a crushing weight. It was as if the inspiration of their early years had left her heart to turn into a wall of silver bricks . . . between her and her husband. He seemed to dwell alone within a circumvallation of precious metal' [p. 522]. As a result of this movement from idea to matter, Gould becomes a figure of almost inhuman coldness, described by those who know him as 'the embodied Gould Concession' whose 'impenetrability' has its 'surface shades' [p. 203].

The destructive transformation of Charles Gould reveals that the whole idea of incarnation is a trap. Lord Jim had failed because he had been prevented from ever completing this act, but Gould's defeat is a direct result of his initial period of success. Paradoxically, his very ability to inform matter with conscious-ness and to make the mine an expression of a spiritual principle only leaves his consciousness more susceptible to the darkness. While Jim finds himself constantly rebuffed in his attempts to establish a substantial being and must remain the eternal youth, Gould's fate is precisely the opposite. The gradual emergence of 'material interests' leaves him imprisoned in his own creation. Like a symbol in which the vehicle has destroyed the tenor, the San Tomé mine is no longer the 'true expression' [p. 107] of Gould's self but rather its tomb, a tomb in which he remains as fixed and immobile as one of Stein's butterflies. It is this same gradual process in which incarnation becomes imprisonment that is at the center of Nostromo's story.

The reader is introduced to Nostromo through a series of descriptions of what might be called his public figure. We see him first through the eyes of Captain Mitchell as a man 'above reproach' [p. 13], then as the rescuer of Viola where he is one whose 'mere presence in the house would have made it perfectly safe' [pp. 19–20]. Throughout the early narrative, he appears in his role as Capataz de Cargadores, the locus of power among the common people of Sulaco just as Gould is among the upper classes. Yet whereas the reader is given access to Gould's subjectivity immediately, during the long account of Gould's relation to the San Tomé mine, he encounters Nostromo through 'the spell of that reputation the Capataz de Cargadores had made for himself by the waterside, along the railway line, with the English and with the populace' [p. 20]. Until late in the novel, the reader never penetrates the surface of this public image.

There is a reason for this. It is because Nostromo's consciousness is completely defined by its surface. Nostromo's life is one 'whose very essence, value, reality, consisted in its reflection from the admiring eyes of men' [p. 525]. Like Willems's existence in Macassar, Nostromo is an example of a man whose entire identity lies in its relation to those outside himself. The key to Nostromo lies in his naïve and unconscious acknowledgment of this principle, his unquestioning acceptance of the fact that his being is defined entirely by his social context. His world is limited entirely to this one dimension, and things only have meaning for him if they manifest themselves on this level. As Decoud observes, 'the only thing he seems to care for . . . is to be well spoken of. . . . He does not seem to make any difference between speaking and thinking' [p. 246]. His acceptance of this principle is symbolised by his acceptance of his name, 'Nostromo', from the English. 'This is our Nostromo!' remarks Signora Teresa, 'What a name! What is that? Nostromo? He would take a name that is properly no word from them' [p. 23].

Nostromo's acceptance of this principle governs the parallel between him and Charles Gould. Unlike the Englishman, Nostromo is not committed to the realisation of an abstract ideal, a theory of rational liberty. But he is, in a similar way, committed to the perfect fulfilment of his public role. Although Captain Mitchell accepts Nostromo as the embodiment of virtue, the more perceptive Decoud realises that Nostromo is, in reality, 'made incorruptible by his enormous vanity, that finest form of egoism which can take on the aspect of every virtue' [p. 300]. In a way, Nostromo's allegiance to the Gould Concession is arbitrary. He could as well have thrown his lot with Montero. Nostromo does not think of himself, any more than he does of other people, as having an innate nature apart from his role in society. His egoism is without content. It manifests itself in his attitude to playing this role, for having accepted one he feels compelled to fulfill it completely. 'Since it was the good pleasure of the Caballeros to send me off on such an errand', he says of his attempt to rescue the silver, 'they shall learn I am just the man they take me for' [p. 267]. His gift of his last dollar to an old lady, performed without witnesses, has 'still the characteristics of splendour and publicity' [p. 414]. Like his efforts to make himself indispensable to his employers and his talent for the picturesque, for the act which strikes the imagination, this gift is the expression of his attempt to give his reputation the widest possible currency and to maintain its total consistency. Nostromo understands clearly, if only intuitively, that, given his assumptions, the validity of his person lies in the consistency of this public image. For Nostromo, identity finds its strength and source not in its internal dedication to some principle but in the extent to which it gives itself a social reality. 'It concerns me', he tells Viola's wife, 'to keep on being what I am: every day alike' [p. 253].

In this sense, then, Gould and Nostromo are parallel figures: both are attempting to achieve the incarnation of an ideal in society, although for Gould this ideal is a substantial theory of political liberty and for Nostromo it is a radically different conception of personal renown. In the opening chapters of the novel, we meet Nostromo at the high point of his success. His life to the moment when he undertakes the rescue of the silver has been 'in complete harmony with his vanity' [p. 414]. The nature of this success, however, suggests not only the similarities between these two figures but also important differences. Like Gould's early achievements, Nostromo's are based on the power of silver. It is not only in the last episodes after he has stolen the treasure that Nostromo is associated with silver. This association is constant throughout the novel, although the terms of the association change in a significant way. Nostromo rides a 'silver-grey mare' [p. 22] and wears a sombrero 'with a silver cord and tassels . . . enormous silver buttons . . . silver plates on headstall and saddle' [p. 125]. He seems 'to disdain the use of any metal less precious than silver' [p. 225]. The scene in which he gives the silver buttons to Morenita is an illustration of the way in which his reputation is based, as firmly as Gould's political power, on the force of material interests. 'But young or old', he tells Decoud, 'they like money, and will speak well of the man who gives it to them' [p. 247]. Like Gould at the beginning of his career, Nostromo is interested in the silver only as a means. He uses it to establish his reputation in Sulaco in the same way that Gould uses it to establish his ideals of political stability and justice. Dr Monygham makes the analogy explicit when he remarks to the chief engineer that Nostromo has 'not grown rich by his fidelity to you good people of the railway and the harbour. I suppose he obtains some – how do you say that? – some spiritual value for his labours, or else I don't know why the devil he should be faithful to you, Gould, Mitchell, or anybody else' [p. 321].

Although both employ the silver in this way, however, they approach their tasks in much different frames of mind. Gould's involvement with the San Tomé mine flows from his awareness of its destructive effects on his father. He understands clearly the nature of the forces he plans to use. Nostromo's relation to the silver, on the other hand, is characterised initially by that same quality of unconsciousness which appears also in his acceptance of the terms of his identity in Sulaco. His character, as Decoud notes, is at once naïve and 'practical' [p. 246], and Nostromo falls in that class of characters who are protected against the effects of the darkness, as Conrad himself once was, by a kind of blessed lack of sophistication.

It is in the context of this essential difference between these two 'racially and socially contrasted men' [p. xi] that we should consider the change which overtakes Nostromo when he awakens on the morning after his unsuccessful attempt to escape with the silver, for this change is explicitly a movement to another level of awareness:

Nostromo woke up from a fourteen hours' sleep. . . . Handsome, robust, and supple, he threw back his head, flung his arms open, and stretched himself with a slow twist of the waist and a leisurely growling yawn of white teeth, as natural and free from evil in the moment of waking as a magnificent and unconscious wild beast. Then, in the suddenly steadied glance fixed upon nothing from under a thoughtful frown, appeared the man.                                        [pp. 411–12]

The key to the particular form this new awareness takes for

Nostromo is in the way his partial failure to rescue the silver affects his public existence. To this point, Nostromo has lived on the surface of life, a surface which he has defined as the two dimensional world of overt actions and attitudes. Wherever he has turned in this world, he has seen the 'perfect form of his egoism' [p. 301] in the 'reflection from the admiring eyes of men' [p. 525], and in keeping with all of Conrad's characters who are protected by their unconscious naïveté he has never thought to question the solidity of this surface. He is like Jim who before the collision accepts the apparent peace of the ocean as a stable medium on which to project his dreams of adventure.

The real effect of Nostromo's failure is not so much in his inability to escape with the silver but in the way in which the attempt compromises him in Sulaco and thus separates him for the first time from this surface. His last act before leaving Sulaco, the gift of a dollar to an old lady, had still, we remember, 'the characteristics of splendour and publicity' and as such was in keeping with the tenor of his life. It is exactly these qualities which are denied him now. 'But this awakening in solitude, except for the watchful vulture, amongst the ruins of the fort', the narrator remarks, 'had no such characteristics. His first confused feeling was exactly this – that it was not in keeping. It was more like the end of things' [p. 414].

The effect of his failure on Nostromo is, therefore, similar to the effect of the collision on Jim. It serves to drive a wedge between self and world, to effect that detachment which causes both to realise the instability of the surface of things. Just as at the moment of collision the visible surface of nature, hitherto stable, appears to Jim 'formidably insecure' in its immobility, Nostromo is here made aware of the insubstantiality of the surface of society which is the foundation of his own existence. 'The necessity of living concealed somehow, for God knows how long, which assailed him on his return to consciousness', we are told, 'made everything that had gone before for years appear vain and foolish, like a flattering dream come suddenly to an end' [p. 414].

The destruction of his unconscious acceptance of the surface world is experienced by Nostromo not simply in negative terms as the fragility of what he had thought real, but more positively as the discovery of an alien force behind this apparent solidity. Nostromo's awareness of this alien force appears as a sudden recognition of the antagonistic subjectivity of others. The flight of the Europeans and the manoeuverings of Gould, acts which destroy the social fabric of Sulaco, appear to him acts of personal infidelity. His sense of betrayal expresses his feeling that he has been used without an understanding of his real nature. Nostromo's resentment at being chosen to rescue the silver has its source in the same realisation. His entire reputation hangs on the success or failure of this mission. He is, Nostromo tells Decoud, 'going to make it the most famous and desperate affair of my life' [p. 265]. Yet he understands clearly that he has been asked to risk what is, in effect, the foundation of his existence though those who have asked him have not understood what was involved. 'Those gentlefolk', he tells Decoud, 'do not seem to have sense enough to understand what they are giving one to do' [p. 280]. This same sense that he has not been understood, and that, because of this, his identity has been violated, lies behind his feeling of betrayal on this morning:

His imagination had seized upon the clear and simple notion of betrayal to account for the dazed feeling of enlightenment as to being done for, of having inadvertently gone out of his existence on an issue in which his personality had not been taken into account. A man betrayed is a man destroyed.                                                         [p. 419–20]

Nostromo's realisation of the worlds of subjectivity behind the social surface of life, worlds in which he himself exists only as a surface, an object to be used, is a revelation of the fragility of his former existence. It is this realisation which governs his reaction to Dr Monygham in the long exchange which takes place between them in the Custom House. The essence of this encounter lies in the tension between the reactions of these two characters to their unexpected meeting, in the way in which 'the diversity of their natures made their thoughts born from their meeting swing afar from each other' [p. 431]. This tension, however, is more than a simple statement of individuality. It is a function of the way in which men, impelled by their particular fixed ideas, reduce others to the level of objects. Nostromo and Dr Monygham meet at the precise point when each has been claimed by such a fixed idea. For Nostromo it is the silver, for Dr Monygham, it is the 'unlawful wealth' [p. 481] of his devotion to

Emma Gould. In his desire to save her, Dr Monygham accepts the return of Nostromo without question, interested in him only as a necessary part of his plan:

Nostromo's return was providential. He did not think of him humanely, as of a fellow-creature just escaped from the jaws of death. The Capataz for him was the only possible messenger to Cayta.          [p. 431-2]

During the extended conversation which follows, Nostromo waits in vain for some expression of interest in the most desperate affair of his life, interest which will assure him that he has, in fact, been taken into account. The narrator moves continuously from one consciousness to another, contrasting Dr Monygham's obsession with Mrs Gould to the way in which Nostromo experiences this lack of interest in himself as a kind of death. Meeting Dr Monygham, the narrator tells us, Nostromo felt 'communicative. He expected the continuance of that interest which, whether accepted or rejected, would have restored to him his personality – the only thing lost in that desperate affair. But the doctor, engrossed by a desperate adventure of his own, was terrible in the pursuit of his idea' [p. 434].

This scene confirms the validity of Nostromo's awakening to the insubstantiality of his former existence. If it is true that his real life lies in the place he occupies in the thoughts of others, then he is continually at the mercy not only of the darkness which lies at the center of his own being, but of the irrationality which is at the center of theirs as well. To become, for another, an object in the way Nostromo does for Dr Monygham is to die. For this reason, the narrator returns again and again to the figure of Hirsch which hangs with 'the immobility of a disregarded man' over this conversation. The 'persistent immobility of the late Señor Hirsch' is a symbol for the kind of death Nostromo experiences at the hands of Dr Monygham:

And the Capataz, listening as if in a dream, felt himself of as little account as the indistinct, motionless shape of the dead man whom he saw upright under the beam, with his air of listening also, disregarded, forgotten, like a terrible example of neglect.          [p. 435]

By seeing Nostromo's new awareness as resulting from an experience of mortality different in form but essentially the same as Gould's we can understand Nostromo's destructive relation to the silver in the last third of the novel. In this final section, he attempts to create a new identity, that of Captain Fidanza, to replace the one he has lost:

Nostromo, the miscalled Capataz de Cargadores, had made for himself, under his rightful name, another public existence, but modified by the new conditions, less picturesque, more difficult to keep up in the increased size and varied population of Sulaco.                    [p. 527]

In one sense, this new identity is, like the old, a 'public existence'. 'Captain Fidanza was *seen*', the narrator remarks, and 'the generation that would know nothing of the famous ride to Cayta was not born yet' [p. 527]. But its real source, the foundation of Fidanza's image, is the San Tomé treasure. Before, Nostromo had used the power of silver in much the same way to support his public existence, but he had done so unaware of the insubstantiality of this existence. Now, his attempt suggests the more conscious strategy of Gould. Flowing, too, from an experience of vulnerability, Nostromo's actions in the last chapters are best seen as an illustration of what can only be called the jealousy which man has for matter's completeness of being. Like Gould's desire to grapple with the mine, Nostromo's urge to 'subjugate in unquestioned possession' [p. 529] this treasure is ultimately a desire to share in this completeness, to found his identity as Captain Fidanza in an unshakable source.

   As it did for Gould, however, the act of incarnation becomes a trap for Nostromo. Although he is successful in protecting the secret of the silver and in maintaining his new identity, Nostromo finds that his new life is one increasingly dominated by material interests. He, too, is afflicted with that fixed idea which is like madness, and suffers continually, the narrator tells us, 'from the concentration of his thought upon the treasure' [p. 523]. Beyond his madness, Nostromo discovers that the moment in which he 'welded that vein of silver into his life' [p. 526] results in a bondage to the darkness which finds him 'chained to the treasure' [p. 495] and 'imprisoned in silver fetters' [p. 546]. Despite his apparent success, Nostromo, like Gould and, in fact, the entire population of Sulaco, falls victim to the weight of the San Tomé mine. 'The feeling of fearful and ardent subjection', the narrator remarks, '. . . weighed heavily upon the independent Captain Fidanza, owner and master of a coasting schooner whose smart appearance . . . [was] so well known along the western seaboard of a vast continent' [p. 526–7].

The lives of both Gould and Nostromo trace a pattern in which consciousness rises above and masters the darkness only to be reabsorbed into it. The inevitability of this pattern makes the adventurer's attempt to return to the source of life and ground his self in his control of this source futile. Even if momentarily successful, such an attempt leads at best to the imprisonment suffered by these two characters.

In *Nostromo*, however, the implications of this pattern are not confined to the lives of individuals. The novel suggests that a similar logic is operative in the whole range of human activity. The process by which Gould's idealistic visions of rational justice are born in reaction to the moral darkness of Costaguana and then are, in turn, transformed into only another manifestation of this darkness is symbolic not only of the law which ordains his personal fate but of the law which has determined the whole history of his country.

In the years immediately before Charles Gould, Costaguana had witnessed another such self-defeating attempt. Beginning in the general South American revolt against Spanish rule led by Bolivar in the 1820s, it resulted, in Costaguana, in the period of Federation.[7] Like the Separatist movement of Charles, the Federation is led by a Gould, by his uncle Henry, who also takes up the banner of reason and liberty:

Just as years ago, calmly, from the conviction of practical necessity, stronger than any abstract political doctrine, Henry Gould had drawn the sword, so now, the times being changed, Charles Gould had flung the silver of the San Tomé into the fray. The Inglez of Sulaco, the 'Costaguana Englishman' of the third generation, was as far from being a political intriguer as his uncle from a revolutionary swashbuckler. Springing from the instinctive uprightness of their natures their action was reasoned. [p. 142]

The period of Federation, however, results not in the establishment of political liberty but first in the tyranny of Guzman Bento and finally in the chaos of greed and corruption which destroy Gould's father. The references to the growing tyranny of the San Tomé mine, then, suggest that, in solidifying into autocracy, the movement supported by Gould is only mirroring the fate of many earlier revolts. And Father Corbelàn's prophecy of a time when 'the people, prevented from their aspirations, should rise and claim their share of the wealth and their share of the power' [p. 510] points to yet another uprising of the spirit against its bondage to material interests.

For Marlow at the opening of *Heart of Darkness*, the progress of all civilisation has been marked by the steady conquest of the darkness by the idea, of matter by form, of emotion by reason. From this point of view, the history of man is a logically sequential progression beginning in the darkness and pointing toward the light. To Captain Mitchell, who is the spokesman in *Nostromo* for this 'historical' point of view, the career of the Gould Concession describes such an upward curve and he speaks confidently in the closing chapters of the 'great future' of the Separatist movement which has saved the San Tomé mine 'intact for civilisation' [p. 483]. It is this assumption of progress, and of the fulfillment of Gould's ambitions to turn the power of the mine to the service of the idea, which determines the form of Captain Mitchell's long narrative in the last chapters of the novel. Mitchell accepts the chronological order of history, speaks of the statue of Charles as an 'anachronism' [p. 482], and follows the natural order of events because this linear progression expresses to him the reality of the historical process. The structure of Mitchell's narrative reflects the assumptions of all those who accept the validity and success of the humanising work of civilisation and who see history as the record of this irreversible process.

The narrator, who frames the story of Gould against the darkness which is at once its source and end, sees that Mitchell's sense of historical progress is an illusion. The real movement of history for him is not linear but cyclical. It traces not a rise from the darkness but repeats the pattern of Costaguana politics in which revolution is inevitably transformed into an autocracy, which in turn gives rise to revolution. The narrator undermines belief in historical progress not only by making the senile Captain Mitchell its spokesman and placing his monologue at a time when the reader is able to see clearly the distance between Captain Mitchell's confident assertions of historical improvement and the real effect of the San Tomé mine on Costaguana. More than this, he presents the monologue itself as a prepared speech which is given to each important visitor. In this context, Mitchell's carefully rehearsed program, 'relentless, like a law of Nature' [p. 481], loses its linear quality and takes on a certain circularity. The Captain's constant repetition of this history of the revolution ironically images the constant repetition of the revolution in history, and the narrator emphasises this by referring to 'the cycle' [p. 486] of Mitchell's monologue – remarking at its end, for example, that 'the coxswain's voice at the door, announcing that the gig was ready, closed the cycle' [p. 489].

The narrator's vision of the landscape thus frames not only the lives of Gould and Nostromo but the whole movement of human history. From this point of view, all civilisation is destined to be reabsorbed into this landscape to become, like the efforts of the Spanish conquerors of Costaguana, 'heavy stonework' or 'some ruinous pile' [p. 89]. This rejection of civilisation and, by implication, of the adventure as it represents man's attempt to control the darkness, echoes and affirms the ironic stance of *Lord Jim*'s anonymous narrator. If it is true that the adventure is inevitably unsuccessful, then the detachment of these narrators would seem to be the only logical alternative. To commit oneself to realising the dream is to invite the destruction which envelops Gould and Nostromo. It is to become, like the two gringo adventurers who go in search of the treasure of the Azuera, the prisoner of the darkness. In forsaking the adventure and taking his stance outside the dream, the narrator of Nostromo protects himself against this fate. *Nostromo*, it seems, presents man with two choices: one a way into the darkness, one a way to survival. Apparently the only strategy left to Conrad is a succession of novels in which the world of men is created only to be denied.

SOURCE: chapter v of *The Metaphysics of Darkness* (Baltimore, Md., and London, 1971), pp. 109–31.

NOTES

[These have been slightly revised and renumbered, from the original –
Ed.]

1. Edward Garnett (ed.), *Letters from Joseph Conrad, 1895–1924*
(London, 1928; repr. New York, 1963), p. 143.
2. [Ed. – Page references in square brackets relate to the text of the
novels as published in the Doubleday 'Canterbury' edition of Conrad's
Works (New York, 1924): the American version of Grant's edition
(London and Edinburgh, 1924.)]
3. Garnett, loc. cit.
4. In 1923 Conrad wrote to Ernest Bendz that 'Nostromo has never
been intended for the hero of the tale of the Seaboard. Silver is the pivot
of the moral and material events': G. Jean-Aubry, *Life and Letters*, II,
296. In this sense the real subject of the novel lies not in the story of any
one character but in the relation of mind to matter. Both Eloise Knapp
Hay, *The Political Novels of Joseph Conrad* (Chicago, 1963), pp. 101–2,
and Albert Guerard, *Conrad the Novelist* (Cambridge, Mass., 1958), pp.
177, 183, note that the central theme of the novel is the process of
idealisation itself.
5. Garnett, *Letters*, pp. 84–5.
6. Ibid., p. 85.
7. On the underlying consistency of the chronological structure of
*Nostromo*, see B. Kimpel and T. C. Duncan Eaves, 'The Geography and
History in *Nostromo*', *Modern Philology*, LVI (August 1958), 45–54.

# *C. B. Cox*     'Shifting Perspectives' (1974)

> The hills are shadows, and they flow
>    From form to form, and nothing stands;
>    They melt like mist, the solid lands,
> Like clouds they shape themselves and go.
>
> TENNYSON, *In Memoriam*

Sir John, chairman of the railway company, arrives at night at
the surveying camp in the hills, just too late to see the last dying

glow of sunlight upon the snowy flank of Higuerota, the highest mountain. The chief engineer, as he waits for the expected diligencia, responds in a conventionally romantic way to the magnificent sunset, which he compares to 'a piece of inspired music'. Afterwards, late at night, the two men pace to and fro discussing their work, both confident they can overcome all the problems, natural and human, that beset the railway. But as they stand, dwarf-like, beneath the basalt walls of precipices, we are reminded of the insignificance of man in the universe. 'We can't move mountains!' declares the chief engineer:

Sir John, raising his head to follow the pointing gesture, felt the full force of the words. The white Higuerota soared out of the shadows of rock and earth like a frozen bubble under the moon. All was still, till near by, behind the wall of a corral for the camp animals, built roughly of loose stones in the form of a circle, a pack mule stamped his forefoot and blew heavily twice.

This incident illustrates in simple form the problems of reading *Nostromo* (1904). In *The Turn of the Novel*, Alan Friedman argues that in much of Conrad's fiction 'form might be defined as the arousing and confusing of desires'.[1] In a letter to Richard Curle of 1923, Conrad explained how he was trying to compose fluid narratives, 'depending on grouping (sequence) which shifts, and on the changing lights giving varied effects of perspective'.[2] In the description of the meeting between Sir John and the chief engineer, we begin with a conventional attitude to natural beauty – 'inspired music' –and then proceed to the faith of these practical men of affairs that they can conquer all natural obstacles in the service of material interests. This confidence is already cast in an ironic light because we have been told of the subsequent riots in Sulaco; it also seems misplaced in the setting of the mountains, which throughout the novel symbolise the indifference of Nature to the futility of man. This is straightforward enough, but what are we to make of the comparison of Higuerota to a frozen bubble? The perspective suddenly shifts once again, and we see that under the moon, in the immensity of space, all the forms of Nature are insubstantial, as transient as a bubble. Then immediately our perspective is drawn back to the particular scene, to the pack-mule stamping and blowing, one detail among the hundreds that give a rich actuality to Conrad's creation of Costaguana.

In this short scene, therefore, our visual perspective rapidly changes, and this reflects shifting attitudes to man, society and Nature. The sequence is 'fluid' in that we are not allowed to settle for any one point of view. Positive actions, colourful people, warm feelings, are constantly framed in a vision which seems to negate their existence; the narrative creates different and opposing areas of value, but offers no final reconciliation.

This is one reason why the last two chapters are so unsatisfactory. A linear sequence of events, describing Nostromo's courtship of Giselle, ends with his death, shot by her father, Giorgio Viola. This gives a false appearance that the story is concluded, and the clash of values resolved. In Alan Friedman's view, Conrad is divided against himself, involved in a struggle between his technical effort to close the experience, and his refusal to do so. His true imaginative vision is represented by the early sections, which bewilder and disturb the reader. The novel falls down when Conarad allows himself to be trapped in space and time. At his best his imagination feeds on ironic evasions. The chronological dislocations give a sense of the richness of history and the multiplicity of events; at the same time they place the reader in what Albert Guerard has called a vertiginous stance.[3] The first part of the novel frustrates the normal objectives of the reader to an astonishing degree, not allowing him to identify himself with one character or to locate himself firmly in time or place.

*Nostromo* presents at least two irreconcilable points of view. At one extreme there is a profound scepticism which pervades the descriptions of landscapes and people, and which seems akin to that of Decoud when he commits suicide; at the other extreme this pessimism is countered by the human and moral claims most finely represented by Mrs Emilia Gould. . . .

SOURCE: extract from *Joseph Conrad: The Modern Imagination* (London, 1974), pp. 60–2.

NOTES

1. A. Friedman, *The Turn of the Novel* (New York, 1966), p. 97.
2. G. Jean-Aubry, *Life and Letters*, II, 317.
3. A. J. Guerard, *Conrad the Novelist* (Cambridge, Mass., and London, 1958), pp. 214–15.

## III UNDER WESTERN EYES

*Douglas Hewitt*      'Animus and Irony'
(1952)

. . . *Under Western Eyes* [was] finished in January 1910. The title is
a significant one; the narrator is an English teacher of languages
in Geneva who comes in contact there with many Russian
émigrés, but who, in the opening pages, denies his competence to
tell the story because he has 'no comprehension of the Russian
character'. This is clearly not intended to be taken merely as a
modest and ironical disclaimer, for it is repeated in varying forms
throughout the book in contexts which show that the teacher
speaks for Conrad himself.

I will only remark here [he says a little later], that this is not a story of
the West of Europe. . . . It is unthinkable that any young Englishman
should find himself in Razumov's situation. This being so it would be a
vain enterprise to imagine what he would think. The only safe surmise
to make is that he would not think as Mr Razumov thought at this crisis
of his fate.                                                   [p. 25][1]

This inability of Western minds fully to understand and
sympathise with Russian characteristics and motives is what the
language teacher stresses more than anything else. Russia is
unlike the West:

In its pride of numbers, in its strange pretensions of sanctity, and in the
secret readiness to abase itself in suffering, the spirit of Russia is the
spirit of cynicism. It informs the declarations of statesmen, the theories
of her revolutionaries, and the mystic vaticinations of prophets to the
point of making freedom look like a form of debauch, and the Christian
virtues themselves appear actually indecent.              [p. 67]

. . . Conrad makes use of his narrators in a number of ways, and it is quite clear that the teacher of languages resembles the Marlow of *Chance* rather than the Marlow of *Heart of Darkness*. He is not personally involved in the fate of Razumov; nothing new in his own character is brought to the surface by his knowledge of the Russian's treachery and remorse. Nor is he another Captain Mitchell, whose naïve optimism stands ironically in contrast to our deeper knowledge of the real issues of *Nostromo*. Whatever irony is directed against him is very mild. A hint of it – but no more – is implied in a phrase like 'my mind, the decent mind of an old teacher of languages' [p. 66]. There is a certain fussiness about him but there is no indication that his incomprehension is a personal inadequacy, because there is no deeper knowledge against which to measure it. There is no view *sub specie aeternitatis* to compare with the view under western eyes. There can be no doubt that Conrad is in general agreement with his judgements. And it is strange to find the creator of Mr Kurtz, the explorer of the tangle of idealisms and basenesses of *Nostromo*, underwriting such statements as:

. . . this is a Russian story for Western ears, which, as I have observed already, are not attuned to certain tones of cynicism and cruelty, of moral negation and even of moral distress already silenced at our end of Europe. [p. 163]

or

. . . this narrative where the aspects of honour and shame are remote from the ideas of the Western world. [p. 293]

The division of mankind into the camp of the good and the camp of the bad, which I have indicated as one of the characteristics in Conrad's later work, is seen here in a special form. The morass of mistaken loyalties, tyranny, deception and shame is, we are constantly informed, a particularly Russian phenomenon. To a great extent, in fact, evil is given a local habitation and a name in Russia. The emphasis throughout is that we – the West – are not tainted by this form of evil. The possessor of the western eyes of the title sees, a little uncomprehendingly, the strange torments of the Russian conscience and the Russian guilt, and we share with him his sense of 'enormous remoteness from their captivity within the sombre horizon of Russian problems' [p. 345].

The subject of Russia was one which engaged Conrad's feelings most violently. In letters he gives free rein to his hatred in such remarks as: 'Russians who (nobody would believe me in 1914) are born rotten'.[2] He speaks in a different tone in the 'Author's Note' to the Collected Edition, however, of

The obligation of absolute fairness . . . imposed on me historically and hereditarily, by the peculiar experience of race and family. . . .

The repression of Poland by Tsarist Russia – a repression felt so strongly by the landowning gentry to which Conrad's family belonged – and the exile and death of his parents were sufficient to excuse almost any bitterness, and his realisation of the need to overcome it stirs our admiration; but we cannot feel that he achieves the detachment which would be necessary before he could treat the subject of Russian bureaucracy and tyranny in a work of art.

It is not our task to reproach him with intolerance, but it is essential that we should see the significance of this lack of detachment. His animus against Russia – his belief that it is fundamentally more evil than the rest of Europe – has been introduced into the novel as it stands in his mind and not subjected to any process of imaginative re-creation. There is, as a result, an incalculable and incomprehensible quality in any evaluation of motives and characters – Russianness.

The minor characters are dealt with very much from the outside; the comment in the 'Author's Note', though written some years after the book, catches the spirit in which they are conceived: 'Peter Ivanovitch and Madame de S. are fair game. They are the apes of a sinister jungle and are treated as their grimaces deserve'.

Razumov, however, is treated differently; we see the world, for a good deal of the book, through his eyes and, whatever Conrad may do later, in the first part he cannot take up towards him an attitude such as he does towards Peter Ivanovitch or Julius Laspara or any of the other revolutionists. He cannot be merely a 'flat' character, a person in a drama whom we see acting upon others but into whose mind we cannot enter, for he is presented as the point upon which are focused the moral issues and the pressures of Russian society which are Conrad's theme.[3] Yet the effect of many passages – and especially of those dealing with Razumov's walk through the streets after Haldin has asked for shelter, and his conversation with Haldin before the latter goes out to be arrested – is that of melodrama, over-written and exaggerated. 'His forehead broke out in perspiration while a cold shudder ran down his spine' – 'A leaden sleep closed his eyelids at once' – 'Sudden fear sealed Razumov's lips'; clichés like these betray the essential unreality of Razumov's plight. The whole passage, especially in Razumov's obsessional dwelling on details like 'the power of goggle eyes and grey whiskers' [p. 60] is heavily indebted to Dostoevsky. And we are asked, in effect, to accept this melodrama as part of a 'Russianness' which we cannot understand, as part of the 'generous indignations and . . . extreme sentiments, too poignant, perhaps, for a non-Russian mind to conceive' [p. 175]. Our inability to form a concrete and deeply realised picture of Razumov's mind is to be seen as a positive success. We are not asked to understand; we can only join the narrator in his uncomprehending observation in what he calls 'my character of a mute witness of things Russian, unrolling their Eastern logic under my Western eyes' [p. 381].

One of the most obvious characteristics of this work is Conrad's use of irony – more especially the irony of situation. This is brought about, as it is in *Nostromo*, by the arrangement of the sections of the story, by the breaking of the chronological sequence of events. But the effect achieved is very different from that of *Nostromo*. In that book we know, for instance, that the idealism of Charles Gould and his wife will lead eventually to the coming of the chairman of the railway company and his triumphant proclamation of the success of material values. We therefore consider every manifestation of the Goulds' idealism with a deeper knowledge; a criticism of their motives is enforced by our knowledge of the results which are to come. In *Under Western Eyes* we find the opposite process of arrangement at work. We know from the first part what has happened to Haldin and what have been the actions of Razumov, and during the rest of the book we listen to the utterances of people who do not. The irony which results is typified by Natalia Haldin's repetition of her brother's description of Razumov as one of the 'unstained, lofty, and solitary existences' [pp. 135, 148], and Sophia

Antonovna's: 'You are feeding on some bitterness of your own'
[p. 255].

The difference is fundamental. The method of *Under Western
Eyes* does not make the issues any clearer; it enforces no
judgements which have not already been made. There is, indeed,
something rather heavy and repetitive about a good deal of Parts
Two and Three. The narrator is seen as constantly groping
towards knowledge which is already in our possession and, since
its effect on him is not of importance, since it leads to nothing but
horror and incomprehension, no fruitful effect is achieved by
such passages as:

He stared at me so queerly that I hardly know how to define his aspect.
I could not understand it in this connexion at all. What ailed him? I
asked myself. What strange thought had come into his head? What
vision of all the horrors that can be seen in his hopeless country had
come suddenly to haunt his brain? If it were anything connected with
the fate of Victor Haldin, then I hoped earnestly he would keep it to
himself for ever.                                              [p. 196]

   SOURCE: extract from *Conrad: A Reassessment* (Cambridge, 1952;
   Philadelphia, 1953), pp. 80–4.


                              NOTES

[These have been slightly revised and renumbered from the original –
Ed.]

   1. [Ed. – Page references in square brackets relate to the text of the
1911 edition reprinted by Dent in 1923.]
   2. In a letter to Sir Sidney Colvin, 12 November 1917.
   3. See a letter to John Galsworthy, 6 January 1908: 'I think that I am
trying to capture the very soul of things Russian –*Cosas de Russia.*'

# *Thomas Moser* 'Conrad's Treatment of Women' (1957)

. . . *In Under Western Eyes*, last of the political novels and of the major, full-length novels, Conrad manages his love story only by restricting it to less than ten per cent of the novel's pages. Originally, Conrad intended to make Razumov's love for Natalia Haldin, sister of the man he betrayed, the center of the novel. He wrote Galsworthy on 6 January 1908 that he had finished the first part:

2nd in Génève. The student Razumov meeting abroad the mother and sister of Haldin falls in love with that last, marries her and, after a time, confesses to her the part he played in the arrest of her brother.

The psychological developments leading to Razumov's betrayal of Haldin, to his confession of the fact to his wife and to the death of these people (brought about mainly by the resemblance of their child to the late Haldin), form the real subject of the story. (*Life and Letters*, II, 65.)

In view of Conrad's usual bad luck in trying to dramatise courtship and marriage, we must admit that he was probably wise to scrap these plans. Instead, Razumov and Natalia appear in only three scenes together, of seven, four and nineteen pages respectively, and the narrator quotes four pages from Razumov's diary which refers to his love for Natalia. In the first two of these scenes, Razumov suffers so from embarrassment and remorse that he scarcely speaks. The third scene, though very important in terms of the meaning of the novel, proves to be an artistic failure.

The characters who enact that last scene play the familiar roles of hero, heroine, and rival. Razumov, an authentic Conradian vulnerable hero, engenders a good deal of interest throughout the novel as the center of a moral and political drama, but as a lover he fails badly. Although Conrad may have hoped that Natalia Haldin would develop into another Mrs Gould, she remains little more than a speaker of noble sentiments, with a frank, healthy walk and a virile handclasp. Conrad deliberately plays

the 'rival', the English professor of languages, in a low key,
minimising his interest in the much younger Natalia. Conrad's
restraint here is certainly a relief from Cornelius (in *Lord Jim*),
but the characterisation is so restrained that the reader may find
the professor interesting only in his technical role as the obtuse
narrator. The three enact a very stereotyped, very unconvincing
scene together toward the end of the book in which almost every
word of the dialogue rings false. The flaw is particularly serious
here since it involves Razumov's confession of guilt as well as his
love for Natalia. Conrad insists too much upon the importance of
the scene and tries futilely to make of Natalia's mother a heroic
figure.

Miss Haldin stopped, and pointed mournfully at the tragic immobility of her mother, who seemed to watch a beloved head lying in her
lap.
That gesture had an unequalled force of expression, so far-reaching
in its human distress that one could not believe that it pointed out
merely the ruthless working of political institutions.

The hero accepts his dismissal from the heroine, picks up the
object she has dropped to the floor, and runs away. ' "That
miserable wretch has carried off your veil!" I cried, in the scared,
deadened voice of an awful discovery.' Natalia says that her heart
feels 'like ice'. The inferiority of this scene can be readily felt by
comparing it with the excellent last two scenes of *Under Western
Eyes*, Razumov's confession to the revolutionists and his punishment, and Sophia Antonovna's account, two years later, of the
whereabouts of all the characters.
Though the love affair does little for the novel, one of the minor
characters, curiously enough, turns the stereotyped gesture of
male abasement before the female into one of the most entertaining scenes in the book. Peter Ivanovitch, a political prisoner in
chains, becomes a feminist when a pale-faced girl smuggles to
him the file she had intended to give her lover before he died.
With the file, Peter Ivanovitch manages to free one leg. 'He was
going to begin on his other leg when he was overtaken by a
terrible misfortune. He dropped his file.' He gropes for it in the
dark, cannot find it, and almost despairs. Then he feels ashamed
of his weakness. 'To fail would have been a sort of treason against

the sacredness of self-sacrifice and womanly love.' To prove his devotion to Woman, he trudges across Siberia carrying his chains. Providence rewards him when the next human being to speak to him proves to be the young bride of a blacksmith. Peter Ivanovitch describes the scene of his liberation in his autobiography (translated into seven or more languages) and Conrad's narrator comments:

'My fetters' – the book says – 'were struck off on the banks of the stream, in the starlight of a calm night by an athletic, taciturn young man of the people, kneeling at my feet, while the woman like a liberating genius stood by with clasped hands.' Obviously a symbolic couple.

Never did Conrad more effectively satirise his own tendency to sentimentalise women . . .

> SOURCE: extract from *Joseph Conrad: Achievement and Decline* (Cambridge, Mass., and London, 1957), pp. 94–6.

# *Tony Tanner*     Nightmare and Complacency: Razumov and the Western Eye (1962)

I

In *Karain: A Memory* Conrad enforces a crude but significant confrontation, an arresting contrast between a group of sober western seamen and the native Karain who is literally haunted by the ghost of the man he once betrayed and killed. The seamen come from 'the land of unbelief, where the dead do not speak, where every man is wise, and alone, and at peace'. Karain appears to them as 'that problem from outer darkness', an incomprehensible 'slave of the dead'. The story might seem to have been written according to a crude formula of reason versus superstition – until we come to the end. There the narrator tells how, years later, he met up with one of the crew who was with him the night they listened to Karain telling his terrible story out in the Eastern Archipelago. This man, Jackson, reminds him of Karain and his weird story of a demonic companion, and then adds:

'Do you know, I sometimes think that – . . . Yes . . . I mean, whether the thing was so, you know . . . whether it really happened to him. . . . What do you think?'

The narrator is shocked.

'My dear chap', I cried, 'you have been too long away from home. What a question to ask! Only look at all this.'

There follow two pages describing the Strand:

. . . the broken confusion of roofs, the chimney stacks . . . the sombre polish of windows . . . the big wheels of hansoms . . . a clumsy string of red, yellow, and green omnibuses rolled swaying, monstrous and gaudy . . . a ragged old man with a face of despair yelled horribly in the mud the name of a paper, while far off, amongst the tossing heads of horses, the dull flash of harnesses, the jumble of lustrous panels and roofs of carriages, we could see a policeman, helmeted and dark, stretching out a rigid arm at the crossing of the streets.
    'Yes; I see it', said Jackson slowly. 'It is there; it pants, it runs, it rolls; it is strong and alive; it would smash you if you didn't look out; but I'll be hanged if it is yet as real to me as . . . as the other thing . . . say, Karain's story.'

Which is *real*: the western world of mechanical efficiency, dominated by the tick-tock of the chronometer, guarded by pavements and roofs, summoned to sanity by the rigid arm of the policeman; or that remote and disturbing world where, against all the rules and tenets of an enlightened rational age, a man can be seen grappling for his life with a ghost? Conrad does not want us to answer this question: he wants us to be worried by it. His style is one which introduces questions, raises doubts, sets undermining ironies into play. It is not hostile to civilisation, but it makes against certain dangerous forms of civilised complacency. Perhaps this makes it clear why a narrator was so indispensable a part of Conrad's technique, for the introduction of a narrator makes possible the challenging interplay of two frames of reference, two schemes of values, two worlds of experience. Marlow is one kind of narrator, the one who involves us with his dangerous material. But there is another kind in Conrad's work: the narrator who tries to impress on us the remoteness, the alienness, the regrettable primitiveness of his material. He will represent the virtues of decency, moderation, a sort of polite if bemused tolerance of what is unusual, plus an uncompromising belief in the bourgeois-liberal tradition of the West: he is, to use one of Conrad's terms, an image of 'befogged respectability'. To make such a reasonable man recount to us some deeply irrational occurrence, to make the nightmarish material pass through the complacent filter, to make the western eye strive to get into focus some seemingly unwestern form of experience – this is to achieve a double irony. (We could compare Thomas Mann's ironic strategy in *Doctor Faustus* where he makes 'the demonic strain pass through an undemonic medium' as he describes it in *The Genesis of a Novel*.) The narrator may convince us of the undesirability and remoteness of his material, but his material may convince us of the inadequacy of the narrator's complacent virtues. The fame delimits and places the picture, but the picture can challenge and even ridicule the frame. In *Karain* Conrad can be seen groping towards the ironic narrative situation which he exploits with maximum effect in *Under Western Eyes*. A liberal western narrator describes with amazed non-comprehension the effects of a betrayal on a man whose imagination and conscience have been fashioned by another, wilder, culture. Instead of the seaman he uses a middle-aged language teacher, instead of Karain he creates Razumov, and instead of the shift from the East to the Strand, there is a shift from Russia to Geneva. Too much insensitive criticism has charged the book with being a crude and embittered anti-Russian tract, but this is to confuse Conrad the conservative essayist with Conrad the profound novelist. The former was the inheritor of Poland's grievances and the recipient of England's hospitality: the latter felt that truth was to be found only at the bottom of the abyss and not in the world-proof lives of the police-protected tradesmen of the west. Anybody who reads *Under Western Eyes* as an anti-Russian polemic has not learned to respond to the full range of Conrad's wide-ranging irony and scepticism, nor to the depths of his insight into the human mind.

II

Let us look, first, at the narrator. He disclaims the gift of imagination, and confesses that he has 'no comprehension of the Russian character'. Their illogicality and their loquacity alike bewilder him. When he comes to transmit Razumov's 'tumult of thoughts' he apologises for their shocking impropriety and stresses that 'this is not a story of the West of Europe'. His 'decent mind' is constantly disengaging itself from the material in hand and there are several reassuring reminders about 'we occidentals'. Too smugly he affirms that 'it is unthinkable that any young Englishman should find himself in Razumov's situation'. He almost qualifies for Yeats's remark about Emerson – he has no vision of evil. With unwarranted confidence and impenetrable complacency he speaks as though the West has managed to eradicate the irrational and tragic elements out of life once and for all; on the other hand everything Russian seems incomprehensible to him – even Haldin's handwriting looks 'cabalistic'. It is not surprising that his advice to Natalia Haldin is all in favour of non-involvement, of renouncing Russian experience and declining to risk any sort of contact with it. A typical remark in his narrative is: 'But I did not want to meditate very long on the inwardness of this peculiar episode.' And yet it is precisely Razumov's inward agony which is most intensely brought home to us, so that by the end of the book it is his experience which seems authentic and real, while the impercipient, incredulous narrator dwindles and draws away from us into unreality. He becomes, as he always appears to Razumov, a vague peripheral fatuous presence. He refers to himself as 'a helpless spectator' and though he has a ready sympathy and shows a decency which Conrad would value plus a scepticism as to the benefits of revolution which was Conrad's own, by the end of the book he seems to us almost stupid in his imperviousness to the profound significance of Razumov's experience and the tremendous effort of character involved in his final confession. He is scrupulously fair in his handling of evidence, but he never achieves any sympathetic insight into Razumov's inner predicament. He is honest and objective because that is his western code: but he is, to use Sartre's word, utterly 'impermeable' in his complacent disavowal of any human relationship with the events he recounts. We could recall Conrad's description of the coast-hugging 'world-proof' citizen: 'generally honest, invariably stupid'. The narrator starts off by disdaining and distancing his dark material: by the end the material has disdained and distanced him – and with him the whole nexus of western common-sense and complacency he represents. One major effect of the book is to secure a qualifying judgement on the myopia of those western eyes. The structure of the book reinforces that judgement. The first part takes place in Russia and inside Razumov. In Part Two there is a switch to the comforting consoling familiarity of Geneva and the narrator's orderly account of life there up to the time of Razumov's arrival. In the third part we are back inside Razumov who this time, however, is here in Geneva. The final part brings out the full horror of Razumov's past predicament and present anguish and ends with that shattering physical attack and accident which so disturb the quiescent uninquiring orderliness of a Geneva day. This complex shifting structure succeeds overwhelmingly in depicting a distant Russian experience which then draws suddenly closer until finally it bulks so large that it is the Western scenery that has taken on the quality of artificiality. It is worth pointing out how severely the stronghold of western civilisation is challenged and belittled throughout the book. On this point the narrator sometimes speaks with uncharacteristic mordancy: some of Conrad's sharp contempt disturbs the bland geniality of the language master. He refers to 'the orderly roof-slopes of that town, comely without grace, and hospitable without sympathy'. Towards the end of the story, as Razumov's crisis approaches, the town is more often noted: 'the emptiness of the quays, the desert aspect of the streets, had an air of hypocritical respectability and of inexpressible dreariness'; 'we turned into the Boulevard des Philosophes, more wide, more empty, more dead – the very desolation of slumbering respectability'; 'the town indifferent and hospitable in its cold, almost scornful, toleration'; 'the main forces of the thunderstorm remained massed down the Rhone valley as if loath to attack the respectable and passionless abode of democratic liberty'. Seen through Razumov's eyes the town is even more contemptible: 'the very perfection of mediocrity attained at last after centuries of toil and culture': dull people in dull environments surrounded by scenery which has for him 'all the marvellous banality of the picturesque made of painted cardboard'. It is of course a fine additional irony that he chooses as the place to write his confessions a little island named after Rousseau and supervised by a statue of that optimistic author of the *Social Contract*. In his inward agony and utter isolation Razumov is a living rebuke to the whole Rousseauistic concept of man. The island itself where Razumov commits to paper the frantic details of his disordered life is 'a perfection of puerile neatness'. Knowing what we do, we too feel that 'there was something of naïve, odious, and inane simplicity about that unfrequented tiny crumb of earth named after Jean Jacques Rousseau'. The Swiss people are of a piece with their environment. There is that idle workman sleeping on a bench who excites Razumov to mutter: 'Elector! Eligible! Enlightened! . . . A brute all the same.' Or that 'solitary Swiss couple, whose fate was made secure from the cradle to the grave by the perfected mechanism of democratic institutions in a republic that could almost be held in the palm of one's hand. The man, colourlessly uncouth, was drinking beer out of a glittering glass; the woman, rustic and placid, leaning back in the rough chair, gazed idly around'. This is really Conrad's contempt: the narrator should be more approving of the achieved security of democratic civilisation. In fact the juxtaposition of Razumov with these untroubled Swiss citizens exemplifies Conrad's severe dichotomy of the human race. In a letter to Madame Poradowska he wrote: 'One must drag the ball and chain of one's selfhood to the end. It is the price one pays for the devilish and divine privilege of thought; so that in this life it is only the elect who are convicts – a glorious band which comprehends and groans but which treads the earth amidst a multitude of phantoms with maniacal gestures, with idiotic grimaces. Which would you be: idiot or convict?' Razumov is a real convict dragging his burden through a phantom town of idiots. And at the end that image becomes the actuality with the deafened Razumov lying shattered in a phantom world peopled with gaping, gesticulating mutes. The relationship between Razumov and the west in general is pointed up for one moment when he starts to shout to the group of anarchists in the garden of the Château Borel. No one passing notices. 'Only a specimen of early tourist in knickerbockers, conspicuous by a brand-new yellow leather glass-case, hung about for a moment, scenting something unusual about these four people within the rusty iron gates of what looked like the grounds run wild of an unoccupied private house. Ah! If he had only known what the chance of commonplace travelling had suddenly put in his way! But he was a well-bred person; he averted his gaze and moved off . . .' The western eye, despite its expensive binoculars, does not inquire too curiously. It sticks to the surface of things. Yet how close it is to the abyss if it did but know it, if it could but see it. There is something quintessentially Conradian in that short scene. The tourist and Razumov, the idiot and the convict – within touching distance, yet worlds apart.

III

Now let us turn to the 'reality' of the book: Razumov's experience. The first section of the book – one of Conrad's most impressive pieces of writing – describes Razumov's initial situation, the sudden appearance of the anarchist murderer Haldin, and Razumov's internal state which leads to his betrayal of Haldin. At the outset Razumov is 'as lonely in the world as a man swimming in the deep sea'. Being a disowned bastard he is perpetually in that unfettered, unmoored, alienated state which Conrad found the crucial testing time for a man. (We could compare Durkheim's concept of 'anomy' in his classic analysis of the causes of suicide.) Not being firmly linked and locked into the community, the social tapestry if you like, he has two desires. One is a necessity: he has to 'keep an instinctive hold on normal, practical, everyday life'. The other is an ambition to win the Ministry of Education essay prize, the silver medal. That medal is important: it is what Razumov takes his compass readings by, it affords him direction and focus. As well as representing the badge of membership, the charismatic pass to society, it helps him to plan an orderly future. When he looks at the medal in his imagination he can foresee a logical, purposeful sequence of days. Razumov is a man with no ties, no emotional footholds: no anchors afford him a consoling tug, reminding him of a deep and necessary centre to which he belongs. He has to locate himself in the world: he has to find a significance in the reassuring pressure of the contingencies of routine, he has to make his work give his life some meaning although 'his success would matter to no one'. The only way he can invest his discernible future with a sense of consequence is by drawing a line between himself and that magical token of social approbation and recognition: the silver medal. (The medal is mentioned again towards the end of his confessions – this time as a symbol of a lost normality of life.) From the start, then, Razumov is in an extremely precarious situation, mentally if not physically.

He is also an intelligent man to whom perception, analysis deduction and imagination are habits. He is not a dumb, unthinking, enduring natural object – like Singleton (in *The Nigger of the 'Narcissus'*) who, one feels, could never for a moment get out of step with nature's profoundest rhythms. Thought, as Conrad as well as Lawrence and Hardy insisted, dislodges a man from his natural context: it corrodes those crude confidences and certitudes which enable a majority of mankind to keep a grip on their lives: it dissolves the universe in doubt. The combination of isolation and intellect is directly responsible for Decoud's remarkably described suicide in *Nostromo*: it is this combination which is Razumov's daily lot. He maintains a sort of working sanity by never disturbing the established normalness of things, by orienting himself by his guiding star, the silver medal.

And suddenly into this man's precariously maintained existence erupts the most dangerous, extreme opposite type: a fanatic with the unshakable confidence of a creed and the reassuring support of a loyal group, an irresponsible irrational anarchist, a man dedicated to destroying the established order of things, a man completely at peace with his soul who scatters complicity wherever he goes. Razumov, for his mind's sake as well as his security, had always kept his life clear and clean. 'He was always accessible, and there was nothing secret or reserved in his life.' And it is this man who returns one evening to find the most wanted criminal in Russia standing in his room like an apparition. It is part of Conrad's irony that this occurs on an evening when Razumov felt in particularly good form to work on his essay for the silver medal. Haldin literally comes between him and his planned future. 'All black against the usual tall stove of white tiles gleaming in the dusk, stood a strange figure, wearing a skirted, close-fitting, brown cloth coat strapped round the waist, in long boots, and with a little Astrakhan cap on its head. It loomed lithe and martial. Razumov was utterly confounded.'

This is a key moment, the unexpected intrusion which Razumov denounces with such vehemence on subsequent occasions. Mentally, as when he says to himself: 'Fatality enters your rooms while your landlady's back is turned; you come home and find it in possession bearing a man's name, clothed in flesh – wearing a brown cloth coat and long boots – lounging against the stove. . . . You cannot shake it off any more. It will cling to you for ever.' And vocally in his protest to Mikulin:

'What is a sober man to do, I should like to know? To cut oneself entirely from one's kind is impossible. To live in a desert one must be a saint. But if a drunken man runs out of the grog-shop, falls on your neck and kisses you on both cheeks because something about your appearance has taken his fancy, what then – kindly tell me? You may break, perhaps, a cudgel on his back and yet not succeed in beating him off.'

That there are uninvited, forced and fatal alliances is a basic Conradian feeling. Willems, in *An Outcast of the Islands*, had felt 'something monstrous and depraved, forcing its complicity upon him'. Or take the reasonable, honourable General D'Hubert in *The Duel*. At that point when his life finally seems safe and secure, on the very eve of his marriage, he is suddenly accosted by representatives from his maniacal pursuer Feraud. And note the image: 'they stood before him lank and straight, as though they had been shot up with a snap through a trap door in the ground'. General D'Hubert's whole life is endangered by 'these serious phantoms standing in his way'. Or think of the sudden visitation of Jones, Ricardo, and Pedro to Heyst's island of renunciation and contemplation in *Victory*. 'Think what it was to me to see them land in the dusk, fantasms from the sea – apparitions, chimaeras! And they persist. That's the worst of it – they persist. They have no right to be – but they are.' It must be added that there are hidden aspects of Willems's, D'Hubert's, and Heyst's characters which make such impositions and visitations possible, no matter how surprising. Razumov might curse fate, but in fact it is his loneliness and accessibility which make him peculiarly vulnerable. Conrad was not a crude fatalist, though he certainly thought life was more illogical and absurd than reason could ever comprehend or allow for. Razumov's intelligence is insufficient defence against an unintelligible world. As he realises: 'An absurdity may be the starting-point of the most dangerous complications. How is one to guard against it? It puts to rout one's intelligence. The more intelligent one is the less one suspects an absurdity.'

Razumov's aloneness and accessibility leave him open to unsolicited and incompatible claims on his allegiance. When he was summoned to meet his aristocratic father, the remote Prince K, he was surprised to be offered a soft white hand. 'But the most amazing thing of all was to feel suddenly a distinct pressure of the white shapely hand just before it was withdrawn: a light pressure like a secret sign.' There is an incipient tie. Then Haldin bursts into his life because he has 'confidence' in Razumov. That is another pressure on his uncommitted soul. And Razumov cannot tell Haldin to go away, cannot break this imposed alliance, cannot dismiss the obstructing phantom. It is in this helpless state that the 'naked terror' of his utter loneliness comes home to him; he even thinks of rushing back to Haldin and embracing him and his cause. Then he recalls that earlier unspoken claim. The father he had never really had represents the harmony of the established order, that great palace of status and security into which he aspires to be admitted. Haldin on the other hand stands for 'horrible discord' not only in Russia but in Razumov's pre-cariously maintained routine existence. In succumbing to the unspoken claim of his father Razumov is following a profound emotional need. His subsequent conservative political ideals are rationalisation. But after Haldin has also made his claim on him his mind is never at rest. 'I want to guide my conduct by reasonable convictions, but what security have I against something – some destructive horror – walking in upon me as I sit here?' Haldin's phantom is forever before him, always to be walked over. He can be killed but he cannot be dismissed.

With the state and Haldin wrestling for his allegiance Razumov might seem like a character in a morality play, except that neither of the opponents are angels, simply forces making his

life impossible. Between them they drag Razumov into the moral
arena, to that testing moment when choice is both unavoidable
and damning. Razumov's mind sides with the state, but it is
Haldin's phantom which refuses to vanish. Once Razumov flings
himself on the bed on which Haldin had lain, awaiting
deliverance or burial at Razumov's hands. ' "It's you, crazy
fanatic, who stand in the way." He flung the pillow on the floor
violently, tore the blankets aside. . . . Nothing there.' At first
Razumov tells himself: 'This will pass and leave no trace. . . . I
am all right'; but near the end as he is sitting with Haldin's
mother in Geneva he realises that phantoms cannot so easily be
exorcised. 'It was impossible to get rid of him. "It's myself whom
I have given up to destruction", thought Razumov. "He has
induced me to do it. I can't shake him off." ' Razumov makes a
discovery similar to that of Harry in Eliot's *The Family Reunion*:

> Now I see
> I have been wounded in a war of phantoms,
> Not by human beings – they have no more power than I.
> The things I thought were real are shadows, and the real
> Are what I thought were private shadows.

## IV

I now want to scrutinise more carefully Razumov's inner
experience and to get at this it will be profitable to ask ourselves
two questions. Exactly why does he betray Haldin: and having
done so why is he driven to confess the deed to the anarchists?
After all, he has an intellectual belief in the necessity of the
stability of the state and an emotional distaste and contempt for
the revolutionaries. Why then does his first act so dislocate and
disorder his life and why does his suicidal confession bring relief?
To attempt some sort of an answer to these questions is to
penetrate to the depths of some of Conrad's profoundest insights
into man's 'riddling, perplexed, labyrinthical soul' or, if Donne's
phrase is too theological, we could say with the careful narrator
'that part of Mr Razumov which was not his body'. The moment
that Haldin expresses his 'confidence' Razumov is lost. 'This
word sealed Razumov's lips as if a hand had been clapped on his
mouth. His brain seethed with arguments.' The honorific appeal

stifles external complaint but stimulates an unprecedented
inward activity, not least of the imagination. 'Razumov saw
himself shut up in a fortress, worried, badgered, perhaps ill-used.
He saw himself deported by an administrative order, his life
broken, ruined, and robbed of all hope. . . . He saw himself
creeping, broken down and shabby, about the streets – dying
unattended in some filthy hole of a room, or on the sordid bed of a
Government hospital.' Imagination always represents a threat to
orderly conduct in Conrad because it causes the mind to slide
away from the 'saving facts' of life and indulge in graphic,
immobilising fantasies of terror or glory. Lord Jim is one
'imaginative beggar', Almayer another, Razumov a third –
though his imaginings are more justifiable than those of any
other Conrad character. However, being unable to protest, he
sets out to find the driver Ziemianitch feeling weak and sick. He is
both sustained and distracted by fear: the nightmarish
townscapes, peopled by silently looming phantoms, correspond
to his internal state (as well as anticipating his end), while his
distracting terror of 'sinking into the lowest social depths amongst
the hopeless and the destitute' as a result of this illicit errand is
aptly dramatised by his sudden discovery that he has walked into
a snowdrift 'up to his knees'. Fear gives way to rage, rage to hate.
And then, meditating on his isolation and lostness he discovers
the 'sacred inertia' of Russia, a concept which provides him with
a mental rallying point, a logic with which to fend off the
encroaching disastrous claims of the idealistic revolutionaries.
'The grace entered into Razumov' – a deep Conradian irony. In
one sense the idea of aligning himself with the inert status quo of
his country is a 'grace' because it gives his mind something to
organise itself around. It brings into play 'the clear grasp of my
intellect', 'my cool superior reason': yet there remains a residual
unease, unamenable to the strictures of reason, which gives the
grace a poisonous taint; and we remember perhaps that significant moment in Judas's life: 'And after the sop Satan entered
into him.' Razumov's sop, we might say, was the pressure of his
father's hand: the satanic grace is his rationalised justification of
the idea of betrayal. His mental faculties, scattered by the sudden
intrusion of Haldin, now marshal themselves behind the emerging notion of an intelligent (not impulsive) renunciation of all
that Haldin stands for. Yet just as his mind approaches this

'courageous' conclusion, two sledges collide near Razumov and he starts when he hears a cry: 'Oh, thou vile wretch'. We may recall that Jim, refusing to admit his guilt, nevertheless spins round when he hears a voice in a crowd yell: 'Look at that wretched cur'. In both cases something deeper than the mind remains ashamed and undeceived: if the conscience is like a worm then it is at this point in Razumov's life that it starts to turn and writhe. Seconds later he has his first collision with Haldin's phantom. Minutes after that he 'discovered what he had meant to do all along'.

He made a few steps and muttered through his set teeth – 'I shall give him up.'
    Then for some twenty yards or more all was blank. He wrapped his cloak closer around him. He pulled his cap well forward over his eyes. 'Betray. A great word. What is betrayal? They talk of a man betraying his country, his friends, his sweetheart. There must be a moral bond first. All a man can betray is his conscience. And how is my conscience engaged here; by what bond of common faith, of common conviction, am I obliged to let that fanatical idiot drag me down with him? On the contrary – every obligation of true courage is the other way.'
    Razumov looked round from under his cap.

Sound ratiocination – but why then that last, incomparably vivid, furtive gesture. Is there some inward pressure which the mind can neither convert nor dismiss? Does some part of him recognise that a bond has been made'– uninvited but ineradicable, not political but creatural? If so then no matter how justified by exigencies and convictions his intellectual decision is, a part will forever contest it. That precious inward equilibrium which was indispensable to Razumov in his isolated unsupported state has gone forever. And that there is such a part to Razumov he reveals by his equivocal shriek to Haldin: 'I am responsible for you'. In that cry is the horror of recognising that fatal bond which the mind denies.
    Razumov's walk, which concludes with his betrayal of Haldin, is indeed 'a nightmare of a walk' and from his point on all his energies will be devoted to an attempt to keep his life from turning into a phantasmagoria. One might compare these lines from *The Spanish Tragedy*:

> There is a path upon your left-hand side,
> That leadeth from a guilty conscience
> Upon a forest of distrust and fear,
> A darksome place, and dangerous to pass.

or the 'phantasma' experienced by Brutus, or the disturbance of perceptual sanity by Macbeth's inward insurrection. All these great betrayers are not tortured by fear of future punishment so much as they are unnerved by a series of dislocations in their ability to apprehend material reality. What worries Macbeth about the dagger he sees before him is not that it reflects his murderous intentions, but that he cannot be sure if it exists or not. Just as Razumov is not sure whether Haldin is or is not an actual presence in his room.

A longer study than this could show how life for Razumov changes into a grotesque pantomine, a hideous farce, a monstrous puppet-show, a nightmare – anything but normal reassuring reality. Two quotations must serve to point up the sort of transformation his life undergoes. As he returns home after the betrayal he argues consolingly with himself.

After he had gone a little way the familiarity of things got hold of him. Nothing was changed. . . . Nothing would change. . . . The sense of life's continuity depended on trifling impressions. The trivialities of daily existence were an armour for the soul. And this thought reinforced the inward quietness of Razumov as he began to climb the stairs familiar to his feet in the dark, with his hand on the familiar clammy banister. The exceptional would not prevail against the material contacts which make one day resemble another. To-morrow would be like yesterday.

But after Haldin has gone down into the street (into the police trap) Razumov suffers from nausea, tries but utterly fails to work, and is reduced to despair by the discovery that his watch has stopped. That last touch tellingly indicates an interruption to, perhaps an end of, the well-regulated normality of his life. From now on his time is not normal society's time. And tomorrow is revoltingly unlike yesterday.

The light coming through the window seemed strangely cheerless, containing no promise as the light of each new day should for a young

man. It was the awakening of a man mortally ill, or of a man ninety
years old. He looked at the lamp which had burnt itself out. It stood
there, the extinguished beacon of his labours, a cold object of brass and
porcelain, amongst the scattered pages of his notes and small piles of
books – a mere litter of blackened paper – dead matter – without significance or interest. . . . An incredible dullness, a ditch-water stagnation
was sensible to his perceptions as though life had withdrawn itself from
all things and even from his own thoughts. . . . He did nothing all that
day; he neglected even to brush his hair. The idea of going out never
occurred to him – and if he did not start a connected train of thought it
was not because he was unable to think. It was because he was not
interested enough.

The usual significances have drained out of the objects of the
phenomenological world: matter from now on becomes horrific
in the unpredictable, disconcerting way it works on Razumov's
senses, senses disordered from within. (Compare Sartre's *Nausea*
in which matter without meaning becomes monstrous.) It is not
long before a normal fellow-student has become 'a vision out of a
nightmare': not long before he is hysterically complaining to
Councillor Mikulin that 'the whole affair is becoming . . . a
comedy of errors, phantoms and suspicions': not long before a
compulsive incoherent loquacity is threatening the imperative
lucidity and control of his speech and behaviour. He extricated
himself from his appalling predicament by the use of his
intelligence, and he banked on that intelligence to see him
through. But the betrayal recoils in a way he never anticipated –
not in the form of conventional remorse, nor the routine
interference of the police, nor even the shaming presumption of
his heroism among the students. The new and unexpected threat
is the malfunctioning of his dislodged mental faculties.

'Impossible to think of anything else', muttered Razumov to himself.
'I'll become an idiot if this goes on. The scoundrels and the fools are
murdering my intelligence.' He lost all hope of saving his future, which
depended on the free use of his intelligence.

It is this inward state as much as outward circumstances which
reduce him to the state in which he has to seek understanding
company, even if it is only police company, the state in which he
wishes vaguely to 'retire' but can only go where the police direct.

The terrible plight summed up by Councillor Mikulin's question 'Where to?' is not that of a man to whom all other lands are barred, but rather that of a man condemned to perceive the whole world through a fractured and aggrieved mind. The external effects of this inner imbalance are presented to us through the uninvolved, objective eyes of the narrator in Part Two. This switch of perspective is very effective. Suddenly we see a strange, haunted figure who seems to be parched, suffocating, and terribly unsteady on his feet. The general ominousness of his presence is added to by the chilling inconsequentiality of his sudden staccato outbursts of speech. And above all there is the awful sleeplessness of those eyes. 'He looked as though he had not slept very well of late. I could almost feel on me the weight of his unrefreshed, motionless stare, the stare of a man who lies unwinking in the dark, angrily passive in the toils of disastrous thoughts.' The narrator brings home to us the physical symptoms with a calmness that makes those very symptoms stand out in arresting relief. 'And he produced a faint, rasping voice quite like a man with a parched throat. . . . He shrugged his shoulders so violently that he tottered again. . . . At the moment he looked to me convincingly tired, gone slack all over, like a man who has passed through some sort of crisis.' (Macbeth, too, finds that he has murdered sleep, and we should think of that other undone character in An Anarchist who 'complained that sleep fled from him'.) But one of the most telling physical details comes from Miss Haldin who tells the narrator how Razumov reacted when she spoke her brother's name to him. 'He was quite overcome. I have told you my opinion that he is a man of deep feeling – it is impossible to doubt it. You should have seen his face. He positively reeled. He leaned against the wall of the terrace. Their friendship must have been the very brotherhood of souls.' No matter how convinced and prepared Razumov's mind is, his body reels under the impact of these terrible unanticipated ironies and reminders – for there had been a bond even if he had disavowed it. Cain and Abel were after all brothers. Later, when the narrator suggests that Haldin might have been betrayed, Razumov suddenly sits down, and when he suggests that it will not cost Razumov any effort to go and comfort Haldin's mother Razumov turns violently away and leans on the parapet of a bridge. In Part Two it is above all the picture of a man incomprehensibly staggering, stumbling, gasping, and suddenly turning away from people that we receive. 'Possessed' is too strong a word and with too simple a notion of Razumov's 'perplexities and complex terrors': it is the occasional physical lapse that is so telling, the momentary failure of co-ordination as though he can no longer perfectly bring his body under the control of his mind. Memorably, this section of the book leaves him staring into the 'rush of the blue water under the arch'. As though the very turbulence of natural forces pacifies him.

In Part Three we are pulled right back into the inward centre of Razumov's anguish: we overhear his 'silent thinking, like a secret dialogue with himself'. The atmosphere of this section of the book can perhaps be hinted at by another quotation from *The Family Reunion* (and in my opinion the extent of Eliot's debt to Conrad has not yet been appreciated). The guilty and tormented Harry describes how it feels to be haunted:

> The sudden solitude in a crowded desert
> In a thick smoke, many creatures moving
> Without direction . . .
> The partial anaesthesia of suffering without feeling
> And partial observation of one's own automatism
> While the slow stain sinks deeper through the skin
> Tainting the flesh and discolouring the bone . . .
>                 One thinks to escape
> By violence, but one is still alone
> In an over-crowded desert, jostled by ghosts.

The difference is that Conrad's insights into guilt are psychological more than theological: he studies what happens to the senses under stress. Thus the description of Razumov's visit to the Château Borel shows him again losing control of his conversation, recoiling at unexpected ironies, subject to sudden mad impulses of violence (he imagines stabbing Ivanovitch), suspecting Madame de S of an ability to read his thoughts, desperately arranging his anguished face in the mirror in an effort to formulate to himself 'reassuring excuses for his appearance marked by the taint of some hereditary disease'. His aim is still sensory sanity, not redemption: 'He was calming down, getting hold of the actuality into which he had been thrown'. Yet that actuality appears to him as a puppet world devoid of human

significance. Madame de S, for instance, seems to him 'a wooden
or plaster figure of a repulsive kind'. And the precious calmness
never lasts long. He is driven to blurting out remarks which at
once reveal and conceal his guilt. It is as though whatever he
starts saying his words coil back to pick at his past. 'I've seen a
phantom once', he stammers out compulsively: 'I was irresistibly
drawn – let us say impelled, yes, impelled; or, rather, compelled –
driven – driven', he shouts to the chief revolutionary, as though
finding some bitter relief in such masochistic ironies. His state
after he has finally emerged from the castle is brought home to us
by a masterly mixture of physical symptoms and inner
reflections:

. . . he lifted his hat and wiped his damp forehead expelling his breath
with force to get rid of the last vestiges of the air he had been breathing
inside. He looked at the palms of his hands, and rubbed them gently
against his thighs. He felt, bizarre as it may seem, as though another self,
an independent sharer of his mind, had been able to view his whole
person very distinctly indeed. 'This is curious', he thought. After a while
he formulated his opinion of it in the mental ejaculation: 'Beastly!'

This sort of incipient schizophrenia experienced by people under
stress is a recurring theme in Conrad, but never had the danger
and stress been as great as for his character Razumov to whom
absolute self-mastery and lucid integration are necessary for
survival. This is what gives his sudden doubts such piercing force.
' "Is it possible that I am but a weak creature after all?" he asked
himself in sudden alarm. "Eh! What's that?" He gave a start as if
awakened from a dream.'

Throughout this section he hovers on the edge of that weakness
which is beyond the jurisdiction of the mind. The sheer effort of
skirting this area of himself makes him perspire and gasp, makes
him feel utterly weary, immensely remote, and eternally
imprisoned – banished forever from free air. His nerves are
inhumanly knotted in the imperative effort 'to preserve a clear
mind' when everything conspires to cloud and disrupt it. His
conversation with Sophia Antonovna, 'the respectable enemy',
with her tremendous integrity, reveals the full extent of his
hopeless plight. At first he is calm and in control, but as the talk
runs on and the woman's questions and insights start to unravel

his precariously maintained composure he comes to a terrible realisation. ' "I shall never be found prepared", he thought with despair.' The perversity of things inside him, the unpredictability of the world outside him together strain his mind unbearably. It has to fight on too many fronts at once. ('They don't understand what it is to be awake, To be living on several planes at once', says Harry in *The Family Reunion*.) An example of the unexpected outward attack is Sophia Antonovna's sudden question about his behaviour on the morning of the assassination. 'An appreciable fraction of a second elapsed before the real import of the question reached him, like a bullet which strikes some time after the flash of the fired shot. Luckily his disengaged hand was ready to grip a bar of the gate. He held it with a terrible force, but his presence of mind was gone. He could make only a sort of gurgling, grumpy sound.' It is then that, in an amazing passage, he literally takes on Haldin's personality and relives the events through remembered hints of what Haldin had said. He identifies with the murdered 'brother', he becomes the very ghost that is haunting him. 'The stairs were dark. I glided up like a phantom.' But this moment of identification turns into nightmare, and a mixture of haunting reminiscence and black hallucination overwhelm him. 'Have you ever listened to the pit-pat of a man running round and round the shaft of a deep staircase.' When Haldin ran to his death down the staircase of betrayal he also wound himself down into the depths of Razumov's memory and being. This is why Razumov often starts talking lucidly enough and finishes up 'like a man who has been dreaming aloud'. The nightmare seeps up into his mind like smoke, just as the falseness of his position threatens to suffocate him. 'The choking fumes of falsehood had taken him by the throat – the thought of being condemned to struggle on and on in that tainted atmosphere without the hope of ever renewing his strength by a breath of fresh air.'

Conrad then gives the final ironic twist to the screw, for Razumov now hears about the suicide of Ziemianitch and the universal belief that this was done out of remorse for betraying Haldin. Razumov is now safe from all external suspicion and accusation. 'His mind was at ease; ease such as he had not known for many days, ever since that night . . . the night.' But even at this moment of security his mind slips away from him and he finds himself speculating on the depth of the lake. He drags his mind back to meditate on his impregnable position – 'All this fitted with marvellous aptness' – but he is distressed to find himself unable to remember some important thing he had intended to do that day. And just at the moment when he is thinking with relief, 'no more need for lies', another revolutionary, Julius Laspara, crosses his path bringing home to Razumov his inextricably involved state. All these instances serve to dramatise 'that incorrigible tendency to escape from the grip of the situation' which is Razumov's most serious threat: when his mind is not tugging back into the nightmare it is leaking away in uncontrolled and distracting irrelevances. It is this curious state that leads him to the shocking thought: 'Is it possible that I have a conventional conscience?' The luck of being provided with a perfect alibi brings home to Razumov with novel force that what is making his life impossible is not external threats and suspicions (as he had thought) but some deep inner activity which can scarcely be named and never fully controlled. The very advent of that question – 'Is it possible that I have a conventional conscience?' – although he dismisses the idea with intellectual contempt, means that the issue of the book is never in doubt. He has not got to dodge something from without, but disgorge something from within.

The last section returns to describe how he was drawn into his activities as a police spy and how, back in Geneva, he is 'betrayed into truth'. It dwells again on his isolation – 'as if in a desert' – and how he is tormented by 'the dark prestige of the Haldin mystery' which 'clung to him like a poisoned robe it was impossible to fling off'. It re-emphasises the dream-like nature of all his subsequent experiences, especially his journey from Russia to Geneva. So that when we suddenly return to Razumov writing his confessions on the island we realise again how strange his life must feel, how it has both dwindled to dream and expanded to nightmare. So his first meditation is curiously apt. 'Perhaps life is just that . . . a dream and a fear.' And so is the narrator's impression of him: 'he had the expression of a somnambulist struggling with the very dream which drives him forth to wander in dangerous places'. The disgorging process – the written confession, the confession to Miss Haldin 'in the glaring light, between the four bare walls', his confession to the revolutionaries as he stands fully exposed dripping with the rain which 'washes him clean' (in the one overtly redemptive hint in the book) – all this follows with a precipitous down-hill inevitability. But it is important to note that his last entry in his confessions denies any change of political conviction. It is rather that he has discovered that there is a truth of state and a truth of self and that he cannot live without the latter. 'Victor Haldin had stolen the truth of my life from me, who had nothing else in the world' – this is one of the most moving entries in his note-book. A life without personal truth is a life without air, hence his dizziness and recurring feelings of suffocation. Once he has decided to "confess, go out – and perish" even though it means the end of everything he had schemed for, his self-preservation, his career, his possible marriage, he feels the intense relief of having regained the priceless truth of his life. 'Now I have done it; and as I write here, I am in the depths of anguish, but there is air to breathe at last – air!' The act of confession which effectively destroys his life, gives him back that without which life cannot be sustained: for once his life is free from suspicion he discovers that it must also be 'free from falsehood'. Eliot's lines are again relevant, for Harry also discovers:

> And in the end
> That is the completion which at the beginning
> Would have seemed the ruin.

Razumov betrayed Haldin in a desperate effort to keep his life normal, to *retain* his sanity by expunging an unbalancing presence which had thrust itself into his life: he confesses to *regain* the sanity which his first act did not preserve as he thought it would. 'The mysterious force' which tears the truth out of him – against all the concealing efforts and stratagems of his intellect – is a profound need for inward truth without which the senses run amok and turn the world into nightmare. The only way to cleanse himself of the completely irrational pollution and untruth which has invaded his life since the betrayal of Haldin is to submit himself to a like fate. He re-enacts what he once made Haldin do, running out of his house at midnight, straight into the den of his judgers, straight into the brute Nikita who handles him with the mutilating violence which his deepest instincts require. Thus this intelligent man who had tried to direct his life according to the dictates of a clear-sighted and calculating mind, turns out to be 'a puppet of his past'. Such is the curious ferocity and profound subtlety of Conrad's brand of determinism. Yet Razumov acquires great stature, not only because of what he suffers, but because in the depths of that suffering he discovers that no matter what is in the balance he cannot live a lie. 'There's character in such a discovery' pronounces Sophia Antonovna. Character, not Christian salvation. Conrad's characters live in a remorselessly terrestial world. Razumov's reward is limited to that peace which lies on the other side of nightmare and which is perhaps all we can hope for in an unredeemed world. Not heaven, but the calmness of a heart at rest and a regained sanity of the senses.

## V

*Under Western Eyes* is the tragedy of 'a man with a mind'. Razumov says to Miss Haldin: 'I have had the misfortune to be born clear-eyed' and the last words in his confession are 'I am independent – and therefore perdition is my lot.' Razumov differs from other Conrad characters in these two particulars: he has a lucid active mind, and that is *all* he has. Thus he complained to Haldin: 'I am just a man. . . . A man with a mind. . . . I have no domestic tradition. I have nothing to think against.' It is by scrutinising the divorced intelligence as it grapples with external irrationality and internal unintelligibility that Conrad makes some of his most profound discoveries about man and his place in the universe. Razumov tries to regulate his life according to his intelligence – he has to, it is all he has got. But he discovers that sanity and inner peace are not products of the reason, cannot be purchased by the deductions of the aware intelligence. Therefore – life is absurd: absurd in the sense to which we are only now accustoming ourselves. Compare this from one of Conrad's letters. 'What makes mankind tragic is not that they are victims of nature, it is that they are conscious of it.' Razumov is not damned by any wrathful divinity for his eminently 'reasonable' betrayal of Haldin: it is the terrible chaos in his consciousness which passes judgement on him.

'It is from weakness, unknown but perhaps suspected, as in some parts of the world you suspect a deadly snake in every bush – from weakness that may lie hidden, watched or un-watched, prayed against or manfully scorned, repressed or maybe ignored more than half a lifetime, not one of us is safe.' (*Lord Jim.*) To those who would maintain that Razumov's experience is outside the area of the probable or who insist that Conrad was here discharging an anti-Russian loathing, to those and indeed to the narrator of the book I would quote Eliot's lines, again from *The Family Reunion*: lines which possibly have their origin in Conrad's own work and which certainly would have earned his approval. Harry, haunted like Razumov, turns on his respectable, incomprehending family.

You are all people
To whom nothing has happened, at most a continual impact
Of external events. You have gone through life in sleep,
Never woken to the nightmare. I tell you, life would be unendurable
If you were wide awake.

*Under Western Eyes* is the compelling account of a man forced into wide-awakeness, a man unwillingly made intimate with the nightmare which hovers forever just under the complacencies of civilised existence. The power and profundity of this novel make it unique in English literature.

SOURCE: essay in *Critical Quarterly*, IV, No. 3 (1962), 197–214.

# H. M. Daleski      'Dispossession and Self-Possession' (1977)

I

Possibly following the unusual example of E. M. Forster, who the year before had used the words of one of his own characters as the epigraph to *Howards End*, Conrad in 1911 quoted 'Miss Haldin' in his epigraph to *Under Western Eyes*: 'I would take liberty from any hand as a hungry man would snatch a piece of bread.' However, whereas Forster's 'Only connect . . .' is not only 'the whole of [Margaret Schlegel's] sermon', but the theme of the novel, Conrad's highlighting of Natalia's dictum has no such obvious relation to the apparent drive of his work. But the remark, in its acceptance of the use of any means to achieve a commendable end, does relate Natalia to an earlier idealist in the Conrad canon, to Charles Gould [in *Nostromo*]. He (it will be recalled) was ready to use 'such weapons as could be found at once in the mire of corruption' in Costaguana in order to safeguard 'law, good faith, order, security'; and his belief that 'a better justice' would 'come afterwards' is parallel with her assertion, which follows the announcement of her credo, that 'the true progress must begin after' [p. 135].[1] The epigraph also relates Natalia to a character such as the Professor [in *The Secret Agent*], who similarly has no scruples as to the means to be used in bringing about a desired new order. Her remark thus brings to mind the moral nihilism that pervades the societies depicted in both *Nostromo* and *The Secret Agent* – and would seem further to imply that a moral opportunism is the distinguishing mark of anyone brought up in the Russia of *Under Western Eyes*, even as positive (and generally idealised) a character as Natalia Haldin.

This is the judgement the novelist would appear to wish us to make in regard to both the sides engaged in the political conflict which is the background to the main action of the novel, for it emerges as a constant amid shifting views of that struggle. Victor Haldin, who initiates the main action when he assassinates the

Minister-President, may be regarded as representative of the revolutionists at their best and acts in the name of the liberty so dear to his sister; we note that he does not hesitate to kill at the same time an unspecified number of innocent bystanders – not to mention his fellow-conspirator [pp. 9–10]. The narrator holds this assassination to be 'characteristic of modern Russia', and adds that, in its perversion of admirable qualities, it is 'still more characteristic of the moral corruption of an oppressed society where the noblest aspirations of humanity, the desire of freedom, an ardent patriotism, the love of justice, the sense of pity, and even the fidelity of simple minds are prostituted to the lusts of hate and fear, the inseparable companions of an uneasy despotism' [p. 7]. Razumov, when he is faced with the fact of the assassination, decides that 'Haldin means disruption', and (associating him with 'volcanic eruption') concludes it is 'better that thousands should suffer than that a people should become a disintegrated mass, helpless like dust in the wind' [p. 34]. The revolutionists, that is to say, figure as the same kind of morally corrupt and disintegrative force as the anarchists in *The Secret Agent* – and indeed Natalia, in the conversation with the narrator from which the epigraph is taken, voices a similarly explosive demand for a clear space: 'The degradation of servitude, the absolutist lies must be uprooted and swept out. Reform is impossible. There is nothing to reform . . .' [p. 133]. At the same time, since the narrator says it is 'an uneasy despotism' that provokes 'the lusts of hate and fear', the autocratic regime opposed to the re-volutionists is itself seen as the source of corruption, and is itself shown to be an anarchic force. As is the case between anarchist and policeman in *The Secret Agent*, there is nothing to choose, morally, between revolutionist and autocrat; and Conrad for-cibly insists on this in his Author's Note: 'The ferocity and imbecility of an autocratic rule rejecting all legality and in fact basing itself upon complete moral anarchism provokes the no less imbecile and atrocious answer of a purely Utopian revolutionism encompassing destruction by the first means to hand, in the strange conviction that a fundamental change of hearts must follow the downfall of any given human institutions' [p. x].

Despite the narrator's reiterated assertion that the materials of his narrative are utterly alien to the western world, we thus cannot help noticing that the Russia of his tale is not notably different from the England of *The Secret Agent*. It is clear, moreover, that the novelist's imagination seized on the Russian experience in terms that are remarkably close to those employed in the English novel: London, we remember, the 'monstrous town', is said to be 'a cruel devourer of the world's light'; the narrator's vision of the 'gigantic shadow of Russian life' would seem to be related to the London image, for he visualises it as 'deepening around [Natalia] like the darkness of an advancing night' which will 'devour her presently', and considers her mother to be another 'victim of the deadly shade' [p. 202]. The narrator's insistent comments make the imagery of darkness significant in this novel too: he maintains that the 'shadow of autocracy' lies on 'Russian lives in their submission or their revolt' [p. 109], and that the 'true, kindly face' of Russia is hidden under a 'pestilential shadow' [p. 184]; and, when Natalia has heard Razumov's confession, he notices the 'shadows [seem] to come and go' in her eyes 'as if the steady flame of her soul [has] been made to vacillate at last in the cross-currents of poisoned air from the corrupted dark immensity claiming her for its own, where virtues themselves fester into crimes in the cynicism of oppression and revolt' [p. 356]. The darkened world depicted by the narrator of *Under Western Eyes*, indeed, makes contact too with that of *Heart of Darkness* – and in a way that suggests there is little to choose not only between the autocrat and the revolutionist but also between the supposedly civilised and the savage: 'It seems that the savage autocracy, no more than the divine democracy, does not limit its diet exclusively to the bodies of its enemies. It devours its friends and servants as well' [p. 306].

Though political conflict is the immediate stuff of the novel, *Under Western Eyes* is perhaps even less of a 'political novel' than *Nostromo* or *The Secret Agent*, one indication of this being that the final impression made on us is of a Russia dwarfed by Razumov, whereas Costaguana and the monstrous city bulk at least as large as the spiritual dramas enacted in them. Conrad himself said (in his Author's Note) that his work was 'an attempt to render not so much the political state as the psychology of Russia itself' [p. vii]; but just as he thought of Jimmy Wait as 'the centre of the . . . collective psychology' of the crew of the *Narcissus*, so, presumably, he must have regarded Razumov as a prototypical Russian – Razumov, it may be noted, wildly says on one impassioned occasion: 'But Russia *can't* disown me. . . . I am *it!*' [p. 209]–for it is the psychology of Razumov that we are actually given.[2]

The immediate clue to Razumov's psychology is that he is alone in the world:

> Officially and in fact without a family . . ., no home influences had shaped his opinions or his feelings. He was as lonely in the world as a man swimming in the deep sea. The word Razumov was the mere label of a solitary individuality. There were no Razumovs belonging to him anywhere. His closest parentage was defined in the statement that he was a Russian. Whatever good he expected from life would be given to or withheld from his hopes by that connexion alone. This immense parentage suffered from the throes of internal dissensions, and he shrank mentally from the fray as a good-natured man may shrink from taking definite sides in a violent family quarrel.          [pp. 10–11]

As lonely 'as a man swimming in the deep sea', Razumov, we infer, is concerned exclusively with keeping himself afloat, but it is further suggested that in Russia the limiting condition of such a concern is not only utter isolation but also complete detachment from 'the throes of internal dissensions'. The plot of the novel, however, at once makes it clear that in this Russia it is impossible to maintain such detachment: slipping into Razumov's rooms after the assassination, Haldin silently demonstrates that one cannot close one's door on dissensions in the street. When Razumov returns to his rooms, Haldin's presence there confronts him with a choice between fidelity to an individual and loyalty to the state, a choice which is analogous, as we have seen, to that faced by the captain-narrator once he takes Leggatt aboard in *The Secret Sharer*. It is a choice which has been repeatedly posed in the large struggles of our time, and Conrad, as in so much of his best work, was foreshadowing a distinctively modern dilemma.[3]

Whereas the captain-narrator in *The Secret Sharer* comes to identify himself more and more closely with Leggatt and staunchly stands by him, Razumov's most vital 'connexion' (we have been authoritatively told) is with Russia. The fact, moreover, that his 'closest parentage' is his country is not merely an indication of the bitterness of his illegitimacy; it suggests also that he is heir to the 'moral corruption' which pervades Russia. Caught between the moral nihilism of Haldin and that of the state, Razumov succumbs as if to a moral plague, betrays Haldin, and becomes a spy. In the end it is with Verloc, the secret agent, that Razumov has an unexpected affinity. Though connections between *Under Western Eyes* and *The Secret Agent* are manifold, Conrad is concerned in the Russian novel with the effects of moral nihilism on the individual psyche rather than on the body politic, as he was in the earlier work. *Under Western Eyes* is, specifically, a study of the psychology of betrayal, its causes and consequences; and the nature of the theme is clearly relevant to the fact that Razumov is Conrad's most profound and subtle characterisation.[4] It is perhaps worth noting, furthermore, that whereas it is Dickens who unofficially presides over *The Secret Agent*, informing its sense of the interconnectedness of society, it is to Dostoevsky that *Under Western Eyes* does unconscious homage as it probes a soul[5].

Conrad's theme has a bearing too on his narrative method. His use of the teacher of languages as his narrator at the outset of the novel leads us to believe that we will throughout see events through his (western) eyes, and that consequently the point of view will be limited, defined and fixed. This, however, does not prove to be the case. In Part First the teacher of languages swiftly dissolves as a narrating presence, and though in this section there are some instances of commentary which should properly be attributed to him, he is largely forgotten. Instead the device of Razumov's journal (which comes into the narrator's possession) ensures not only that we see events through the Russian's eyes but that he serves as a centre of consciousness for most of this section – as the following representative passage indicates:

Razumov wondered why he had not cut short that talk and told this man to go away long before. Was it weakness or what?
He concluded that it was a sound instinct. Haldin must have been seen. . . .
Everybody Haldin had ever known would be in the greatest danger. Unguarded expressions, little facts in themselves innocent would be counted for crimes. Razumov remembered certain words he said . . .– it was almost impossible for a student to keep out of that sort of thing. . . .
Razumov saw himself shut up in a fortress, worried, badgered, perhaps ill-used. He saw himself deported by an administrative order, his life broken, ruined, and robbed of all hope. . . .      [pp. 20–21]

In Part Second there is an abrupt shift in point of view. Razumov, making his appearance in Geneva, is no longer the centre of consciousness; instead he is seen consistently in this section from the outside through the eyes of the narrator or of Natalia, as in the following instance which describes his first meeting with Haldin's sister:

> She had stood before him speechless, swallowing her sobs, and when she managed at last to utter something, it was only her brother's name – 'Victor – Victor Haldin!' she gasped out, and again her voice failed her.
> 'Of course', she commented to me, 'this distressed him. He was quite overcome. I have told you my opinion that he is a man of deep feeling – it is impossible to doubt it. You should have seen his face. He positively reeled. He leaned against the wall of the terrace. Their friendship must have been the very brotherhood of souls! . . .        [p. 172]

The shift in point of view in this section is accompanied by a very special sort of time-shift. In Part First the narrative is clearly retrospective, and the narrator, having read Razumov's journal, is in possession of all the facts relating to his story; in Part Second the narrative is non-retrospective, and the narrator's earlier knowledge of Razumov is simply suspended (though in a few cases it is disconcertingly noted: 'I could almost feel on me the weight of his unrefreshed, motionless stare, the stare of a man who lies unwinking in the dark, angrily passive in the toils of disastrous thoughts. Now, when I know how true it was, I can honestly affirm that this *was* the effect produced on me. It was painful in a curiously indefinite way – for, of course, the definition comes to me now while I sit writing in the fullness of my knowledge. But this is what the effect was at that time of absolute ignorance' [p. 183]. The immediate effect of the shift in point of view is the creation of a powerful dramatic irony, for we know what Natalia and the narrator do not know, and given our knowledge, the outer view of Razumov is strikingly suggestive of his inner condition.

In Part Third there is a shift once again to Razumov's point of view and consequently in the long scenes between him and Peter Ivanovitch or Sophia Antonovna the narrative is filtered through his consciousness. In this section there are also instances of a doubling-back, so that incidents previously witnessed through

the eyes of Natalia or the narrator are now reviewed by
Razumov:

> 'It's here!' he thought, with a sort of awe. 'It is here – on this very
> spot . . .'
> He was tempted to flight at the mere recollection of his first meeting
> with Natalia Haldin. He confessed it to himself; but he did not move,
> and that not because he wished to resist an unworthy weakness, but
> because he knew that he had no place to fly to. . . . Slowly he ascended
> the stairs of the terrace, flanked by two stained greenish stone urns of
> funereal aspect.                                                    [p. 204]

Finally, in Part Fourth there is no single or steady point of view.
In the first part of this section, with the time-shift to the events in
Russia that immediately preceded Razumov's arrival in Geneva,
the point of view is that of Razumov; when we return to the
fictional present in Geneva, the narrator takes over once more,
and we continue to see things through his eyes up to and
including the scene of Razumov's confession to Natalia (though
the retrospective account of Razumov's interview with Mrs
Haldin is presented from the young man's point of view);
Razumov is again the centre of consciousness in the scene of his
public confession; in the last chapter of the novel the point of view
is that of the narrator.

It is clear, therefore, that Conrad has contrived to handle a
nominally fixed point of view and a seemingly chronological
narrative in such a way as to effect constant switches in
perspective, Part Fourth serving in this respect as a model of the
method employed throughout. The form of the novel, that is,
forces on us the sense of shifting perspectives, and so serves to help
us focus the theme, for what Conrad traces in his psychological
study of Razumov is his changing view of the act of betrayal. It is
more than a quirk of form that Razumov's ultimate repudiation
of the act should be recorded in Part Fourth, where all is fluid,
and the novelist, seemingly giving way to a narrative abandon,
veers from one view to another.

II

Haldin is drawn to seek the aid of Razumov by the sense he has of his strong self-containment: he tells Razumov that, as he 'dodged in the woodyard down by the river-side', he thought of him as a man with 'a strong character', as one who 'does not throw his soul to the winds' [p. 15]; and he declares, furthermore, that Razumov is 'collected – cool as a cucumber. A regular Englishman' [pp. 21–2]. It is one of the biting ironies of the novel, however, that Haldin should be deceived by Razumov's apparent self-possession. The product of circumstances which deny him the moral autonomy that grows out of a secure past, Razumov has only a tenuous identity, and his very name is to him no more than a 'label'. Like Jim he gives himself to daydreams of the glories that await him, seeking to fix an identity in ambitious projections of his future. But in the present his hold on himself (as is soon shown) is dependent on his hold on routine: 'Razumov was one of those men who, living in a period of mental and political unrest, keep an instinctive hold on normal, practical, everyday life' [p. 10]. It is Razumov's tragedy, as it is Jim's, that the everyday should break on unsuspected wrecks, and that, though safe in his own rooms, 'the Revolution' should seek him out 'to put to a sudden test his dormant instincts, his half-conscious thoughts and almost wholly unconscious ambitions . . .' [p. 294]. Though he remains outwardly controlled, his inner response to the predicament he finds himself in is revealing:

> Razumov had listened in astonishment; but before he could open his mouth Haldin added, speaking deliberately, 'It was I who removed de P— this morning.'
> Razumov kept down a cry of dismay. The sentiment of his life being utterly ruined by this contact with such a crime expressed itself quaintly by a sort of half-derisive mental exclamation, 'There goes my silver medal!'                    [p. 16]

Razumov's imagination, like that of Jim or Jukes, is readily susceptible to intimations of disaster: he at once accepts that 'the sentiment of his life' is 'utterly ruined' and that his silver medal is lost, the former being his determination to 'convert the label Razumov into an honoured name' by the sort of 'distinction' that would begin to accrue to him on his securing the latter for his prize essay [pp. 13–14]. His immediate response, that is, is despairing, but it is also entirely self-centred; and though he

begins to build an elaborate ideological structure to justify and
rationalise his eventual betrayal of Haldin, it is clear from the
outset (as has been remarked) that it is founded on self-interest.[6]

As it turns out, it is his betrayal of Haldin that ruins the
sentiment of his life since the autocratic regime to which he
betrays him will not readily relinquish Razumov to his studies;
but he persists in believing that it is Haldin who, with 'the self-
deception of a criminal idealist', has '[shattered] his existence like
a thunder-clap out of a clear sky' [p. 258], and 'robbed' him of his
'hard-working, purposeful existence' [p. 358]. Since his hold on
such a hard-working existence is his sole support in the deep sea
into which he has been cast, Haldin's irruption into his peaceful rooms is viewed as striking at his very life, and he feels that
his 'solitary and laborious existence [has] been destroyed – the
only thing he [can] call his own on this earth' [p. 82]. If
Razumov, therefore, feels – like Nostromo – that he has gone out
of his existence, it is because inwardly he loses possession of
himself in the crisis. Subsequently, he tries to contain himself
when he discovers that Ziemianitch is drunk, 'biting his lip till
blood came to keep himself from bursting into imprecations' [p.
28]; but he finally lets go when it appears that not even repeated
kicks can wake the drunken driver, whom he has come to
summon to Haldin's aid:

He picked up the lantern. The intense black spokes of shadow swung
about in the circle of light. A terrible fury – the blind rage of self-
preservation – possessed Razumov.
   'Ah! The vile beast', he bellowed out in an unearthly tone which
made the lantern jump and tremble! 'I shall wake you! Give
me . . . Give me . . .'
He looked round wildly, seized the handle of a stablefork and rushing
forward struck at the prostrate body with inarticulate cries. After a time
his cries ceased, and the rain of blows fell in the stillness and shadows of
the cellar-like stable. Razumov belaboured Ziemianitch with an
insatiable fury, in great volleys of sounding thwacks. . . .      [p. 30]

Razumov's outward loss of control here, so clearly manifested in
his wild cries and looks and in the frenzied 'rain of blows', decides
his fate. Losing his self-possession, he becomes 'possessed' by 'the
blind rage of self-preservation'. Thereafter his main actions until
his confession to Natalia are determined by the force which has

now taken hold of him. Razumov, that is to say, is – like Jim – an inglorious victim of his own instincts, of the rage for life.[7]

Razumov continues to beat Ziemianitch until the stick he is using breaks in half:

> He flung from him the piece of stick remaining in his grasp, and went off with great hasty strides without looking back once.
>
> After going heedlessly for some fifty yards along the street he walked into a snowdrift and was up to his knees before he stopped.
>
> This recalled him to himself; and glancing about he discovered he had been going in the wrong direction. He retraced his steps, but now at a more moderate pace. . . .
>
> Ziemianitch's passionate surrender to sorrow and consolation had baffled him. That was the people. A true Russian man! Razumov was glad he had beaten that brute – the 'bright soul' of [Haldin]. Here they were: the people and the enthusiast.
>
> Between the two he was done for. Between the drunkenness of the peasant incapable of action and the dream-intoxication of the idealist incapable of perceiving the reason of things, and the true character of men. It was a sort of terrible childishness. But children had their masters. 'Ah! the stick, the stick, the stern hand', thought Razumov, longing for power to hurt and destroy.                                    [p. 31]

The symbolism here, as always when Conrad is at his best, is a natural outgrowth of the action. Up to this point Razumov has been trying to save himself by saving Haldin; with the urge to protect himself made more imperative as a result both of his surrender to that which has now taken possession of him and of the evident failure of his mission to Ziemianitch, he 'discovers' that he has been 'going in the wrong direction', that the way he has chosen leads only to an impasse. When he 'retraces his steps', Razumov begins unconsciously to move towards betrayal. The unconscious springs of his thought are strikingly suggested when he begins at once to reflect on the necessity for 'the stick' and a 'stern hand' in dealings with a man such as Ziemianitch: since he views the driver as 'a true Russian man' and representative of 'the people', he tacitly aligns himself here with the authoritarian forces of autocracy – and unconsciously begins to ready himself for the betrayal of Haldin on ideological grounds.[8] Conrad's understanding of Razumov's psychology is subtle indeed: he wishes us to regard his authoritarian views as ideologically sincere, a reflection both of the cast of his mind and of his intellectual integrity when confronted with the revolutionary enthusiasm of a man like Haldin; but the novelist also makes it clear that Razumov's views are triggered by less disinterested forces, of which he remains consciously unaware. The same applies to his emotions. When the Prince takes him to the General and he repeats his story about Haldin, he makes up his mind 'to keep Ziemianitch out of the affair completely':

To mention him at all would mean imprisonment for the 'bright soul', perhaps cruel floggings, and in the end a journey to Siberia in chains. Razumov, who had beaten Ziemianitch, felt for him now a vague, remorseful tenderness.                                    [p. 48]

Razumov's feeling of remorse and tenderness, though 'vague', is no doubt sincere, but, having determined to betray Haldin and suppress any mention of his attempt to aid him to escape, there are other reasons for his deciding to keep Ziemianitch out of it.

After turning back from the snowdrift, Razumov reflects that having Haldin in his rooms is 'like harbouring a pestilential disease that would not perhaps take your life, but would take from you all that made life worth living – a subtle pest that would convert earth into a hell' [p. 32]. Both Nostromo and Decoud, we recall, believe that their 'possession of [the silver] is very much like a deadly disease for men situated as [they] are'; and the reminiscence suggests that, if Razumov finds himself called on to safeguard Haldin as they the silver, any corruption attendant on such an effort will be likely in his case – as it was in theirs – to be worked from within, not without. His system, as we know, has already been undermined; and, casting round for ways of saving himself, he contemplates killing Haldin on his return home, only to reject that course: 'The corpse hanging round his neck would be nearly as fatal as the living man' [p. 32]. Ironically, of course, Razumov's betrayal of Haldin hangs his corpse round his neck just as fatally; and like the Ancient Mariner, Razumov carries that corpse with him – until it drops from his neck when he confesses. The literary association here provides a frame for the ensuing drama of guilt and expiation, and also points ahead to the change of perspective required for release.

Before he can bring himself to decide to give Haldin up,

Razumov experiences an epiphany – and an hallucination. Continuing to make his way home, he suddenly looks up and sees 'the clear black sky of the northern winter, decorated with the sumptuous fires of the stars', and receives 'an almost physical impression of endless space and of countless millions'. This impression brings with it an image of the snow covering 'the endless forests, the frozen rivers, the plains of an immense country, obliterating the landmarks, the accidents of the ground, levelling everything under its uniform whiteness, like a monstrous blank page awaiting the record of an inconceivable history' [p. 33]. Razumov's vision of the snow is not unlike that of Gabriel Conway at the end of Joyce's story 'The Dead', but whereas Gabriel is led by his vision to a melancholy acquiescence in the blurring of lines between the living and the dead on whom the snow falls alike, Razumov is roused to a sense that what the 'immense country' needs is 'a will strong and one . . . not the babble of many voices, but a man – strong and one!' [p. 33]. He is strengthened still further, that is, in the authoritarian position he has taken up, the vision leading him indeed to 'the point of conversion', for it would seem to be only a strong man who could leave his mark on the 'monstrous blank page' that is Russia. At the same time the epiphany provides him with an emotional as well as ideological ground for the betrayal since, under the immense and level snow, the human is blotted out and the individual life made to seem utterly insignificant. It is a further irony of the betrayal that his own life is reduced by it to an insubstantial blankness: within a month of the betrayal he recognises that 'his existence [is] a great cold blank, something like the enormous plain of the whole of Russia levelled with snow and fading gradually on all sides into shadows and mists' [p. 303].

Though Razumov contemptuously contrasts 'the luridly smoky lucubrations' of Haldin with 'the clear grasp' of his own intellect, and determines that, if he is to suffer, it should be for his convictions, not for 'a crime' that his 'cool superior reason' rejects, he is still not emotionally ready for the betrayal: the moment he '[ceases] to think' he becomes the prey of 'a suspicious uneasiness' that seems to well up from the depths, an 'irrational feeling that something may jump upon [him] in the dark – the absurd dread of the unseen' [p. 35]. It takes the hallucination to complete the process by which he is led to ignominy:

Suddenly on the snow, stretched on his back right across his path, he saw Haldin, solid, distinct, real. . . . The snow round him was untrodden.

This hallucination had such a solidity of aspect that the first movement of Razumov was to reach for his pocket to assure himself that the key of his rooms was there. But he checked the impulse with a disdainful curve of his lips. He understood. His thought, concentrated intensely on the figure left lying on his bed, had culminated in this extraordinary illusion of the sight. Razumov tackled the phenomenon calmly. With a stern face, without a check and gazing far beyond the vision, he walked on, experiencing nothing but a slight tightening of the chest. After passing he turned his head for a glance, and saw only the unbroken track of his footsteps over the place where the breast of the phantom had been lying.

Razumov walked on and after a little time whispered his wonder to himself.

'Exactly as if alive! Seemed to breathe! And right in my way too! I have had an extraordinary experience.'

He made a few steps and muttered through his set teeth –

'I shall give him up.'

Then for some twenty yards or more all was blank. . . .

'Betray. A great word. What is betrayal? They talk of a man betraying his country, his friends, his sweetheart. There must be a moral bond first. All a man can betray is his conscience. And how is my conscience engaged here; by what bond of common faith, of common conviction, am I obliged to let that fanatical idiot drag me down with him? On the contrary – every obligation of true courage is the other way.'                                                                [pp. 36–8]

Razumov, the son of reason, lives up to his name here, and is satisfied he 'understands' how his 'thought' has brought about the 'extraordinary illusion'. We see, however, that the hallucination is the product of an emotional necessity, of his need to prove to himself that he *can* walk over Haldin, as it were, for his decision to give him up, though unconsciously in the making from the moment he finds Ziemianitch drunk, is consciously formulated only after he demonstrates this to himself. It is notable, moreover, that he gazes 'far beyond the vision' when he walks over it, for in so doing he enacts his version of the betrayal, averting his eyes from the trampling on Haldin which the betrayal entails and fixing them on that which lies 'beyond' him – on the ostensible 'act of conscience' [p. 38] undertaken for the larger welfare of his country. Razumov, that is to say, is trapped in the familiar dilemma of means and ends; and the hollowness of his moral position is indicative of the nullity to which he is reduced when he first loses possession of himself. For there *is* 'a moral bond' between Haldin and himself, the bond of fellowship or brotherhood which Haldin asserts in turning to him for help (and indirectly affirms when he constantly refers to Razumov as 'brother'), the bond of their common humanity whose obligations are as strong as those of a 'common faith' or 'common conviction'. That Razumov deliberately walks over 'the place where the breast of the phantom had been lying' brings out the human implications of the betrayal, the willed denial of feeling that it is; just as the fact that he sees Haldin lying 'right across his path', 'right in [his] way', is expressive of his view of Haldin as an obstacle to his own progress –and so of the base self-centredness of his public concern.

Crushingly aware of his own 'moral solitude' and desperately longing for 'moral support' in the position he has taken up [p. 39], Razumov exploits the opportunity of turning to Prince K—, his unacknowledged father, with his tale of Haldin. The Prince treats him considerately, but will have nothing more to do with him; and the betrayal, which is formally committed at this point, accordingly only intensifies Razumov's sense of moral isolation. Not that he is left without his ghosts, for the sights and sounds of Haldin's trusting departure from his rooms remain to haunt him:

> Gazing down into the deep black shaft with a tiny glimmering flame at the bottom, [Razumov] traced by ear the rapid spiral descent of somebody running down the stairs on tiptoe. It was a light, swift, pattering sound, which sank away from him into the depths: a fleeting shadow passed over the glimmer – a wink of the tiny flame. Then stillness.
>
> Razumov hung over, breathing the cold raw air tainted by the evil smells of the unclean staircase. All quiet. [p. 63]

Haldin's descent into 'the deep black shaft', with its sounds sinking away 'into the depths' and 'the tiny flame' disappearing in shadow, becomes for Razumov an image of his descent to death. And what Razumov breathes into his deepest being is an air which is 'tainted' not so much by 'the evil smells of the unclean staircase' as by the corruption of betrayal.

III

When Razumov begins to attend lectures again after the
betrayal, he is said to be 'quite sufficiently self-possessed for all
practical purposes', but 'his new tranquillity' in fact is 'like a
flimsy garment' that seems 'to float at the mercy of a casual word'
[p. 71], exposing his more profound loss of self-possession. Almost
at once he begins to be plagued by dreams which reveal his
unconscious perception of what he has brought on himself by the
betrayal:

Still-faced and his lips set hard, Razumov began to write. When he
wrote a large hand his neat writing lost its character altogether –
became unsteady, almost childish. He wrote five lines one under the
other.

> History not Theory.
> Patriotism not Internationalism.
> Evolution not Revolution.
> Direction not Destruction.
> Unity not Disruption.

He gazed at them dully. Then his eyes strayed to the bed and remained
fixed there for a good many minutes, while his right hand groped all
over the table for the penknife.

He rose at last, and walking up with measured steps stabbed the
paper with the penknife to the lath and plaster wall at the head of the
bed. This done he stepped back a pace and flourished his hand with a
glance round the room.

After that he never looked again at the bed. He took his big cloak
down from its peg and, wrapping himself up closely, went to lie down on
the hard horse-hair sofa at the other side of his room. A leaden sleep
closed his eyelids at once. Several times that night he woke up shivering
from a dream of walking through drifts of snow in a Russia where he was
as completely alone as any betrayed autocrat could be; an immense,
wintry Russia which, somehow, his view could embrace in all its
enormous expanse as if it were a map. But after each shuddering start his
heavy eyelids fell over his glazed eyes and he slept again.     [p. 66]

When Razumov writes his manifesto (which so impresses
Councillor Mikulin), he formulates a mature, intellectual justification of the betrayal, but the 'almost childish' hand in which it is
written reveals the emotional immaturity in which the betrayal is

rooted. The quoted passage is further suggestive of the way in which a secret sharer makes subversive comments on his conscious intentions. When Razumov 'stabs' the paper to the lath and plaster, he pins his colours to the wall, so to speak, with a gesture which defiantly proclaims both his acceptance of responsibility for having disposed of Haldin, who had lain on the bed, and the finality of the deed, for 'after that he never [looks] again at the bed'. But his dream indicates that Haldin is not so easily disposed of. In evoking the totality of his isolation in the immense Russia for which he has betrayed Haldin, it expresses more than his unconscious perception of the degree to which he has cut himself off from his fellows by his own act; since it is he – the man who has just spelt out his anti-revolutionist position – who is 'as completely alone as any betrayed autocrat could be', the dream is also an early intimation that, in betraying Haldin, he has in fact betrayed himself. It is precisely at this point in the narrative that the narrator draws attention to the necessity of finding a 'key-word' as an aid 'to the moral discovery' which, he says, 'should be the object of every tale'; thinking of Russia as a whole, he advances the word 'cynicism' since he sees it as 'the mark of Russian autocracy and of Russian revolt' [p. 67], but the moral discovery Razumov slowly makes is that betrayal means self-betrayal, which is as good a key-word as any in his story.

During his first interview with Mikulin, Razumov experiences a waking dream which is further revelatory of the implacability of his unconscious vision:

At that moment Razumov beheld his own brain suffering on the rack – a long, pale figure drawn asunder horizontally with terrific force in the darkness of a vault, whose face he failed to see. It was as though he had dreamed for an infinitesimal fraction of time of some dark print of the Inquisition. . . .
He was indeed extremely exhausted, and he records a remarkably dream-like experience of anguish at the circumstance that there was no one whatever near the pale and extended figure. The solitude of the racked victim was particularly horrible to behold. The mysterious impossibility to see the face, he also notes, inspired a sort of terror.
. . .                                                             [p. 88]

This experience links up with one that immediately follows Haldin's departure from his rooms when, with 'his mind [hovering] on the borders of delirium', Razumov suddenly hears himself saying, 'I confess' – 'as a person might do on the rack' – and thinks to himself, 'I am on the rack' [p. 65]. The two experiences are an accurate if appalling forecast of the mental torture to which he has condemned himself, a self-torture which continues until a confession is indeed wrung from him: his confession of the betrayal to Natalia. The vision in Mikulin's office, moreover, vividly communicates the main causes of his suffering. As in his earlier dream of the wintry Russia, the fact of his solitude, his apparent abandonment by those who might have been near him, is a specific cause of anguish; but though this is 'particularly horrible', it does not seem to be as terrible as his inability 'to see the face' of the figure on the rack (though he knows it is 'his own brain suffering' there) for this inspires 'a sort of terror'. Ironically, he has lost face neither with the revolutionists nor the government officials, but the loss of face is his own harsh judgement on himself, and points to his loss of even a tenuous identity which is one of the most damaging consequences of his loss of the full possession of himself. When he betrays Haldin, he ceases to be the man he was, as is quietly dramatised in his encounter with a friendly professor, whom he used to visit: 'How is it we never see you at our Wednesdays now, Kirylo Sidorovitch?' the professor asks; and he is 'too astonished to be offended' when Razumov meets his advance 'with odious, muttering boorishness' [p. 299]. Realising he has attracted 'the eye of the social revolution', Razumov consciously envisages the possibility that 'he no longer [belongs] to himself' [p. 301]. This is true in more ways than he realises; and it is not without significance that the narrator (on the day of Razumov's confession) remembers his 'extraordinary hallucined, anguished, and absent expression' [p. 320].[9]

Initially, however, he simply tries to deny the change. He is most himself at home, though the narrator notes his room might have been expected to be 'morally uninhabitable'. He sets to work again, 'at first, with some success', and his 'repaired watch' (dropped on the night of the betrayal), which is to be heard 'faintly ticking on the table by the side of the lighted lamp', seems to assert the continuity of the life he has taken up again at the point Haldin interrupted it – just as the lamp would seem to banish the vision of the dark staircase. But his 'unwillingness' to

leave the place where he is 'safe from Haldin' grows so strong that
in the end he ceases 'to go out at all', thus demonstrating that, if
betrayal is a denial of the bonds of fellowship, its logical
consequence is complete isolation. And indeed whenever he has
previously gone out, he has 'felt himself at once closely involved
in the moral consequences of his act', for it is 'abroad' that 'the
dark prestige of the Haldin mystery' falls on him, clinging to him
'like a poisoned robe it [is] impossible to fling off' [pp. 299–300].
That Razumov is implicitly associated with Hercules here
suggests he is the victim of his own poison: once he becomes
habituated to keeping up false pretences with the friends and
sympathisers of Haldin, he is morally ready – sufficiently
poisoned – for the role Mikulin wishes him to play. Mikulin,
indeed, who asks the unanswerable question 'Where to?' by way
of answer to Razumov's announced intention 'to retire' [p. 99],
believes he is in effect made ready by the betrayal itself. He points
out to Razumov that his desire to return to his old way of life, to
assert 'his attitude of detachment', is untenable, given the kind of
commitment he has made [p. 294]. Having asserted the primacy
of the state over the individual where Haldin was concerned,
Razumov cannot claim exemption for himself in this respect;
and, if the moral consequence of the betrayal is further betrayal,
both of himself and of those on whom he will be set to spy, the
political consequence is his transformation into a secret agent. It
is Razumov's loss of self that leaves room, as it were, for the false
self that is foisted on to him.

But his loss of self also makes room for other visitants, it being a
capacious gap that has to be filled, and (after he has confessed to
Natalia) Razumov shows in his journal that he is fully aware of
what happened to him spiritually as a result of the betrayal:

> I was given up to evil. I exulted in having induced that silly innocent
> fool [i.e. Kostia] to steal his father's money. He was a fool, but not a
> thief. I made him one. It was necessary. I had to confirm myself in my
> contempt and hate for what I betrayed. . . .　　　　　　[p. 359]

Razumov analyses his own condition here in terms both of a
psychology and a theology. The gullible Kostia, naively ready to
do his bit for the Revolution and so for the gallant Razumov, is
savagely exploited by him. Razumov sees clearly that he was led

to corrupt Kostia, to make him (and anyone else connected with Haldin) contemptible, in order to justify his own behaviour to himself, and so to enable him not only to live with the betrayal of Haldin but undertake further betrayals as a spy. The fact that he 'exulted' in Kostia's corruption, however, suggests that it was not psychological need alone that drove him; and he sees that he behaved as he did also because he was 'given up to evil', that, in giving Haldin up, he had in effect given away his soul. In a manner that is reminiscent of Kurtz, Razumov must be seen as having abandoned himself to a passion of evil: 'Natalia Victorovna', he writes in his journal, 'I embraced the might of falsehood, I exulted in it – I gave myself up to it for a time' [p. 360]. Razumov, that is to say, is not possessed by the rage of self-preservation alone; having given himself to falsehood, he comes to think of himself in a more traditionally orthodox way as having been 'possessed'. He confesses in his journal that he was tempted to steal Natalia's soul by setting out to win her love:

Perhaps no one will believe the baseness of such an intention to be possible. It's certain that, when we parted that morning, I gloated over it. I brooded upon the best way. The old man you introduced me to insisted on walking with me. I don't know who he is. He talked of you, of your lonely, helpless state, and every word of that friend of yours was egging me on to the unpardonable sin of stealing a soul. Could he have been the devil himself in the shape of an old Englishman? Natalia Victorovna, I was possessed! . . .                        [pp. 359–60]

Razumov is also taken up, of course, with his spying. But on the day he writes his first report to Mikulin he experiences a strong revulsion from the kind of existence that has been forced on him:

The futility of all this overcame him like a curse. Even then he could not believe in the reality of his mission. He looked round despairingly, as if for some way to redeem his existence from that unconquerable feeling. He crushed angrily in his hand the pages of the notebook. 'This must be posted,' he thought.                                        [p. 316]

The 'curse' by which Razumov is overcome here would seem to be not so much the 'futility' of spying as the spiritual despair into which his life as a spy has driven him – and which imprints itself in his looks when he drops his guard. But if his sense of futility is 'unconquerable', his feeling of despair is not, for though he looks round 'despairingly', it is 'as if for some way to redeem his existence'. Conrad's depiction of a way to redemption is the crowning triumph of the novel.

IV

Even before he has actually betrayed Haldin but after he has decided to do so, Razumov is held for a moment by the possibility of confession. In order to escape from the terrible 'moral solitude' in which he finds himself, he '[embraces] . . . the delirious purpose of rushing to his lodgings . . . to pour out a full confession in passionate words that would stir the whole being of [Haldin] to its innermost depths'; and he imagines how such a confession would end in 'embraces and tears' and in 'an incredible fellowship of souls – such as the world had never seen' [pp. 39–40]. It is the fellowship that Razumov craves, and it is unfortunate for both Haldin and himself that 'the glimpse of a passing grey whisker' at this point evokes for him the image of Prince K— since it deflects the craving to him – and his only access to the Prince is by way of the betrayal.

The contact with the Prince is short-lived, but it leads to his meeting with Mikulin. After his first meeting with the councillor Razumov suddenly begins to think of him as a unique fellow-soul – and he once again envisages confession as a means of cementing a relationship:

Go back! What for? Confess! To what? 'I have been speaking to him with the greatest openness', he said to himself with perfect truth. 'What else could I tell him? That I have undertaken to carry a message to that brute Ziemianitch? Establish a false complicity and destroy what chance of safety I have won for nothing – what folly!'

Yet he could not defend himself from fancying that Councillor Mikulin was, perhaps, the only man in the world able to understand his conduct. To be understood appeared extremely fascinating.

On the way home he had to stop several times; all his strength seemed to run out of his limbs; and in the movement of the busy streets, isolated as if in a desert, he remained suddenly motionless for a minute or so before he could proceed on his way. He reached his rooms at last.

[pp. 297–8]

Razumov's sense of his moral solitude is excruciating: at best, we remember, he is 'as lonely in the world as a man swimming in the deep sea'; now, after the betrayal, and with less apparent chance of survival, he is 'isolated as in a desert'. When he stops in the street and 'all his strength [seems] to run out of his limbs', it is to despair that he momentarily succumbs, his condition once again recalling that of Jim on board the *Patna*, for after Jim has decided there is nothing he can do in the emergency, this seems 'to take all life out of [his] limbs'. It is the intensity of his need for human contact that accounts for the irrationality of Razumov's urge to return to Mikulin and confess to him. It turns out to be significant that in these two initial instances the idea of confession should be associated with something like sudden abandon.

In the absence of vital human relationships Razumov begins to keep a journal, which the narrator describes as 'the pitiful resource of a young man who had near him no trusted intimacy, no natural affection to turn to', but it is perhaps even more to the point that he calls the journal a 'mental and psychological self-confession' [pp. 308–9]. Razumov, that is to say, is in the end driven to self-communion, and even this is assayed by way of confession. But the journal is more than a pitiful resource:

The record, which could not have been meant for any one's eyes but his own, was not, I think, the outcome of that strange impulse of indiscretion common to men who lead secret lives, and accounting for the invariable existence of 'compromising documents' in all the plots and conspiracies of history. Mr Razumov looked at it, I suppose, as a man looks at himself in a mirror, with wonder, perhaps with anguish, with anger or despair. Yes, as a threatened man may look fearfully at his own face in the glass, formulating to himself reassuring excuses for his appearance marked by the taint of some insidious hereditary disease.

[p. 214]

The self-communion, we see, is in fact, a self-scrutiny, a necessary part of Razumov's self-discovery; and if he looks in the glass to reassure himself, he does at least register the fact of the insidious disease. We may regard the journal, indeed, as the one place in which he relaxes his repressive hold on his secret sharer, the shadow (it will be recalled) that informed his dreams, and which he quickly dispels when it otherwise rises into his conscious mind: after he has left Peter Ivanovitch and his 'painted Egeria', for instance, he feels 'as though another self, an independent sharer of his mind', is able 'to view his whole person very distinctly indeed'; though he formulates 'his opinion of it' – presumably, his person, that is – in the 'mental ejaculation: "Beastly!"', his 'disgust' quickly vanishes 'before a marked uneasiness', and he simply concludes it is 'an effect of nervous exhaustion' [p. 230].

The journal, furthermore, is the means by which he composes himself:

Alone in his room after having posted his secret letter [i.e. his first report to Mikulin], he had regained a certain measure of composure by writing in his secret diary. He was aware of the danger of that strange self-indulgence. He alludes to it himself, but he could not refrain. It calmed him – it reconciled him to his existence. . . .          [p. 339]

Razumov's calmness and composure suggest that in his writing of the journal he regains a modicum of the self-possession he has lost. Since this would seem to be the product of his self-confession, it is clearly intimated how he might reconcile himself to his existence not alone in his secret writing but in the public world outside his room. And his self-possession, we note moreover, seems also to be the product of his readiness to let go, to relax the tight hold on himself that, as a spy, he has successfully managed to maintain, for he is 'aware of the danger of that strange self-indulgence', but cannot and does not refrain from it.

The person who sparks his confession in the outside world is, of course, Natalia. She reports to the narrator how Razumov was 'quite overcome' and 'positively reeled' when they met for the first time:

'I was grateful to him for that emotion, which made me feel less ashamed on my own lack of self-control. Of course I had regained the power of speech at once, almost. All this lasted not more than a few seconds. "I am his sister," I said. "Maybe you have heard of me."'

'And had he?' I interrupted.

'I don't know. How could it have been otherwise? And yet . . . But what does that matter? I stood there before him, near enough to be touched and surely not looking like an impostor. All I know is, that he put out both his hands then to me, I may say flung them out at me, with the greatest readiness and warmth, and that I seized and pressed them, feeling that I was finding again a little of what I thought was lost to me for ever, with the loss of my brother – some of that hope, inspiration and support, which I used to get from my dear dead. . . .'      [pp. 172–3]

The intensity of Razumov's emotion when he chances on Natalia, the degree to which he is overcome, suggests something more than the shock which he might be expected to feel in such a situation; it would seem to be expressive, rather, of a quite involuntary and genuine feeling of remorse. He may be taken to imply later that, when he thereupon flings his hands out at her, he launches his exercise in Satanism, for he confesses in his journal that it was then he finally decided to steal her soul: 'When we met that first morning in the gardens, and you spoke to me confidingly in the generosity of your spirit, I was thinking, "Yes, .[Haldin] himself by talking of her trustful eyes has delivered her into my hands!" If you could have looked then into my heart, you would have cried out aloud with terror and disgust' [p. 359]. Razumov may well have felt that his best defence against Natalia's trusting innocence was to attack and violate it, but the 'readiness and warmth' with which he puts out his hands to her are patently sincere and betoken, rather, his own deep desire for human connection in response to what her emotion seems to proffer.

Razumov, that is, falls in love with Natalia despite himself, as is quite apparent by the night of his confession:

He raised his face, pale, full of unexpressed suffering. But that look in his eyes of dull, absent obstinacy, which struck, and surprised everybody he was talking to, began to pass away. It was as though he were coming to himself in the awakened consciousness of that marvellous harmony of feature, of lines, of glances, of voice, which made of the girl before him a being so rare, outside, and, as it were, above the common notion of beauty. He looked at her so long that she coloured slightly.

[pp. 342–3]

His love, we see, has grown to such an extent that it seems to fill his inner emptiness, for it dispels the 'absent' look in his eyes. And love's alchemy would seem, too, to posit that the lost self may find itself, for it is as though he 'comes to himself' in his feeling for her. The narrator realises Razumov has discovered that he 'needs' her [p. 347], but that creates another need, the need, in the fullness and sincerity of his love, to confess his betrayal of her brother –

and renounce her: 'I felt', he writes, 'that I must tell you that I had ended by loving you. And to tell you that I must first confess. Confess, go out – and perish' [p. 361].

Razumov's confession, however, is actually triggered by his one and only meeting with Haldin's mother, during which he makes some further discoveries:

The fifteen minutes with Mrs Haldin were like the revenge of the unknown: that white face, that weak, distinct voice; that head, at first turned to him eagerly, then, after a while, bowed again and motionless . . . had troubled him like some strange discovery. And there seemed to be a secret obstinacy in that sorrow, something he could not understand; at any rate, something he had not expected. Was it hostile? But it did not matter. Nothing could touch him now; in the eyes of the revolutionists there was now no shadow on his past. The phantom of Haldin had been indeed walked over, was left behind lying powerless and passive on the pavement covered with snow. And this was the phantom's mother consumed with grief and white as a ghost. . . . He had said all he had to say to her, and when he had finished she had not uttered a word. She had turned away her head while he was speaking. The silence which had fallen on his last words had lasted for five minutes or more. What did it mean? Before its incomprehensible character he became conscious of anger in his stern mood, the old anger against Haldin reawakened by the contemplation of Haldin's mother. And was it not something like enviousness which gripped his heart, as if of a privilege denied to him alone of all the men that had ever passed through this world? It was the other who had attained to repose and yet continued to exist in the affection of that mourning old woman, in the thoughts of all these people posing for lovers of humanity. It was impossible to get rid of him. 'It's myself whom I have given up to destruction', thought Razumov. 'He has induced me to do it. I can't shake him off.'

Alarmed by that discovery, he got up and strode out of the silent, dim room with its silent old woman in the chair, that mother! He never looked back. It was frankly a flight. But on opening the door he saw his retreat cut off. There was the sister. . . .          [pp. 340–1]

The 'strange discovery' Razumov makes as he confronts 'that figure of sorrow' [p. 340], as he takes in the fact of a 'mother consumed with grief', has such a forceful effect on him because it is of something he has never known – the power of a mother's love. It is in that enduring love, he suddenly realises, that

Haldin – though walked over and dead – 'continues to exist', as
he does too 'in the thoughts' of the revolutionists, despise them
though he may; and this realisation brings with it the bitter
reflection that it is he himself who is 'given up to destruction',
that it is he – in his unmitigated isolation – who will be utterly
destroyed. This discovery is followed by another, to which he is
led by Mrs Haldin's 'incomprehensible' silence. She has intuitively divined that he is lying – the narrator tells us later that
'she had not believed him' [p. 372] – and her silence, not
understood but quite unexpected, unnerves him. He has come to
speak to Mrs Haldin and her daughter only after having been
informed of Ziemianitch's suicide and having heard Sophia
Antonovna's explanation of it, an explanation which fortuitously
clears him of all suspicion 'in the eyes of the revolutionists'.
Finding Mrs Haldin alone, he attempts finally to lay the ghost of
Haldin, secure in the belief that 'nothing [can] touch him now',
but her silence denies him the confirmation of his safety. Instead,
as his 'old anger against Haldin' stirs in response, he is made
sharply aware that 'the phantom of Haldin' has in fact not been
'left behind', that indeed he cannot 'shake him off', that his
corpse is still hanging round his neck. If Razumov's departure is
'frankly a flight', it is as much from his own insights as from that
intimidating silence that he flees, from the devastating sense of his
isolation and from the knowledge that he will always have to bear
the burden of the betrayal. When his 'retreat' is 'cut off' by the
advent of Natalia, he stands firm, but – facing up to his new
knowledge – gives in to an overwhelming need to shake the
corpse from his neck and break out of his isolation. 'You are
going, Kirylo Sidorovitch?' she asks, and he answers: 'I! Going?
Where? Oh yes, but I must tell you first . . .' [p. 346]. Razumov's
'Where?' recalls Mikulin's 'Where to?' and suggests that, if the
logic of betrayal leads in political terms to his spying, it leads – in
spiritual terms – to his confession. It leads, that is, since he is safe
from all suspicion when he confesses, to what is actually a self-
betrayal (though it proves to be redemptive), thus symbolising
what has been implicit all along. It leads also, in the end, to an
affirmation of that need for a human bond which was tacitly
repudiated in the betrayal: 'Do you know why I came to you?'
Razumov asks Natalia. 'It is simply because there is no-one
anywhere in the whole great world I could go to. Do you

understand what I say? Not one to go to. Do you conceive the
desolation of the thought – no-one – to – go – to?' [pp. 353–4].

Strung up to the point of confession, Razumov cannot easily
bring the painful words to his lips; and as he struggles both to
make the confession and keep it back, it is a moot question
whether his urge to let go will prove stronger than his will to hold
on:

The convulsive, uncontrolled tone of the last words [Razumov has just
told Natalia that she is 'a predestined victim', and added that this is 'a
devilish suggestion'] disclosed the precarious hold he had over himself.
He was like a man defying his own dizziness in high places and tottering
suddenly on the very edge of the precipice. Miss Haldin pressed her
hand to her breast. The dropped black veil lay on the floor between
them. Her movement steadied him. He looked intently on that hand till
it descended slowly, and then raised again his eyes to her face. But he
did not give her time to speak.
    'No? You don't understand? Very well.' He had recovered his calm
by a miracle of will. . . .                                    [pp. 349–50]

To Razumov confession is like a dizzying plunge to death
because he knows that it must mean the giving up of Natalia, who
alone has seemed to hold out to him the hope of life, and because
he knows too that it must mean the end of his present existence. It
must mean, furthermore, an abrogation of identity, an irrevoc-
able loss of face in relation to the person (so admiring of him) that
he cares for most; and as he totters 'on the very edge of the
precipice', our minds are taken back to Captain Allistoun of the
*Narcissus*, who – standing firm at all costs once he has confined
Jimmy to his cabin – will not expose himself to a far less
demanding reversal. We are taken even further back to Willems
[in *An Outcast of the Islands*], who – it will be recalled – is said to be
'like one who, falling down a smooth and rapid declivity that
ends in a precipice, digs his finger nails into the yielding surface
and feels himself slipping helplessly to inevitable destruction'. A
great gap divides the tortured Russian from the outcast of the
islands or the tight little captain, but the resemblance is
sufficiently striking to suggest that the path trod by Conrad in
fifteen years of intense creative activity, though taking in larger
and larger areas of experience, is circular and returns – at the end
of this great period – to a point not far removed from that from

which he started. But this is misleading, for if the novelist does come back to such a point, he sets off at once in a very different direction.

Willems lets himself slip – and falls to destruction. At first it seems as if Razumov, though he manages to steady himself on the very edge of the precipice, is to follow a similar fate:

'This man is deranged,' I said to myself, very much frightened.

The next moment he gave me a very special impression beyond the range of commonplace definitions. It was as though he had stabbed himself outside and had come in there to show it; and more than that – as though he were turning the knife in the wound and watching the effect. That was the impression, rendered in physical terms. One could not defend oneself from a certain amount of pity. But it was for Miss Haldin, already so tried in her deepest affections, that I felt a serious concern. Her attitude, her face, expressed compassion struggling with doubt on the verge of terror.

'What is it, Kirylo Sidorovitch?' There was a hint of tenderness in that cry. He only stared at her in that complete surrender of all his faculties which in a happy lover would have had the name of ecstasy.

[pp. 350–1]

At this stage Razumov no longer totters, struggling to keep his hold, but lets go. When he does so, he gives in – the images in this passage vividly suggest – to an abandon that is comparable to the abandon of suicide, for it is as though he has 'stabbed himself' and is 'turning the knife in the wound', and also to the abandon of passion, for it is as though he has surrendered, like 'a happy lover', to 'ecstasy'. To let go, it would seem, is to die, is indeed to lose possession of the self, but the lover's ecstasy, at least, suggests that this may be a happy preliminary to the restoration of self. And this, though rendered in physical terms . . . is evocative of what happens to Razumov in his spiritual crisis.

When Razumov finally confesses by pressing 'a denunciatory finger to his breast with force' and saying that his story 'ends here – on this very spot', he remains looking at Natalia 'with an appalling expressionless tranquillity' (p. 354). It is his apparent lack of feeling that the narrator finds appalling, but his outer tranquillity is the first indication that he has recovered possession of himself. In his journal Razumov seems to grasp this paradox:

It is only later on that I understood – only today, only a few hours ago. What could I have known of what was tearing me to pieces and dragging the secret for ever to my lips? You were appointed to undo the evil by making me betray myself back into truth and peace. You!

[p. 358]

This passage brings to mind Donne's appeal to his three person'd God to break, blow, burn and make him new; for if Razumov is torn to pieces by the secret that is finally dragged to his lips, it is not he that is undone but the evil, and he too is made anew. Or, rather, he recovers the self he has lost, for he is betrayed 'back into truth and peace'. If he finally allows himself to slip over the precipice, it is not to destruction that he falls, for – as he realises – he is 'saved' by Natalia and by the confession she inspires 'from ignominy' and from the 'ultimate undoing' which the exploitation of her love would have meant [p. 361]. In refusing to take advantage of her love and in deliberately and selflessly renouncing her, Razumov not only affirms that need for integrity in personal relations which he had denied in his betrayal of Haldin but demonstrates his own newly achieved wholeness, an integrity of being.

Razumov persists in believing that, after the confession, 'perdition is [his] lot' and that he has 'done with life' [p. 362], but this is not what the journal indicates:

Suddenly you stood before me! You alone in all the world to whom I must confess. You fascinated me – you have freed me from the blindness of anger and hate – the truth shining in you drew the truth out of me. Now I have done it; and as I write here, I am in the depths of anguish, but there is air to breathe at last – air! And, by the by, that old man sprang up from somewhere as I was speaking to you, and raged at me like a disappointed devil. I suffer horribly, but I am not in despair. There is only one more thing to do for me. After that – if they let me – I shall go away and bury myself in obscure misery. In giving Victor Haldin up, it was myself, after all, whom I have betrayed most basely. . . . [p. 361]

The 'one more thing' Razumov says he still has to do is, of course, to make his public confession to the revolutionists, going to them – like Jim to Doramin – to take responsibility for what he has done and court physical retribution. But, unlike Jim, he does

not abandon himself to despair – he is 'not in despair' despite his
anguish – and his spirit remains firm within him. It is true that in
the event his body takes rough punishment, for he is first
deafened by Necator and then crippled by the tramcar he does
not hear, thus having the marks of his experience emblematically
imprinted on him, as it were, his deafness to Haldin's appeal for
help having been the prelude to another sort of crippling – but
none of this can efface what he gains from the confession to
Natalia. His confession to her is, first of all, a liberation, for it
'frees' him from 'the blindness of anger and hate' and marks his
'escape from the prison of lies' [p. 363]. And this, in turn, is a
release into renewed life, for 'there is air to breathe at last',
whereas 'the choking fumes of falsehood' had previously 'taken
him by the throat' [p. 269]. It is a release, furthermore, from that
which has possessed him – from a preoccupation with self-
preservation, as his readiness to expose himself to the revolutionists shows; and from the grip of a demonic evil, as the
curious reference to the narrator's having raged at him 'like a
disappointed devil' suggests, for when he first felt himself
possessed, we recall, it was to wonder whether the devil had not
taken the shape of the 'old Englishman'. Finally, Razumov (like
the captain-narrator in *The Secret Sharer*) comes to the sort of self-
knowledge that is the condition and reward of a full possession of
self – and that to some degree mitigates the miserable existence
which is left him. But it is, after all, no more than a miserable
existence; and it confronts us with the austere bleakness of
Conrad's vision which, though it sees how a Jukes or the captain-
narrator may win through to a steeled heart amid the turmoil of
the sea, seems able to envisage the deprivation of a redeemed
Razumov – or a Monygham – as the only sort of triumph to be
wrested ashore from an engulfing darkness of the spirit.

Razumov, however, is nevertheless the most impressive exem-
plar in Conrad of a self-possession that, paradoxically, may
accrue from a readiness to let go. It is a paradox, as I have tried to
show, that is at the heart of Conrad's work; and, if in the course of
this discussion I have had occasion to make comparisons in one
way or another between Razumov and characters in [other
works of Conrad's] – between him and Captain Allistoun, and
Kurtz, and Jim and Jukes; between him and Nostromo and
Decoud, and Verloc, and the captain-narrator in *The Secret*

*Sharer* – it is because in *Under Western Eyes* Conrad has brought accumulated wisdom to bear on his most complex character. It is wisdom which is the product of his art and runs against one of his own most cherished beliefs: at the end of his ordeal Razumov may violate 'the first condition of good service', but as a result he is spiritually qualified for it.

SOURCE: extract from chapter 7 in *Joseph Conrad: The Way of Dispossession* (London, 1977), pp. 184–209.

NOTES

[These slightly revised, have been renumbered from the original – Ed.]
1. [Ed. – Page references in square brackets relate to the text of the novel as published in Dent's Uniform Collected Edition of *The Works of Joseph Conrad* (London, 1946–55).]
2. Conrad certainly thought of an earlier version of the novel in these terms. [Cites letter of 6 January 1908 to Galsworthy: see excerpt in Thomas Moser's discussion of the novel, above – Ed.]
3. It is a dilemma to which a contemporary of his was to give vivid expression in 1939 when it had its bearing on life in England: 'I hate the idea of causes, and if I had to choose between betraying my country and betraying my friend, I hope I should have the guts to betray my country.'E. M. Forster, 'What I Believe', *Two Cheers for Democracy* (London, 1951; paperback, 1965), p. 76.
4. Jocelyn Baines takes a similar view, maintaining that Razumov is 'the most considerable character that Conrad created'. *Joseph Conrad* (London and New York, 1960), p. 362.
5. Conrad disliked Dostoevsky – J Baines quotes him as referring to the Russian as 'the grimacing, haunted creature' (ibid. p. 360) – but a Polish critic, Wit Tarnawski, has shown the numerous ways in which *Under Western Eyes* is indebted to *Crime and Punishment*: 'Poleska [another Polish critic] quotes the fundamental resemblance, that the heroes of both novels are students psychically shattered by a crime they committed. To this we may add that love is a factor arousing the consciences of both and leading them to the confession of guilt. Resemblances in detail are still more striking: the roles of mother and sister in both novels, the mental derangement of both mothers at the end of the novels, the curious illness of both heroes after committing the crime, the identical roles played by the sledge-driver Ziemianitch and the house-painter, both suspected and at the same time relieving the

hero of suspicion. Finally both writers create a similar final situation for their heroes – freeing them of suspicion so that their confessions may arise from their own free will.' Quoted (from a translation) by E. Knapp Hay, *The Political Novels of Joseph Conrad: A Critical Study* (Chicago and London, 1963), p. 280.

6. Leo Gurko has pointed out that Razumov is 'goaded by his threatened and resentful egotism' into plunging 'into the web of rationalisation that finally persuades him to identify his own interests with the established Russian power'. *Joseph Conrad: Giant in Exile* (New York, 1962), p. 188. Bruce Johnson also remarks that 'there is so much selfish rationalisation in Razumov's suddenly intensified conservatism that we can hardly accept it at face value'. *Conrad's Models of Mind* (Minneapolis, 1971), p. 147.

7. Razumov has frequently been compared to Jim, though usually on the grounds of his being portrayed in a similar drama of guilt and atonement. The most interesting statement of this view is that of André Gide in a journal entry: 'Much interested by the relationship I discover between *Under Western Eyes* and *Lord Jim*. (I regret not having spoken of this with Conrad.) That *irresponsible* act of the hero, to redeem which his whole life is subsequently engaged. For the thing that leads to the heaviest responsibility is just the *irresponsibilities* in a life. How can one efface that act? There is no more pathetic subject for a novel, nor one that has been more stifled in our literature by belief in Boileau's rule: that the hero must remain, from one end to the other of a drama or a novel "such as he was first seen to be".' Quoted from the Justin O'Brien translation of the Journals by R. W. Stallman (ed.), *The Art of Joseph Conrad: A Critical Symposium* (East Lansing, Mich., 1960), p. 5.

8. Conrad's art here is so sure that he can even afford an undercutting irony while presenting Razumov with the greatest seriousness. Razumov may long to wield a stick with a stern hand, but the stick he has used to beat Ziemianitch has broken in his hands and been flung away, a mute intimation of the futility and vanity of authoritarian pretensions. Not that those of the revolutionists are viewed any less ironically:

I do not remember now the details of the weight and length of the fetters riveted on [Peter Ivanovitch's] limbs by an 'Administrative' order, but it was in the number of pounds and the thickness of links an appalling assertion of the divine right of autocracy. Appalling and futile too, because this big man managed to carry off that simple engine of government with him into the woods. . . . It was the end of the day; with infinite labour he managed to free one of his legs. Meantime night fell. He was going to begin on his other leg when he was overtaken by a terrible misfortune. He dropped his file.

'All this is precise yet symbolic . . .'                              [pp. 120–1]

Revolutionary activity, it is indicated, is a filing away in the dark at the fetters of autocracy; moreover, since the revolutionists are not fit for 'the gift of liberty' (which the file is said to be [p. 121], they let it slip through their fingers.

9. Cf. Osborn Andreas, who says Razumov must 'force the image of himself that he presents to the world and the image of himself which he possesses in his own mind to coalesce and become one. He feels that he can no longer endure a situation in which his true self is like a disembodied and invisible ghost which, instead of inhabiting his visible body, merely accompanies him wherever he goes.' *Joseph Conrad: A Study in Nonconformity* (New York, 1959), p. 134.

# SELECT BIBLIOGRAPHY

The following studies, not excerpted in this Casebook (though some are referred to therein), are also of especial interest in the criticism of these three novels.

Jocelyn Baines, *Joseph Conrad: A Critical Biography* (London, and New York, 1960).

Peter G. Garrett, *Scene and Symbol from George Eliot to James Joyce* (New Haven, Conn., and London, 1969).

Peter J. Glassman, *Joseph Conrad and the Literature of Personality* (New York, 1976).

Jeremy Hawthorn, *Joseph Conrad: Language and Fictional Self-Consciousness* (London, 1979).

Eloise Knapp Hay, *The Political Novels of Joseph Conrad* (Chicago, and London, 1963).

Irving Howe, *Politics and the Novel* (New York, 1957).

Frederick Karl, *Joseph Conrad: The Three Lives* (London, 1979).

F. R. Leavis, *The Great Tradition* (London, 1948).

Bernard Meyer, *Joseph Conrad: A Psychoanalytic Biography* (Princeton, N.J., 1967).

J. Hillis Miller, *Poets of Reality* (New York, 1965).

E. W. Said, *Joseph Conrad and the Fiction of Autobiography* (Cambridge, Mass., 1966).

Norman Sherry (ed.), *Conrad: The Critical Heritage* (London, 1973).

Norman Sherry (ed.), *Joseph Conrad: A Commemoration* (London, 1976).

Robert Penn Warren, ' "The Great Mirage": Conrad and *Nostromo*', in *Selected Essays* (New York, 1951).

Ian Watt, *Conrad in the Nineteenth Century* (Berkeley and Los Angeles, California, 1979).

# NOTES ON CONTRIBUTORS

JOHN BUCHAN 1st Baron Tweedsmuir (1875–1940): novelist, essayist and political administrator (Governor-General of Canada, 1935–40).

C. B. COX: John Edward Taylor Professor of English Literature, University of Manchester, and co-editor of the *Critical Quarterly*. His publications include *Joseph Conrad: The Modern Imagination* (1974) and (with A. P. Hinchliffe) the Casebook on *The Waste Land*.

RICHARD CURLE (1883–1968): author of the first book-length study of Conrad (1914), and his other publications include *The Last Twelve Years of Joseph Conrad* (1928) and *Joseph Conrad and His Characters* (1957).

H. M. DALESKI: member of the English Faculty, Hebrew University of Jerusalem. His publications include *The Forked Flame: A Study of D. H. Lawrence* (1965) and *Joseph Conrad: The Way of Dispossession* (1977).

AVROM FLEISHMAN: teaches in the English Department, Johns Hopkins University. His publications include *Conrad's Politics: Community and Anarchy in the Fiction of Joseph Conrad* (1967), *The English Historical Novel: Walter Scott to Virginia Woolf* (1971), and critical studies of Jane Austen and Virginia Woolf.

EDWARD GARNETT (1868–1937): editor, critic, poet and novelist (husband of Constance Garnett, translator of Russian literature, and father of David Garnett, novelist). An important figure in the literary scene of Conrad's day, his books include *Tolstoy: His Life and Writings* (1914), *Turgenev: A Study* (1917), *Friday Nights: Literary Criticism and Appreciations* (1922) and an edited volume of Conrad letters (1928), as well as a novel, *Light and Shadow* (1889).

ALBERT J. GUERARD: teaches in the English Department, Stanford University. His publications include *Conrad the Novelist* (1958) and studies on Thomas Hardy and André Gide.

JAMES GUETTI: teaches at Rutgers University. His publications include *The Limits of Metaphor* (1967).

DOUGLAS HEWITT: teaches English at Pembroke College, Oxford. His publications include *Joseph Conrad: A Reassessment* (1952; 3rd edn 1975) and *Approach to Fiction: Good and Bad Readings of Novels* (1972).

FORD MADOX HUEFFER (1873–1939): novelist, critic and poet, he later changed his name to Ford Madox Ford. He and Conrad collaborated on *The Inheritors* (1901) and *Romance* (1903).

BRUCE E. JOHNSON: teaches in the English Department, University of Rochester, N.Y. He has published *Conrad's Models of Mind* (1971) and articles on *Heart of Darkness* and Hardy's *Tess of the d'Urbervilles*.

JOHN MASEFIELD (1878–1967): poet, novelist, playwright and critic. He was Poet Laureate from 1930 to his death.

THOMAS MOSER: teaches in the English Department at Stanford University. He has published *Joseph Conrad: Achievement and Decline* and articles on *Wuthering Heights*, Thomas Wolfe and Ford Madox Ford (Hueffer).

ROYAL ROUSSEL: teaches English Literature at the State University of New York at Buffalo. His publications include *The Metaphysics of Darkness* (1971).

K. K. RUTHVEN: Professor of English Language and Literature, University of Canterbury, New Zealand. His publications include *A Guide to Ezra Pound's 'Personae'* (1969) and the volume on *Myth* in the 'Critical Idiom' series (1976).

TONY TANNER: Fellow of King's College and Lecturer in English, University of Cambridge. His publications include *The Reign of Wonder: Naivety and Reality in American Literature* (1965), *City of Words: American Fiction, 1950–1970* (1971) and books on Jane Austen and Henry James.

LIONEL TRILLING (1905–75): late Professor of English, Columbia University. His works in criticism and the history of ideas include *The Liberal Imagination* (1950), *The Opposing Self* (1955), *Beyond Culture* (1965) and *Sincerity and Authenticity* (1973).

# INDEX

Figures in italic denote reviews, essays or extracts in Parts One and Two.

Abbreviations: *HD Heart of Darkness; N Nostromo; UWE Under Western Eyes.*